Breaking 80

The life and times of Joe Carr

By Dermot Gilleece
With a foreword by Sir Michael Bonallack

Contents

Foreword
By Sir Michael Bonallack

Some of my most enjoyable times in golf have been those spent in the company of Joe Carr.

I had never seen Joe play prior to 1956, though I was, of course, well aware of his record and was already one of his fans. In that year, I played in my first Amateur Championship at Troon and on studying the draw, I realised that we were both in the same quarter and could possibly meet, subject, of course, to my winning three rounds, as I never doubted that Joe would cruise through to that stage.

My first sight of him was on the practice ground. A tall, lanky man with a white cap which had a green pom-pom on top and who hit the ball further than anyone I had ever seen. My first reaction was the hope that I didn't have to play him, for there was no way I felt I could give him a game.

As things turned out, we both lost in the second round, myself to Joe Golden, an American, and Joe to Matt Alexander whom I seem to remember was a Scottish football player. The following year, much to my surprise, I was selected for the Walker Cup team to play at Minikhada and so, for the first time, I found myself in a team with Joe, to be followed by five further Walker Cup teams as well as two Eisenhower Trophy teams.

As I expected, Joe was the life and soul of the party, and on the long flight to Canada and on our way to the USA, he wasted no time in introducing me to Liar Dice, another game at which he excelled and which I learned the hard way.

The following year, we met each other in the semi-finals of the Amateur Championship on the Old Course at St Andrews. At that time, the semi-finals, as well as the final, were played over 36 holes.

In the morning round, I got off to a good start and, having gone out in 33, found myself three up standing on the 12th tee. As we were waiting to drive, Joe remarked to his caddie in a voice loud enough for me to hear: "Don't worry, the wind's from the left to right now and he can't handle that." Needless to say, he was right and I duly went down by 4 and 3 and Joe went on to win his second Amateur Championship.

Though his "aside" was taken in good humour, I made a mental note that one day I would get my own back. As it turned out, it was 10 years before I got the opportunity.

Meanwhile, two years later I again found myself against him in the quarter-finals of the Amateur at Royal Portrush, and as I still had not mastered a strong left to right wind, Joe won by 2 and 1 and went on to take the final by 8 and 7. In the process, he drove the ball superbly but it has to be said that his putting at that time left a little to be desired.

In the 1959 Walker Cup at Muirfield, he was putting with a rusty-headed, hickory-shafted implement which looked as if it had been found in a rubbish tip. Having missed one or two short putts with it while playing in the foursomes with Guy Wolstenholme, he was walking off the green when an over-eager young spectator, running to get a good view, trod on the putter-shaft and broke it.

Joe was upset, especially as his partner remarked "Thank heavens for that." Thereafter, he putted with a three iron with much better results.

By this time, we were firm friends and usually played practice rounds together, which were always great fun and we also proved fairly successful in relieving some of the US players of their dollars. But things in that area were about to change, as far as Joe was concerned.

In the autumn of 1960, we were both in the Eisenhower Trophy team playing at Merion. Joe, with his usual optimism, challenged Jack Nicklaus to two dollars a shot on their totals for 72 holes. Unfortunately, that happened to be the year when Jack beat Ben Hogan's winning, 1950 US Open score over the same course, by no fewer than 18 strokes.

After two rounds, Jack's total was 133 and Joe's 148, whereupon Joe decided it would be a good idea to double the stakes for the last two rounds. As things turned out, it was anything but a good idea, as Jack proceeded to shoot 136 to Joe's 153. "Not to worry," said Joe. "He thinks he can play poker." Sure enough, Joe soon got his money back, with interest.

While I myself did not really play bridge, Joe was also a scratch player at that game which he loved to play in the evenings after the Amateur Championship practice rounds. He also played poker and we had many happy evenings with some of the other competitors, which was part of the enjoyment of amateur golf at that time.

Joe captained two Walker Cup teams in which I played. The first was in Baltimore in 1965 when, for the first time, a Great Britain and Ireland team were not defeated on American soil, the match finishing tied. This outcome was due largely to Joe's optimism and enthusiasm, which were infectious.

We did not play each other again in the Amateur Championship until 1968 at Troon, by which time Joe was a little past his peak and I had won two Amateurs, in 1961 and 1965. I think both of us were delighted when we found ourselves in the 36-hole final, but I still remembered his "left to right wind" remark of 10 years previously.

On the first tee, the referee asked what ball we were both playing. I promptly said Dunlop 65 number 6, to which Joe expressed shock, saying: "You can't play a number 6; I always play 6s." Whereupon I replied: "So do I." "Well, I've been playing much longer than you have," Joe protested. Determined not to budge, I insisted: "That's got nothing to do with it."

Though the exchange was all in good fun, the match referee was somewhat bemused by it all, especially when Joe said to me as I was addressing the ball: "I hope you lose the f. . . ing thing." Neither of us, nor the spectators, could stop laughing for quite some time, but the match eventually got under way.

We both played well on the front nine but I just got my nose in front. Then, as we stood on the 10th tee, I became conscious that the wind was left to right. By this time, I could play with the wind in that direction while, unfortunately for him, Joe was not now so good with it.

Remembering his remark of 10 years earlier, I said nothing but picked up some grass and threw it in the air. Then I stuck my finger in my mouth before holding it up as a further test of the wind's direction. Joe grinned and called me something unmentionable, but proceeded to aim his tee shot a further 20 yards left, and he then hooked it. The ball finished near a lark's nest from which he got a drop and as he said afterwards with a wry smile, it was the closest he got to a birdie for the remainder of the round.

At the 13th, we were looking for Joe's ball in the gorse when a woman approached him with a collection tin. Though somewhat taken aback, Joe said to her: "I haven't got any money on me and I haven't got any sense either, otherwise I wouldn't be here playing this stupid game and looking for this bloody golf ball." You will gather from these reminiscences that golf with Joe was always an adventure; always fun.

I could not believe my luck when, having been appointed Secretary of the Royal and Ancient Golf Club in 1983, I found Joe was to be Captain of the Club in 1991. This meant that for a year, we would once again be travelling together all over the place, a prospect I looked forward to with immense pleasure.

Nor was I disappointed. Joe was a magnificent ambassador, not only for the R & A but for golf. Just as he had thrown everything into the game as a player, he did likewise as Captain, with the result that he brought a great deal of pleasure to hundreds of people.

I consider myself very fortunate to have played amateur golf in the Joe Carr era. Today's players are probably far better than we were, but I doubt if they enjoy themselves as much as we did. I still have to meet a finer sportsman, who took victory or defeat in the same, cheerful manner.

I am honoured and privileged to call him my friend.

Sir Michael Bonallack,
June 2002.

ÉIRE 　　 IRELAND

Uimh. **M**	3039
No.	3

Deimhniú breithe arna h-eisiúint de bhun na
hAchta um Chlárú Breitheanna agus
Básanna 1863 go 1996

Birth Certificate issued in pursuance of the
Births and Deaths Registration Acts
1863 to 1996

Breitheanna a Cláraíodh i gCeantar / Births Registered in the District of..... **New Kilmainham** ..... i gCeantar an Cháraitheora Maoirseachta do / in the Superintendent Registrar's District of..... **Dublin** ..... i gContae / in the County of..... **Dublin** ..... Éire / Ireland

Uimhir No. (1)	Dáta Breithe Date of Birth (2A)	Túsainmneacha (má tugadh) an Linbh Forename(s) (if any) of Child (3A)	Gnéas Sex (4)	Ainm agus Sloinne an Athar Name and Surname of Father Seoladh an Athar Address of Father (5A)	Ainm agus Sloinne na Máthar Name and Surname of Mother Seoladh na Máthar Address of Mother (6A)	Siniú, agus Cáilíocht an Fhaisnéiseora Signature and Qualification of Informant(s) Seoladh an Fhaisnéiseora Address of Informant(s) (7A)	Dáta an Chláruícháin Date of Registration (8A)	Túsainmneacha má tugadh taréis chlár na breithe iad, agus dáta Forename(s), if added after registration of birth, and date (9)
49	1922 Eighteenth February	Joseph Benedict	male	George Waters 17 Turvey Avenue.	Margaret Mary Waters	Mary Ann McDonough Present at birth 19 Turvey Avenue	Twenty Second March 1922	
	Ionad Breithe Place of Birth (2B)	Sloinne an Linbh Surname of Child (3B)		Sloinne nó Sloinnte an Athar roimhe seo Any former Surname(s) of Father (5B)	Sloinne nó Sloinnte na Máthar roimhe seo Any former Surname(s) of Mother (6B)		Siniú an Chláraitheora Signature of Registrar (8B)	Notaí Notes (10)
	19 Turvey Avenue				McDonough		R	
				Slí Bheatha an Athar Occupation of Father (5C)	Slí Bheatha na Máthar Occupation of Mother (6C)			
				Machinist			Cláraitheoir Registrar	

Deimhním leis seo gur fíor chóip seo thuas de thaifead Uimh. **49** i gClár-leabhar na Breitheanna atá faoi mo chúram.
I hereby certify that the foregoing is a true copy of the Entry No. .... in a Register Book of Births in my custody.

J. M. Hennessy
Cláraitheoir *(Maoirseachta) na mBreitheanna agus na mBásanna.
*(Superintendent) Registrar of Births and Deaths.

Oifig / Office ....

* Scríos amach an focal idir lúibíní mura n-oireann sé. ? Strike out word in brackets if not applicable.

I gCeantar / For the District of..... **Dublin**

Dáta / Date **29/1/0 2**

Is é Bliain na Breithe sa Chóip Deimhnithe thuas ná / The Year of Birth shown in the above Certified Copy is
One Thousand **nine** gCéad Hundred and **twenty-two**

Is cion trom é an deimhniú seo a athrú nó é a úsáid tar éis a athraithe
TO ALTER THIS CERTIFICATE OR TO USE IT AS ALTERED IS A SERIOUS OFFENCE

Joe Carr's birth certificate. His parents were George and Margaret Mary "Missie" Waters of 17 Turvey Avenue, Inchicore. Joe was to be the fifth of their seven children. Missie's sister, Kathleen, and her husband, James Carr, had just returned from India and had taken up positions as steward and stewardess of Portmarnock Golf Club. They were childless and agreed to adopt Joe when he was ten days old. Joe was to meet his natural father on only one occasion.

IV

Prologue

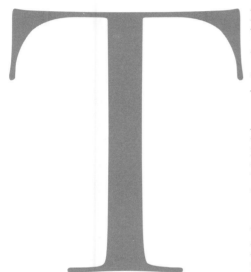he premises at number 4 Bachelor's Walk, Dublin, were ideal for a burgeoning business. Bought from Scannell's Auctioneers, there was space upstairs for a staff of 150 girls who were manufacturing coats, skirts and various other forms of women's clothing. Downstairs, samples of these garments were on display in an equally spacious showroom.

Given the company's humble beginnings in Lower Abbey Street only a few years previously, Joe Carr took understandable pride in what he and his partner, Freddie McDonnell, were achieving. It was early 1949 and with World War II restrictions continuing to ease by the day, all indications were that the future could be faced with considerable optimism.

As he ambled around the showrooms, however, Joe's confidence was suddenly shaken to the roots. For the remainder of his life, he would carry a vivid picture of the man who walked into the premises that day. Though Joe had never seen him before, he looked strangely familiar.

For reasons he couldn't explain, Joe was gripped by a sense of panic as this middle-aged man walked towards him. Modestly dressed in a suit and hat, he had a well-rounded girth and was of average height, several inches smaller than the tall, slim figure of one of the country's leading amateur golfers. As the two of them walked towards each other, the older man smiled. Then, looking directly at Joe, he said quietly: "I'm George Waters and I'm your father."

Joe couldn't think straight. He looked around, stunned. As the man went on to explain that he lived in Birmingham, he wondered anxiously if anyone had overheard. And while making no acknowledgement of what the stranger had said, his only thought was of how he could guide him outside the shop before somebody saw them together.

This was the moment he had dreaded; the reality that he had pushed into the background from childhood. Now, totally out of the blue, it had surfaced and he didn't know what to do.

They left the showrooms and went for a cup of coffee in a café nearby. It was a short meeting and little was said. When they parted, Joe never saw his father again.

Chapter One
In Name Only

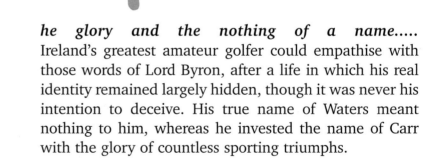

The glory and the nothing of a name.....
Ireland's greatest amateur golfer could empathise with
those words of Lord Byron, after a life in which his real
identity remained largely hidden, though it was never his
intention to deceive. His true name of Waters meant
nothing to him, whereas he invested the name of Carr
with the glory of countless sporting triumphs.

According to popular legend, Joe was born in
Portmarnock clubhouse on February 18th 1922, to James
and Kathleen Carr. In fact, his birth took place on the far
side of Dublin city at 19 Turvey Avenue, his grandmother's house in the suburb of Inchicore, where he was christened Joseph Benedict Waters.

His father and mother were George and Margaret
Mary "Missie" Waters (nee McDonough), who lived at 17
Turvey Avenue, which became the baby's first home. And
when we note that McDonough was also the maiden
name of Kathleen Carr, the background to a remarkable,
family agreement which shaped young Joseph's life,

begins to emerge. While Missie Waters was pregnant with Joseph, who would become the fifth of her seven children, her married sister was nearing the end of a seven-year stay in far-off India where husband, James, was a warrant officer in the 5th Royal Irish Lancers. And, as it happened, Kathleen suffered a miscarriage following the conception of her first child.

The hand of fate was also evident in the fact that only a month prior to Joseph's birth, the Carrs happened to arrive back in Dublin, after James had retired from the army and he and his wife had taken up positions as steward and stewardess at Portmarnock Golf Club. They had answered an advertisement for the positions towards the end of 1921.

"It seems that when I arrived on the scene, the Waters family was pretty strapped for money," said Joe. "So the two sisters arranged that I should be adopted by the Carrs and I understand that I moved into my new home in Portmarnock when I was 10 days' old. My adoptive parents never discussed the matter, but I know that there was no legal adoption. Nothing. It was as simple as that."

So it was that Missie Waters gave up her fifth-born to her childless sister.

As a consequence, when James Carr died in 1939, the chief mourners at his funeral mass at the Church of SS Peter and Paul, Baldoyle, were his widow, Kathleen, and adopted son, Joe, who, by that stage, had acquired the additional, confirmation name of Bartholomew. George Waters, meanwhile, had gone from his job as a railway machinist in Kingsbridge Station (now Heuston Station) and emigrated to England.

One of Joe's sisters, Kathleen, is still alive in a Dublin nursing home, at the time of writing, but he believes that the remainder of his natural family are dead. "I don't know when my father died; maybe that was wrong of me," said Joe. "But I got to know my sister Kathleen, who phoned me in 2001 to tell me that my brother George had died."

He went on: "I also got to know another of my brothers, Michael, who lived in England where he was a member of a golf club in the Birmingham area. In fact, he became a great friend of my brother-in-law, Kevin Hogan, and he also got to know Walker Cup colleagues, Michael Bonallack and Michael Lunt.

"There were times when I thought of asking Kathleen more about my family, but I figured why open a can of worms? She used to call to our showrooms in town, where an employee would inform me 'Your sister's here.' So there was no attempt to keep our relationship a secret. But nothing of this was known in the wider world outside my family, my business and my friends."

Joe added: "Michael, who was married to a girl called Vera, was a fine golfer and I remember one occasion when he came to stay with us at Suncroft (Joe's house in Sutton), I gave him a sweater of mine. And when my next-door neighbour, Mrs Cunningham, remarked that she had seen me out playing golf at Sutton, it was actually Michael she was talking about. We were very much alike."

Though the Carrs attempted to protect their adopted son as best they could, there were times growing up when he was confronted by his true identity. It happened at school and around Portmarnock where unthinking or downright malicious people, children and adults, would taunt him, as if being adopted were some sort of crime.

"When I was about six or seven, I became aware that adoption carried a certain stigma and people weren't slow in telling me about my situation," recalled Joe. "I remember a certain man in the Portmarnock area who would ask me how my aunt and uncle were, referring to the Carrs, my parents as I knew them.

"Because of this, I got to hate meeting that man and would run like a scalded cat when I'd see him. I still don't know how he came about the information and at the time, I didn't much care. Other things like that happened to me, little innuendos from boys at school.

"Eventually, when the evidence piled up that I was, in fact, adopted, I deliberately blocked it out of my mind. To me, dad and mother will always be James and Kathleen Carr. They were the only parents I've known. I understand that my natural mother died some time before 1930.

"I would go visiting to Inchicore, where I remember meeting an aunt and my grandmother. And not so long ago in Sutton, a man came to me and introduced himself as a nephew of mine. It seems that I had been responsible for getting him into Newlands Golf Club about 30 years ago."

As memories came flooding back, Joe continued: "With the passage of time, I knew in my heart of hearts that I was adopted. And the fact that other people didn't seem to think it was right caused me a lot of emotional pain growing up. Initially I tried to block it out, but as I matured, I thought 'To hell with this. I've done nothing wrong.'

"And all the while, my adoptive parents never mentioned it to me, good, bad or indifferent, which was obviously a conscious decision they stayed with, right up to the time they died. It was as if they, too, were determined to block out the real truth. They always gave me the impression that they were my natural parents. I had taken the place of one they had lost and they always treated me as their own. I never tried to analyse why they decided to keep the truth from me. That, too, was blocked out. And I never asked them, because in one way I didn't want to offend them, while there was also an awareness that I really didn't want to know the full truth.

"They were unbelievable parents, both of them, wonderfully kind and caring in the way they looked after me. I can't ever remember being smacked. It was a most loving upbringing and I couldn't have wished for anything better. And they did this while running affairs at Portmarnock Golf Club like a military operation.

"They always took me on holidays with them and I remember a Mediterranean cruise in 1932, when I was a 10-year-old, aboard the SS Van Dyke. It was a wonderful experience, one I'll never forget."

After the death of James Carr, his widow went to live with two maiden aunts in Inchicore, where Joe later set her up in business, selling coats around the neighbourhood and sometimes further afield. Andy Doherty, an employee of Carr and McDonnell, would deliver a whole range of coats which she would sell for a tidy mark-up. She kept this little business going, with the unstinting support of her son, until her death in 1972.

On his 80th birthday, Joe mused: "Looking back over my life, I think how lucky I was to have been adopted by such wonderful people. And there were hidden benefits like the fact that my background made me a loner, so giving me a burning desire to succeed. To prove myself. I became introverted, shutting the outside world off from what was going on in my mind."

Then, of course, there was the fact of being brought up in a marvellous, golfing environment which allowed him, as a five-year-old, to witness George Duncan winning the Irish Open at Portmarnock in August 1927. And of seeing Willie Nolan, the club professional, hitting shots. And there was the progress Joe made at his own game, with a set of hickory-shafted clubs which Nolan had cut down specially for him.

Only one player broke 80 in the third round of the 1927 Irish Open and going into the final 18, Duncan was 11 strokes adrift of his Wentworth assistant, Jack Smith. The weather was horrendous. In fact, a big catering marquee was wrenched from its moorings and torn apart by a ferocious wind which swept at gale force across the expanse of shallow duneland.

A particularly apt description of the conditions was by a correspondent who wrote: "The competitors found that direction was a thing to aim at rather than to achieve." In the quest for some form of protection against relentless rain, Joe recalled how his mother gathered up all the brown paper she could find and gave it to Duncan to wrap in layers around his body.

The Englishman then proceeded to shoot the round of a lifetime, a miraculous 74 which allowed him beat compatriot Henry Cotton by a stroke. It was an effort so remarkable that the American, "Wild" Bill Melhorn, was moved to describe it expansively as "the greatest round, under the circumstances, ever played in the history of golf."

During that, and further trips to Ireland, Duncan gave Joe some valuable tips, as did the gifted Nolan. And with those cut-down clubs, a youthful Joe devised his own, special route to the fairways so as to cope with Portmarnock's formidable carries off the tee, notably at the second, fifth, eighth, 10th and 11th holes.

At the second, for instance, he would place his drive on the path running from the tee to the fairway, to avoid the punishing rough. And by the time he was ready to join a club, he was capable of beating his father, a 12-handicapper, around Portmarnock in a level match.

Against that background, it was hardly surprising that he should have revelled in a move to Sutton, where he became a juvenile member. He was 10 years old and tall for his age. "Given my status as the steward's son, there was no possibility of my becoming a juvenile member at Portmarnock," he said. "That's the way things were back then, and we all accepted it."

Though he was blessed with a wonderfully athletic body from his natural parents, Joe believes that the competitive steel which characterised his golfing career, was the product of his upbringing. And nobody worked harder than he did. Those close to him could hardly believe the amount of effort he put into golf, especially by way of preparation for what would be his second British Amateur triumph at St Andrews in 1958.

"While growing up as Joe Carr and not Joe Waters, I never considered myself a fraud," he insisted. "Still, any time the truth, which I had pushed to the back of my mind, attempted to come to the fore, I pushed it back again. And it is something I continued to do, right up to an advanced stage of my life. So it was that I could read reports about my various golfing successes in the newspapers without feeling that I had done anything deceitful.

"In a way, it was a sort of schizophrenic existence, which, as I have indicated, could be quite painful at times. Like when somebody would come to me and say that they had met my aunt, or my uncle. That would get my stomach in a knot.

"But my situation was helped by the fact that I grew up in changing times. The perceived stigma associated with adoption was becoming less and less a factor. Eventually, it didn't matter a damn, which is how things are in the modern world. It's what you are today, what you've made yourself that matters, not where you came from."

The Christian Brothers at O'Connell's School in Dublin, knew Joe's background but they protected his identity as best they could. Still, there were schoolyard whispers about his origins in Inchicore and how Joe wasn't what he presented himself to be. But he claims not to have been aware of this undercurrent – "it was a part of my life that I blotted out, whatever the environment." Either way, his status was helped considerably by a sporting prowess which made him something of a hero to his peers.

But his attendance, which was "below average" for his final school year, clearly left quite a lot to be desired, and suggested that the Brothers also indulged him. As it happened, he was only in his fifth year at O'Connell's when he partnered Nicky McIntyre to victory in the 1939 Irish Mixed Foursomes Championship at Milltown. Incidentally, it was interesting to see an address of Portmarnock Golf Club after a pupil's name in the attendance book.

One can assume that there were many times when the call of the links often proved to be too strong. Those were the formative years which he spent honing the skills that were to carry him to the pinnacle of golfing success. Days of mitching from school were often covered up by a certain Brother Stapleton, who was very good to him.

In the event, he passed the Intermediate Certificate but on the week that he was due to sit the Leaving Certificate, he was competing in the 1940 Irish Close Championship at Royal Dublin, where he was beaten in the semi-finals by Billy O'Sullivan. One down playing the 17th, he effectively threw away any chance of winning when, after O'Sullivan had driven ruinously right, Joe committed the cardinal sin of following him out of bounds. As it happened, John Burke took the title with a 4 and 3 victory over the Kerryman in the final.

Schoolboy contemporaries think of Joe as a zealous recruiter for the Pioneer Total Abstinence Association. They also remember him as a promising sprinter, winning the 100 yards and 220 Colleges Championship of Leinster, though he never developed that particular talent. He was all-round junior athlete of the year and also played rugby for the school as a wing-threequarter. Then there was the golf.

With a pension from the British army, as well as a salary from Portmarnock GC, Joe's adoptive father took care of the financial needs of his sporting son. Those were the days when a steward's salary was all-found, which meant his parents wouldn't have had serious demands on their money, with food, heat, drink and light all taken care of by the club. They lived quite comfortably, to the extent that Joe cannot recall ever wanting for anything.

By the time he captured the East of Ireland Championship in 1941, the past no longer existed as far as he was concerned. As he put it: "I had earned the right to be called Joe Carr and nobody thought anything more about it. Essentially, I saw myself in simple terms as a product of my upbringing and with nothing to prove to the outside world." But times weren't easy.

After his father (which was how he viewed him) died, he and his mother went to live in Emmett Road, Inchicore, where they shared one room over a butcher shop – quite a change from their fine accommodation at Portmarnock. His mother cooked and they ate and slept, all in the one room.

He recalled: "My mother had only a very small pension which meant that we were effectively surviving on 15 shillings a week at the time, which is what I was earning as an apprentice in Todd Burns in Mary St, where Penneys is now." At the time, the chairman of Todd Burns was Lorcan Sherlock, the high sheriff of Dublin and a member of Portmarnock, who gave his name to the Lorcan Sherlock Trophy at Hermitage GC.

Joe went on: "I can recall three or four very lean years, during World War II. Like the occasions when I would go home from work to have my lunch in Inchicore, so as to save the expense of eating in town. And how I would wait for the number 21 bus on which a good golfer from Newlands, by the name of Joe O'Reilly, used to be the conductor. And he would let me on free and then take me back into town again.

"It was also difficult to continue my golf at Sutton, where I had been a member since 1932. At first, Portmarnock were extremely generous in giving me practice facilities, but there came a time when they wanted to stop me, because of the fact that between each Saturday morning and Sunday evening, I would leave about half an acre of divots behind me."

Meanwhile, his dramatic progress in the competitive arena soon made Joe a victim of his own success, in a manner of speaking. Championship triumphs led to selection on the 1947 Walker Cup team for the first, post-war staging of the event at St Andrews. Which was fine, in that it meant only a short trip across to Scotland.

When he was retained for the 1949 team to play at Winged Foot, however, it meant travelling beyond these islands for the first time in his adult life. Which, of course, meant getting a passport, under the name on his birth certificate – Joseph Benedict Waters. And it struck him that when he went on that luxury cruise with his parents 17 years previously, they must have included him as a child on one of their passports.

"Now, as a 27-year-old, I was confronted with my true identity for the first time," recalled Joe. "And when I applied for the passport, it was the only time in my life that I signed my name as Joseph Waters. It didn't even arise when I married Dor a year previously. I signed the register in the church in Howth as Joseph Benedict Carr. And there wasn't a problem. Dor knew all about my past. I know I told her but she would also have known about it through her brother Kevin, who was a great friend of mine, as well as being very friendly with my brother Michael.

"But I don't think old man Hogan (his future father-in-law) was too pleased about the situation. When I went to him to ask for Dor's hand in marriage in the bakery (Kylemore) they had in North Frederick St, the first thing he said to me was: 'You'll get none of my money.' But we actually became great pals as time went on.

"So, I was picked on the Walker Cup team as Joe Carr but as far as my passport was concerned, I was Joseph Waters. It meant that when it came to queueing for immigration or anything like that, I made sure I was last into the queue, in case anyone happened to look over my shoulder. As things turned out, the immigration people were the only ones who saw the truth."

He went on: "I know that in modern situations, the team manager generally looks after such matters, but Laddie Lucas was our captain and the practice didn't apply in those days. Either way, I held onto my passport for dear life. I wouldn't dare leave it out of my hands. Now the stigma of adoption had reasserted itself in earnest. And it hurt."

In fact, the entire episode caused him so much discomfort that he determined to do something about it on his return to Dublin. So he talked to Jimmy Carroll, his golfing colleague at Sutton where, incidentally, they eventually shared the course record with rounds of 61. Jimmy was a detective garda in Store St station who did the odd bit of work for Carr and McDonnell, where he gained the reputation of being a splendid fixer.

So it was that he solved Joe's identity crisis by having him change his name by deed poll to Joseph Benedict Carr. Everything was taken care of by solicitor, Seamus O'Connor, who happened to be a member of Portmarnock GC.

Against that background, I suggested to Joe that he had married Dor under false pretences; that it was a fraudulent relationship. To which he replied with a hearty laugh: "What about my six kids and my 14 grandchildren? What's to become of them?"

Then, with obvious emotion, Joe went on: "Later in my life, as I thought about those times, I realised how fortunate I was to have been adopted. All the golf I have played in all the countries over the world: it would never have happened if I hadn't been adopted. God knows where I would have finished up.

"There would have been no shame in driving a train or driving a truck, but it couldn't compare with the life I've had, culminating in captaincy of the R and A. Apart from the financial aspect of things, there was the fact that my dad was such a good steward at Portmarnock that we made invaluable friendships among the members.

"I was introduced to a lot of very influential men, like Edwin McGrath, the tea merchant, Willie Fitzsimons of the Educational Company of Ireland, and Geoffrey Power, who was the secretary at Portmarnock since God knows when. They always kept tabs on how I was doing in the various championships.

"I've no doubt that a lot of members of Portmarnock Golf Club must have known my true identity, but nobody ever mentioned it. As for my own children: my daughter Sibeal came to me and told me about it. And John heard it outside. So did Jody. They all heard it. So I called a family meeting and the whole matter was thoroughly aired."

And what were his thoughts now, in his 81st year? With typical candour, he replied: "My thoughts are completely different to what they were. My thoughts now are look, for God's sake, names don't matter a damn. What matters is what's inside a person. What have you done with your life; what friends have you made? Who have you touched going through life? That's what matters today. That's all there is to it.

"As for my adoptive parents: I feel I should be down on my knees every day, thanking God for the wonderful people they were. Because of them, I played golf all over Ireland, England, Scotland and Wales, and in Denmark, Holland, Spain, France, Italy, South Africa, New Zealand, Australia, Canada, the United States and Mexico. Those are things I could never have done if I hadn't been adopted.

"Then again, I might have been a successful runner, or a tennis player. But either way, I never would have seen what I saw through golf."

How did he feel his friends and colleagues in the higher echelons of golf would view these revelations? "My feeling is that in the old days, it would probably have created a bit of a scandal," he replied. "But in this day and age, I would expect people to say: 'Didn't he do very well. Wasn't he a great fellow to beat a way through all of that'."

And what of all the record books which had him listed as the winner of so many golf titles under what was essentially an assumed name until he formalised it by deed poll? Those titles, in the first decade of his championship career, were won by a man called Joseph Waters, not Joe Carr.

Now his voice adopted an intensity, a steel which at a different time and in different circumstances, would have thrown the fear of God into a golfing opponent. "I believed that I had earned the name of Joe Carr," he replied with some emphasis. "And I'm satisfied that I did everything that could conceivably have been asked of me to prove myself worthy of my adopted name. That's my answer."

Did he feel he had cheated people? Again, there was no attempt to dodge the issue. "It often worried me that I was an imposter, even if I never deliberately set out to deceive anyone," he replied. "I suppose I did cheat people, but I have to say that I genuinely thought of myself as Joe Carr, not Joe Waters."

Why was he saying these things so late in his life, on his 80th birthday? "Because it is a chapter that needs to be closed," he said. "I have lived with this for too long. For instance, I have never applied for the old-age pension, nor the free travel, nor a free telephone nor any other state benefit, because of the rigmarole I would have to go through with the Department of Social Welfare over my birth certificate. Isn't that crazy? "

He added: "Throughout my life, it has been my own, personal can of worms, and now the can has finally been opened. And I'm glad."

Chapter Two
His Greatest Prize

Among the congratulatory phone calls which Joe received on the weekend of his 80th birthday, was one from a long-time friend. In a brief but clearly warm conversation, Martin Winston wished him many happy returns.

Through the years, there had been numerous, similar chats between them on a variety of shared interests. But neither man could ever forget a desperately sad call which Martin found himself making to Joe on May 8th, 1976. It was to have a devastating effect on the Carr household, utterly destroying the unity, strength and warmth which had characterised life at Suncroft.

"Golfer's wife found dead", The Irish Times informed its readers on June 24th, in a report of an inquest held the previous day. It detailed a tragedy which had already had a profound impact, both outside and within the golfing community.

According to the report, Dor was found dead in bed in Cameron Cottage on the family's island in Lough Derg, where she had gone for the weekend, as was her custom. It stated that Martin Winston and his wife Joan, who had a residence on Illaunmore Island nearby, were accompanied by an associate, James Tierney, when their grim discovery was made, that evening.

Martin, a Dublin company director, had been fishing close by Cameron Cottage when he and Joan decided to call in on Dor, whom they had known for a long time. Concerned when there was no reply to their knock, they gained access through a window to discover Dor in bed.

A pathologist, Dr J O'Driscoll, later stated at the inquest that death resulted from Dor becoming sick and inhaling her own vomit. The jury returned a verdict in accordance with the medical evidence. She was 52.

Joe and Dor had started out as teenage friends through their membership of Sutton Golf Club. Indeed, the strong links which the Hogan family had with the club are reflected in the fact that Dor's brother, Des, a hospital registrar, was Captain in 1953 (when Joe won his first British Amateur) and again in 1954 when his wife was Lady Captain, while another brother, Kevin, was also a prominent member.

Their father was also deeply involved in the club. Meanwhile, because of the difficulties of getting across the city after he and his mother had moved to Inchicore, Joe was often invited to stay at the Hogan home, "Stonyhurst", backing onto the sea on the Dublin side of the Marine Hotel, close to Sutton Cross.

There were four children, Kevin, Colm, Des and Dor, all of whom are dead now. Des's daughter, Lorna, married Ryder Cup golfer, Peter Townsend, but died prematurely. Colm went to Canada and became Mayor of Alberta and Kevin emigrated to Nairobi where he won the Kenya Amateur Championship.

It was through his friendship with Kevin that Joe became a house guest at Stonyhurst. That, in turn, allowed him to meet Dor who was a nurse in the old Meath Hospital at the time. And on the occasions when Joe stayed overnight, her father, Michael Hogan, would drive him over to Sutton GC in the early morning and wait for the dawn to break before the future son-in-law would start practising.

"From hanging around the Hogan house, it was natural I should be drawn to Dor, who was a very attractive young woman," recalled Joe. "And the upshot was that we fell in love and got married on October 5th, 1948 at the Church of the Assumption in Howth – much against the old man's wishes, I might add. I remember Kit Claffey, who was a great friend of Dor's mother, Dorothy, going to Michael and persuading him to give his daughter a proper send-off on her wedding day."

So he relented and Dor was brought into town where, according to Joe, she was bought sufficient sheets and blankets to last 10 years. And a decidedly swanky reception, paid for by Michael Hogan, naturally, was held at the Gresham Hotel which was then Dublin's grandest. The event generated so much excitement that mounted police were called in to keep the crowds back.

But Joe always had the feeling that her father disapproved of the marriage, presumably because, as a wealthy businessman, he didn't want his only daughter to be depending on a young man who didn't have two pennies to rub together. Granted, as a keen devotee of golf, he greatly admired Joe's skills, but it is important to remember that Dor's beau hadn't made a serious impact on the game internationally at that time.

"I remember I had a Crombie coat, which was the height of fashion," said Joe, "and Colm Hogan gave me the gift of a motor-car, a big Ford V8 which he had got from Metro Motors. Dor wore her mother's hugely-expensive Russian mink coat, which the old man had paid something outrageous like £1,000 for in 1932. And as a wedding gift, old man Hogan brought me down into the offices of his company, Kylemore Bakeries, in Store St and gave me £1,000. Let me tell you that £1,000 was an awful lot of money in 1948."

The honeymoon of Joseph Benedict Bartholomew Carr and Dorothy Mary Hogan, was at Parknasilla in Co Kerry where, by his own admission, Joe was in trouble from the outset. He and Dor played golf on the charming little nine-hole course attached to the Great Southern Hotel, which was fine. But problems arose from the fact that Joe also got involved in some all-night poker sessions which, among other things, meant staying in bed much of the following day.

Then, like steps of stairs, the six children came along. According to Joe, two of them were "mistakes", but he won't say which two. And he considers he and Dor were blessed in having reared six children with no serious problems, unlike some of the horrific, drug-related stories one hears about youngsters these days.

Their first house, a rented property in Belton Park Avenue, Donnycarney, was acquired some months before they were married so as to have it properly prepared. As a married couple, they remained there for about a year before renting another house, 108 Dublin Road, just beside the Esso Garage at Sutton Cross, a few hundred yards up from "Stonyhurst", the Hogan home.

Then Lauder's house came up for sale. This was the family home of Edmund S Lauder, a Scot who came to Dublin in the 1880s to manage the internationally-known photographic firm of Lafayette. He later became a very influential figure at the embryonic Sutton GC and a grand-daughter of his, Nicky McIntyre, partnered Joe to victory in the Milltown Mixed in 1939, when they were both teenagers. Anyway, the Lauder house, opposite the sixth green at Sutton, went for more than £2,500 which was beyond the reach of Joe and Dor at the time. As Joe recalls, they put in a bid which wasn't quite high enough.

As things turned out, it was a fortunate failure. Six months later, when business had improved significantly and his financial situation was very much healthier, Suncroft came up for sale and Joe bought it for £2,800, of which he borrowed £2,000. It was to become the legendary home of Ireland's most famous golfing family.

"From the outset, it seemed to be the perfect house, situated right beside Sutton GC," said Joe. "Yet it was in a very poor state of repair and we had to do quite an amount of work on it. Eight years later, I had cleared off the £2,000 mortgage, yet I still owed £1,900 after all the work had been done."

Part of the work involved the construction of a large, additional room which gave Suncroft the spacious look of a golf clubhouse. From an idea which Joe had picked up in America, there was a large car-port, almost 70 feet long and costing about £15,000, which was serious money in those days. And he had a snooker room installed, to indulge his love of a game at which he had become quite proficient, indirectly through his friendship with Freddie McDonnell. In fact, the table came from Jordans, who were Freddie's in-laws.

Jim Wall was the architect on the Suncroft project which had pine floors and double-glazing: no expense was spared. Apart from the snooker room and a spacious lounge which could accommodate a party of 200 guests, there was an extra bedroom with the latest technology of the time, including electric curtains.

Joe recalled: "Those were marvellous days. Dor was the perfect hostess and we always had plenty of help, not least from her personal friends like Maureen Moran. Having had 17 years at Portmarnock with 200 acres as my backyard, I now had Sutton golf course, all 28 acres of it. It was all mine, to run on, play golf, jog, do almost anything."

When Michael Hogan was killed in a car accident on his way into Dublin, his son Des inherited the bakery business which was later sold for £5.5 million. Dor was left an annuity of £150 for life, which was not to be scoffed at in those days. There was also the matter of her modest share of the business which Des Hogan bought out for

£3,000. Dor Carr was a remarkable woman who made an indelible impact on those with whom she came in contact. As a mother and hostess, we will look at her through her son, Roddy, her daughter Sibeal and through Roddy's friend John O'Leary and, as a golfer, through the assessment of her by Paul MacWeeney, the golf correspondent of The Irish Times during the 1950s and 1960s.

RODDY

"Basically, she managed J B's entire life, making it possible for him to become a successful golfer. In fact, her raison d'etre was to make him a champion, just as Vivienne Player, Barbara Nicklaus, Valerie Hogan, Toots Cotton, Vivien Jacklin, Mary O'Connor and Winnie Palmer did for the men they married.

"This was the situation: she was absolutely dedicated to J B's success and while he looked after business matters from nine to five, mother took care of everything else, right down to the sandwiches which he took to the practice ground with him on Saturdays and Sundays.

"She was in every sense a mother hen, who created a warm, secure, loving nest for the rest of us. She was an extraordinarily gentle woman who always had time for people. I remember my friends would come into the house and in the usual way of teenagers, they couldn't talk to their parents. But they could talk to her. And after a chat, they would emerge totally refreshed, as if they had somehow been cleansed.

"Her greatest pleasure, however, came from J B's success. To be perfectly blunt about it, we didn't have a father in the accepted, family sense. The only time I remember J B having lunch with us was on a Saturday. We never went for a Sunday drive. We rarely saw him. Mother was the heart and soul of everything that happened at Suncroft. The fact that we got 26 pints of milk per day for close on 20 years, gives some idea of the amount of traffic which was drawn into the house by her being what she was.

"John O'Leary came for a weekend and stayed for months; Jimmy Bowen (another Irish international), the same. And there were others, like the writer Pat Ward-Thomas, who would stay for a few days at a time. It was a big family scene, totally controlled by mother. In fact, it became such an open house that strangers sometimes thought it was the Sutton Clubhouse!

"That's true. There were incidents of strangers who played the course and then came into our house and sat down to steak and chips, thinking they were in the clubhouse. It was understandable, in a way, insofar as there were always clubs on the stairs. And one of the girls who worked in the house, Mary Grealish from Connemara, was there to look after them when they came in.

"On one such occasion, Mary asked them after they had eaten: 'Whose friend are you?' To which their embarrassed reply was: 'Is this not Sutton Golf Club?' That's the sort of house it was.

"Meanwhile, J B believed in the Gary Player approach to practice, whereby if you put in more work than anybody else, it had to give you a priceless edge. And most of the time it did, certainly in this country. That's why he drove us all to be like-minded when we chased our own particular goals in the game.

"It meant that J B had nothing to worry about but practising for the next golf tournament. When he came home in the evening his tea was ready, then he was off with the clubs, onto the putting green or the driving range. She wouldn't have had things any other way. She even arranged his diet which was light years ahead of anything his contemporaries were doing.

"Then she would knit those little green tassels which were sewn onto the top of his caps. They became part of the Joe Carr image. When an opponent saw the tassel, it sent a certain message.

"Everywhere he went, either in Ireland or overseas, he was groomed by her as to what to say in his speeches and how to relate to people. And on his return home, mother sent letters of thanks and became friends with influential wives, all aimed at enhancing the international image of Joe Carr. Huge numbers of Christmas cards were sent, with a photograph of the family. And there were numerous charities which were subscribed to and which he knew nothing about.

"I've no doubt that these things were significant in the awards he got, such as the Bobby Jones Award and the Walter Hagen Award, and the fact that he was invited to become a member of Augusta National.

"She travelled with him a lot. Frankly, I don't know how she did it while raising the six of us. I can remember my brother Gerry, who was 12 at the time, being with her at Royal Portrush in 1970 when Johnny Faith beat me in the final of the North of Ireland Championship.

"That was part of the investment she made in trying to help me achieve success in the game. There was another occasion, on the night before the final two rounds of the East of Ireland in 1970, when she massaged my temples to ease away the tension and ensure I'd get a good night's rest. 'Let me rub your head for you,' she said gently. And with that, she eased me to sleep, with the result that I woke up fresh in the morning and went on to win the title.

"But all the while, we were aware that her priority was J B. In a way, it was a classic exercise in management and public relations, the sort of things I went on to get involved with as an employee of Mark McCormack's at IMG. And for his part, it is very much to Pop's credit that I never heard him speak ill of anybody. The only other golfer I could say that about is Des Smyth. And that's remarkable.

"I was aware of great affection for J B among the media and I can honestly say that he never set out deliberately to achieve that. Then again, it's always easier to be nice to people when they're nice to you. All the time."

JOHN O'LEARY *(The Ryder Cup golfer whose tournament victories included the 1982 Irish Open at Portmarnock)*
"Part of the legend of Suncroft is that I went to stay with the Carrs for a weekend and ended up staying two years. Which is not true. The fact remains, however, that I stayed there for two successive summers, about two months in each case.

"I started playing golf when I was 12, at Butlin's Holiday Camp in Co Meath. Jimmy Mahon Jnr, who was Irish Boys' champion at the time, was also there. It was a fantastic couple of weeks; on the golf course from morning till night.

"By the time I was approaching 14 and a junior member at Foxrock, my handicap began tumbling down and I played my first event, which happened to be the Joe Carr Trophy (Under-15) at Laytown and Bettystown. I remember going down there full of expectations and then topping my first tee shot. I think I shot 98, possibly higher.

"But with more practice, I came back a year later – and won the Joe Carr Trophy with a 75. (Joe had a house at Bettystown, where he used to go shooting with a friend, Bobby Cuddy, and it was this association with the area that prompted the club to ask him to present a trophy. In fact, he was a member of Lord Dunsany's shoot of 10 guns and had a German shepherd gun-dog named Trefora). Arising out of that win, I was invited to the Carr household for a day's golf and ended up staying overnight. It was an extraordinary experience: the house was full of young people and everything was beautifully organised by Dor.

"So I stayed overnight and sat down with a dozen other kids for breakfast, including the Carr family of Jody, Roddy, Sibeal, John, Gerry and Marty. I can't remember who the other kids were, except that we were treated royally. And we went out for a run with Joe at about 7.0 in the morning, down to the Claremont Beach. Then we chipped some balls onto the second green at Sutton. Several visits later, this had become a ritual.

"He would say to us: 'Right. What are you going to work on for the day?' And we all went off and played golf and worked on different things. And when he came home from work in mid-afternoon, he would join us for nine holes, encouraging and advising all the time.

"And Dor was extraordinary. As I remember that first summer, I had originally planned to stay a couple of days but it stretched into virtually the entire holidays. My parents had no problem with this, because they knew I was having a ball in a fantastic, golf environment. I remember Suncroft as a radiant, happy house, where youngsters were kept in a positive frame of mind.

"I'm not sure whether I had my own bedroom or if I shared with Roddy. But whenever I sat down to eat, there were never fewer than 12 and sometimes as many as 16 at the table. It seemed that golfers were coming and going all the time, and many of them were strangers to me. I suspect they were Sutton members who dropped in for a cup of tea and a chat. I was never aware of alcohol in the house, as such.

"Joe would spend some time with us in the morning, then we worked on our golf all day. From Suncroft as a base, we would head off to play in competitions while being made aware of the responsibilities of being a successful golfer. There was a lot more to it than simply playing the game.

"And Dor was always there. She had a heart of gold and managed to make everybody completely welcome in her home. And the beautiful thing was that we all learned something from her. Looking back to important occasions such as the aftermath of my Irish Open win at Portmarnock in 1982, I would have no hesitation in saying that much of the responsible attitude I showed in the way I treated people, was down to her.

"In fact, the entire Carr experience was hugely important to me, not least for the fact that I wasn't from a golfing background. I saw my uncle, Mixie Murphy (who was president of the GUI in 1963), only about once a year.

"I tended to be a bit fiery as a youngster and I can remember sitting down with Dor and she'd chat with me about things, like a sort of mother confessor. Just the two of us. In her anxiety to point me in the right direction, she told me stories about Joe in his younger days, about the little mistakes he made along the way. This proved to be a great help in terms of the development of my golfing career. I had a very close relationship with her.

"Then there was the way she supported everything that Joe did. In training, he was so far ahead of everybody else at that time and a lot of it was down to the platform Dor provided for him. On a broader level, she had a remarkable insight into people, which I can only assume came from being so close to somebody who had reached the pinnacle of amateur golf. And her love of the game was palpable.

"I consider myself fortunate in having had the most beautiful parents. And I came to look on the Carr family as an extension of the love and support I received at home. They added immeasurably to what was always a happy childhood for me, to the extent that if I ever see a member of the family nowadays, we normally go straight into each other's arms."

SIBEAL

"One of the things I remember most about my mother was her determination that I would develop as an individual in my own right.

"While everybody in our house seemed to eat, sleep and live golf, I deliberately chose to become a rebel. In fact, the only time I tried the game was out on the second hole at Sutton, when I was 10 years old.

"I remember picking up a driver and walloping the ball towards a green shed in the distance, probably close to 200 yards away. I surprised even myself at how far it went. As it happened, my dad saw this and his reaction was: 'My God, you're a future women's international.' But my response was: 'No way.'

"With that, I left the club down and never picked one up again. The truth is that I found the atmosphere of golf in our house overwhelming at times and this was my way of downing tools, as it were. So, as a golfer, I could be described as a one-shot wonder.

"I remember some of my girl friends wouldn't be allowed over to our house because the boys were so wild. But I grew up being comfortable in boys' company and could fight as dirty as any of them. I certainly knew how to take care of myself.

"Still, my mother felt I needed to be protected, as the only girl. And to that end, she encouraged my interest in horse-riding which I took up at Betty Parker's school, locally. I loved it. I used to ride in gymkhanas and even at the Horse Show, but somewhat at variance with the Carr tradition, I would describe myself as being competent without being a champion.

"Growing up, one of the things I became aware of was how to behave. My mother was a stickler for manners. She also drilled into me: 'You're never better than anybody else; but nobody is ever better than you.' And that's something I have since passed on to my own children.

"And she ensured that my upbringing wouldn't be smothered by my father's golfing success. I was Sibeal, my own person.

"I remember my mother was a very demonstrative woman, gentle, yet strong at the same time. She ruled the roost. I have vivid memories of her writing letters and of stacks and stacks of Christmas cards. It was a ritual that any time she met somebody, socially or otherwise, there would always be a follow-up note from her. And it was instilled into us that we should do the same.

"Some of this activity was clearly geared at furthering my father's career in a public relations sense, but it was also part of who she was.

"All the while, it was obvious to me growing up that my father loved my mother dearly. She always got a kiss on the cheek from him every time he came into the house. And he would always phone her to tell her where he was going. It was generally about four or five in the afternoon but we were never made privy to those conversations: they were strictly between the two of them.

"It was obvious to me that he needed her; that she was very important to him. And he demonstrated this through a deep sense of respect for her, which gave me a great feeling of security. For her part, my mother insisted that my father would always be given his own chair and he was invariably given priority with meals. In fact, she made sure that everything at Suncroft revolved around him."

PAUL MACWEENEY

After Joe had won the Milltown Mixed for the first time with Nicky McIntyre in 1939, and again with her in 1949, when she was Mrs Cunningham, he and Dor won it six times. And while there might be a tendency to view Dor as being very much the fragile half of a formidable partnership, Joe would invariably highlight her wonderful short game.

With a handicap which eased out from nine to a high of 15, Dor was a relatively short hitter, even by women's standards. But she was a wonderful putter and a better-that-average bunker player, largely because of the tremendous work she did on her short game around the second green at Sutton.

At their competitive best, the Carrs were treated like royalty at Milltown. And the red-carpet treatment was shown to be fully justified, in that the tournament never had the same appeal when, for whatever reason, they didn't compete or were knocked out in one of the early rounds. Attendances of up to 3,000 watched the semi-finals and final, especially if local favourite John Nestor happened to be in action with Philomena Garvey.

While Miss Garvey would boom a drive down the second, Dor would have been stretched to make the carry. But in and around the greens, Dor was a match for anyone.

"They were unbelievable times – marvellous," Joe recalled. "And I will never forget that Milltown GC were the first to give me honorary life membership after I had won the Amateur at Hoylake in 1953. In fact, their decision was wired to the Royal Liverpool clubhouse, before I headed back to Dublin."

As a special assignment, away from his work for The Irish Times, MacWeeney wrote a charming piece about the Milltown Mixed which, almost inevitably, featured the Carrs in a dominant role. Describing Dor as always "a competent player", he went on to suggest that it was only when joining Joe in the Mixed that she revealed "such remarkable, temperamental strength."

The scribe went on: "The rearing of a young family, greatly restricted Dor's golfing opportunities until the 1953 golfing season. That was the Carrs' first breakthrough and from then until 1970, what could be termed the Carr-Garvey era (at Milltown), saw each write their names on the honours list six times in the 17 years.

"Having entered for the first time in 1953, the Carrs chalked up three successes in four years, the 'interlopers' being the Hannins in 1954. Dor's handicap varied between nine and 15, according to the demands of domestic life, but she was just as effective on the higher as on the lower figure, for she had precisely the right approach to the tasks confronting her.

"She was not long, but she was straight and she was able to carry out, almost to the letter, her husband's advice as to the best placing of the drives and high irons. She was never tempted to go for carries beyond her strength, but was quite content to play short, or steer clear of trouble, happy in the knowledge that Joe could add more power when needed.

"Her short game was remarkable. She would not have been human had she not fluffed the occasional pitch or chip, but few players of her handicap could have made so few errors under severe strain and under the critical gaze of thousands of eyes.

"'She was a better putter than me,' Joe told me and that really was only the slightest of fond exaggerations. Her accuracy on the greens almost broke the hearts of many opposing pairs and one might well doubt if there could have been a more formidable pair to be found anywhere in a handicap event of this kind.

"As the Carrs were gaining so firm a grip on the proceedings, the crowds mushroomed into thousands each year. When it is remembered that the opportunity for watching, at reasonably close range, the leading man and woman player in Europe (Carr and Garvey) during the 1950s and early 1960s, the tremendous interest was hardly surprising."

Incidentally, most of those victories were celebrated with soft drinks because neither Joe nor Dor drank alcohol until after the Walker Cup in Seattle in 1961. In Joe's words: "I said to Dor, who never had a drink either, and she was 37 by that time, 'We'll have a bottle of wine.'"

He went on: "I'll always remember it. We had travelled from Seattle to San Fransisco and after a bottle of Rose, we went off to a nightclub. To be honest, it was more of a strip joint, which neither of us had ever seen before. There, I had a couple of Drambuies and unused to the stuff, I was soon feeling pretty high.

"To this day, I can still remember myself drinking Drambuie and shouting up at the stage 'Take it off.' Dor must have been mortified because she took a handkerchief out of her bag and covered up the R and A crest on my blazer, for fear anybody would recognise the idiot making a show of himself. The idea was that we were going to have a second honeymoon over there, but I'm afraid the drink took over."

Of their last Milltown success, MacWeeney wrote: "Although it could not be realised at the time, 1967 was the most nostalgic tournament for 14 years, for it was the last of the six victories for the Carrs. By then, Dor was playing very little competitive golf and her handicap was out to 15, and while she still showed that amazing temperament in front of the milling crowds, the physical strain was becoming increasingly evident.

"However, that only spurred on Joe to even greater efforts and duly they worked their way through to the final, against youthful but yet formidable opposition in the persons of Greg Singleton and his sister Vivienne of Donabate, who was to reach international rank. Furthermore, the Singletons had the confidence of a victory over the Carrs in the previous year.

"There was little doubt that the Singletons would have won had they kept the ball on the fairways, but once again, Joe wove his spell over young rivals. Two up after three, they looked to be on the high road, but from the seventh to the 11th, they lost every hole so that from two-up, they plummetted to three-down and there was to be no reprieve.

"Such extended success could not have been expected to last indefinitely, but there might have been general mourning had it been realised that the curtain had fallen on the greatest era in the history of the Mixed.

"Strangely enough, the Carrs had only one direct confrontation with Phil Garvey and any of her partners. That was in 1961, one of their winning years, when they met Phil and a Milltown 12-handicapper, Des Kearns, in the semi-finals. In Joe's opinion, that drew the biggest crowd ever seen on the course – and they got maximum value, for only at the 21st did the Carrs get home.

"Indeed such an outcome seemed improbable when Kearns and Phil went dormie one but, for once, the great Garvey made a vital error, finding deep rough off her drive to the 18th to enable the Carrs to square. Three holes later, they staggered into the final and eventually registered their fourth success."

When Joe and Dor celebrated their silver wedding anniversary in October 1973, the children clubbed together and bought a special medal for their mother, which was inscribed: "For 25 years of service above and beyond the call of duty."

The milestone was also considered by The Irish Times to be worthy of a story headed "My best prize was my wife." Underneath, the piece read: "Casually casting his eyes at an impressive display of hundreds of trophies in a tastefully decorated drawing room, Joe Carr, the great amateur golfer who last night celebrated his silver wedding, said: 'The greatest prize I ever won was my wife, Dorothy Hogan.'

"To mark their silver wedding anniversaries, Joe and his wife invited to their house, Suncroft, Burrow Rd, Sutton, many of their friends, relatives and top sporting personalities.

"In turn, Joe had by his side his greatest admirer, his Dublin-born wife. The Carrs have a family of five boys and one girl, aged from 10 to 24. Roddy Carr perhaps is the most like his father, being particularly useful over a golf links.

"Between intervals of greeting his guests last night, Joe managed to chat with our reporter. He said that with a big increase in his business interests, he quite honestly now had not much time for serious golfing. But he still likes to play for pleasure. He likes also to keep fit and certainly looks it. 'I run two miles over the beach each day,' he said."

❖

By way of background to the fateful weekend on Cameron Island three years later, Joe recalled: "It was a place we bought as a retreat on the Shannon and, in fact, we still have it, though it is now owned by my son, John. Martin Winston owned Illaunmore, which at 210 acres, is the biggest island on the Shannon. Two men lived on Cameron in a small house which they kept adding to until it was extended to five bedrooms. One of them was a great cook and the other was a great gardener. And they had a lovely piano."

He went on: "I used to go down to Martin to do a bit of shooting and we would go over to the other island and have a chat with the two boys. When one of them died, the other one abandoned the place, which meant that it came up for rent. The upshot was that Martin brought me over and I rented the island for about £100 a year. That was 30 years ago.

"Dor would go down there at weekends, sometimes with Mary Grealish, sometimes on her own. Mary was the eldest of a large family in Rosmuc in Connemara - the next stop to America - who were recommended to us by a priest friend, Fr Moran. Mary's father earned a living from gathering seaweed from the beach and work like that.

"I remember driving down to Connemara in the red Jaguar which I had at the time, and I picked up this shy teenager, wearing a beret. And she didn't speak a word of English. But she finished up doing a wonderful job at Suncroft and was followed by her sisters Anne, Barbara, Brid, Nora and Kathleen – six in all. And Dor was absolutely marvellous with them all, teaching them cooking while taking care of their schooling.

"Anyway, on this particular weekend, she went down and Martin Winston rang me. Himself and Joan (Martin's wife) had been there, saw her through the window, rushed in and she was gone. And Martin rang me, and Des (Hogan) and myself drove down."

That was May 8th, 1976. After the funeral, all the family, Joe and the six children, went back down to the island and stayed there for a week. In lighter moments, Joe would remark that there would be no shortage of masses for Dor, given the number of priests throughout the world that she had sponsored, especially in Africa. Money was sent for the education and other needs of these clerics and when the occasion arose, Joe would be called upon to contribute.

SIBEAL

"After my mother died, I stayed on at Suncroft for about a year, before I got married. In the house were my father, Gerry, myself and Kathleen Grealish, youngest sister of Mary Grealish who, incidentally, still called to us.

"It was a very, very difficult time for my father. Hugely difficult. His support, his right arm was gone. It was only when she had departed that I fully appreciated how important she had been in all our lives. And it was obvious to me that my father missed her terribly.

"It was as if the lights had gone out in Suncroft. The house seemed empty. The buzz and babble of kids seemed part of another time. And my father just sat there withdrawn, saying nothing most of the time. Now and again he would express concern that the house would be broken into. He was quite fragile, emotionally.

"For our part, Gerry and I simply tried to get on with our own lives, though I attempted to take over the female role in the house. We didn't talk about my mother's death, either to my father or to each other. It was as if we had settled for an unspoken awareness of the tragedy. Each of us dealt with it in our own way.

"Visitors came to the house but my father gave them no encouragement. I don't think any of us could really imagine what he was going through at that time."

❖

Clearly, life without Dor would never be the same, but Joe's competitive career had taught him to look forward and face the next challenge. As he put it: "I had a good staff looking after me and the kids were still there. There were things to be done and I was still playing golf, though not on a competitive basis at that stage. But life went on."

Then, by way of concluding this chapter of his life, he said of Dor: "As a wife and mother, you couldn't get better. Apart from being tremendously supportive to me in my golf career, she taught the kids wonderfully well. Any time they stayed with anybody, they had to write a note immediately. There are lots of fine qualities I remember about Dor. She was something very special."

In fact, as he had described her on their 25th wedding anniversary, she was the biggest prize of his career.

Chapter Three
A Working Partnership

As a trustee of the Darren Clarke Foundation, Joe is aware first-hand, of the opportunities available to promising young golfers these days, through support from Government and other sources. Things were rather different, however, for an 18-year-old back in 1940. And in the austere environment of World War II, he considered himself fortunate to get a three-year apprenticeship in Todd Burns, a reputable department store in Mary's St, Dublin.

For the first year, he was paid 15 shillings (about 60 cent) a week, which rose to £1 (1.27 Euro) during the second year and on to £1.5s in the third year. And he was employed in the so-called mantle department, selling women's coats, suits and skirts, which would be his stock-in-trade for the remainder of his working life.

The charge-hand was another Dubliner, a sharp, efficient young man by the name of Freddie McDonnell, who was about five years older than Joe. Such an age-gap, as the male sex moves from youth to manhood, can often be unbridgeable. But fortunately for Joe, Freddie didn't view his teenage colleague in such terms.

"From the outset, we found that we got on famously well," he recalled. "This certainly wasn't difficult as far as I was concerned, because Freddie was a superb guy in every way. Indeed I wasn't long at Todds before he was covering for me while I was away somewhere trying to win a golf tournament."

He went on: "I was out on the road, travelling for them, at the time of my East of Ireland win. In fact I would be away for four weeks at a time, in a Ford Prefect car with the back seat taken out so as to accommodate the samples. Then I went on to do general stuff and I had my own driver with this gas thing up on top."

The "gas thing" to which Joe refers, was standard equipment for most cars during the war years when the average motorist was permitted sufficient petrol only to start the engine before it was switched over to a charcoal burner.

Gradually, the friendship strengthened, even after Freddie married Rita Jordan, whose family ran a very popular snooker hall in Abbey St. As things turned out, the marriage of Freddie and Rita was responsible for introducing Joe to the game of snooker. "Freddie was an unbelievable snooker player – a 50 breaker, no problem," said Joe. "And I began to spend a lot of time at Jordan's, playing snooker with him, after hours. In fact, whenever I wasn't playing golf, I was at the snooker table – from one green surface to another."

His fondness of snooker was such that it became his primary sporting outlet for a period of six months, when he had to stay away from golf because of jaundice. And he became so proficient at the game as to be runner-up in the Irish Amateur Snooker Championship at a time when such names as Seamus Fenning, Bobby Brown and Larry Redmond were dominating the sport.

Always game for a fresh challenge, Joe played an exhibition in February 1955 at Cill Dara GC against Jack Rea, who was known at the time as Ireland's Mr Snooker. A native of Dungannon, which would later give Dennis Taylor, the 1985 World Champion, to the game, Rea held the Irish Professional title for 21 years from 1951 until relieved of it by Alex Higgins in 1972.

He was also credited – if that's the appropriate word – with being one of the originators of Irish jokes, in a snooker context. Back in those days of innocence, he would start his exhibition routine with such classics as: "Don't call us Irish stupid. We invented a comfortable toilet-seat until, 200 years later, some stupid Englishman went and put a hole in it."

By way of combining his two, great sporting loves, Joe played golf pool which, for those unfamiliar with the game, involves four or five players, each of whom has a different-colour cue ball and object ball. The aim of the game is to complete all six "holes" of the snooker table in a clock-wise direction, starting at the corner pocket to the left of the black spot.

Anyway, Joe became so good at it that on one occasion he completed all six "holes" at the same visit to the table, working the ball around the blue spot with screw. He also played skittles and with a God-given eye for a ball, had no difficulty in taking care of himself. Apart from the games with Freddie, there were also jousts with his best friend, Kevin Hogan, in the Cosmo, located in a basement on O'Connell St.

Joe recalls an occasion when he and Kevin didn't have the necessary funds to go down to Open Week in Tramore GC. So they rambled into the Cosmo where they met up with a well-known local "shark." Confident of his friend's prowess at the game, Kevin proceeded to bet £50 that Joe would demolish him. This, incidentally, was 20 years before Paul Newman made such activities famous in the movie, The Hustler.

Anyway, Joe devoured the shark. And when they played doubles or quits, he won again. And with £100 between then, they were set fair for Tramore. They actually travelled there by tandem, having sent their clubs by rail. And

Joe recalls that there were stretches of the journey south where he was most definitely pedalling for both of them, a matter which he duly raised with Hogan, in well-chosen words over his shoulder.

Joe's success in that little Cosmo escapade was hardly surprising, given that he was eminently capable of breaks of 90 at snooker when the mood was on him and he got a favourable run of the balls. He also played billiards but only moderately: the quick-fire excitement of snooker with its emphasis on potting, was more to his liking.

As can be gathered, between work and play, he and Freddie were spending quite a bit of time together. And despite a serious problem which arose between them some years later, they were to remain in each other's thoughts right up to the time of writing. Indeed Joe has always talked affectionately of his long-time friend and in appropriate circumstances, would enquire as to his well-being.

With their combined knowledge of the fashion trade and their eagerness to gain some sort of financial independence, it was perhaps inevitable that they should have decided to leave Todd Burns and go out on their own. And as a preparatory move in that direction, they were busily engaged in moonlighting, without their employer's knowledge.

As Joe recalled, design wasn't a major consideration in the fashion industry of that time. Indeed Coco Chanel famously dismissed Christian Dior's "New Look" of the post-war period as "Clothes by a man who doesn't know women, never had one, and dreams of being one." Good taste was the key, not the garishness which, some decades earlier, had prompted Oscar Wilde to remark: "She wore far too much rouge last night, and not quite enough clothes. That is always a sign of despair in a woman."

Whatever their partnership might hold for them, Joe certainly had no intention of spending the remainder of his working life selling garments for Todds. And in a worst-case scenario, he reasoned that he could always join the ranks of professional golfers, in the event of their business going bust.

Meanwhile, markers were already being called in. As Joe put it: "I played with all the mill owners in those early days and they gave me top quality material on very long-term credit. I'm sure it was Carr the golfer not Carr the businessman that did it."

Through his golfing activities Joe had, in fact, made some very good connections in business throughout the country. And he could see that Freddie was what could be described as a marvellous ground man, an anchor, who was happy to stay behind and do the work, while his partner concentrated on selling. As close friends, they readily recognised each other's strengths and were satisfied from the outset that the combination was perfect.

So it was that in 1946, Joe, the more confident of the two, went to their immediate boss, James Clune of Todd Burns, and gave notice for both of them. "Mr McDonnell and myself are leaving", Clune was informed, directly. And a measure of their standing with the company was that Clune expressed regret at their decision and wished them well, clearly realising that there was nothing he could do to stop them.

With that, Joe went to his prospective father-in-law, Michael Hogan, and asked for the loan of £500 which, though a fortune to the aspiring businessman, was a relatively modest sum to the owner of the highly successful Kylemore Dairies and Bakery.

Hogan, as we have indicated, was quite an autocrat who seemed to have difficulty in coming to terms with the idea of a son-in-law, even if the candidate happened to be a champion golfer whom he was prepared to transport to tournaments in his luxurious Ford V8. Anyway Joe, whose courtship with Dor was getting to the serious stage, asked the man who was known as "The Boss" for the necessary cash.

As luck would have it, Hogan happened to be in one of his benevolent moods and took Joe along to the Munster and Leinster Bank in Connell St, Dublin. Indeed this was the same bank where, 20 years later, Joe would be invited to become a director.

With cash in hand, the first deal the new partnership did was at Clery's department store, where Joe was on excellent terms with the buyer. After acquiring a quantity of lining for cash from another Dublin company, Polikoffs, they brought it to Clerys where it was sold on for a handsome profit.

From then on, Joe became so committed to their embryonic business that he turned down what was then a highly lucrative job with V P Phillips, a Dublin firm of insurance brokers. Given his enhanced profile as the reigning Irish Amateur Open champion, they were prepared to offer him a salary of £1,500 per year – splendid money at that time – plus a car. But he turned them down.

The immediate post-war era was notable for the fact that Jewish businessmen, who had dominated the clothes trade, were quitting it in favour of jewellery, money-lending, banking and auctioneering. So, there was a gap in the market. It was then up to Joe and Freddie to prove that there was a market in the gap, especially when famously shrewd operators were looking elsewhere.

A considerable bonus for the likely lads was their youth and enthusiasm. As Joe recalled: "We were determined that nothing could stop us when we settled into our fourth floor offices at 25 Lower Abbey St, down from Wynn's Hotel, on the corner." He went on: "Our manufacturing base was in Gardiner Row but we also farmed out stuff to other people. We became very resourceful hustlers, with a staff of about 18."

In fact they were highly successful by the standards of those days, with their earnings soaring from four pounds a week to £24, almost overnight. Carr and McDonnell were on their way. While Freddie was in charge of production, Joe concentrated on sales. And in the process, he met some great people across the length and breadth of the country, people like Frank and Delia Bennett, who lived in Youghal and operated Bennett's the Bargain Store, a very successful business in Cork.

Said Joe: "I remember I would go down and stay with them every year, playing golf by day and poker by night. And there was a particular evening, at an early stage of our business relationship, when Frank called me aside, handed me five grand and said 'There you are Joe – work off that.' Getting such a large advance carried the stamp of pure friendship, as far as I was concerned. His intention was to make it easy for us to become established and I never forgot it to him."

From humble beginnings, the company would grow eventually to have a staff of 550, with changes of showrooms to Bachelor's Walk and later to 12,000 square feet of premises in Upper Abbey St. But in terms of sales, their most productive premises were the various golf courses throughout the country without which, Joe readily acknowledges, they could never have succeeded.

Whatever the location, the procedure was generally the same. On arrival in the town, Joe would enter the store of an established or prospective customer, whereupon the owner would turn to a member of his staff with the instruction: "Write the order down; we'll be back in three and a half hours." With that, the proud owner would trade golf shots with a national sporting hero and by the time they returned, a substantial order had been written for Carr and McDonnell.

There were extremely modest courses where the greens were surrounded by wire to keep the sheep away. And many of the players were more modest still. But there were no complaints from their distinguished guest. In fact, he would often give them some very useful golfing tips, like making sure to take the club back on the inside and then remembering to kick in the right knee on the downswing. Handicaps were known to tumble while in the process of buying women's fashion wear.

If there was no improvement, at least there were the considerable bragging rights attached to a game with the winner of whatever championship Joe happened to be the holder of at the time. And having started out as business outlets for Carr and McDonnell, these stores became the framework for lasting friendships, which, in Joe's view, would probably not be possible in today's business climate.

"I remember on Mondays, immediately after the end of the War, I used to leave Dublin at six in the morning in a big Austin van, and arrive in Galway at about nine," he said. "There, I would meet with James O'Flynn and his designer, Adamson, from the Galway Woollen Mills.

"Cloth at that time was like gold-dust. You couldn't get it anywhere. But after a quick breakfast and then 18 holes of golf, we'd go into the mill and James would pick up bales of cloth while asking rhetorically, 'Who's that for, Arnotts; who's that for, Clerys; who's that for, Todds.' And each bale would be re-directed into our van. And I'd return to Dublin with 12 or 14 pieces of cloth, all of the finest quality.

"I remember Jimmy Carroll and Freddie meeting me and the three of us hauling the bales up the four flights of stairs to our office before it went on to the factory. Business was a lot friendlier then than it is now. It wasn't as cut-throat."

Carroll's involvement with Carr and McDonnell stemmed from his being stationed as a detective garda at Store St Station. Its proximity to the Kylemore Bakery, meant he became friendly with Michael Hogan and through Hogan, with Joe. Of course they would later become committed team-mates at club and international levels.

In such circumstances, it followed that Freddie would become involved in golf. With Joe's help, he joined Donabate GC where he went on to become one of the club's most respected members, filling the role of captain and then president and lending his name to the McDonnell Cup. Freddie's wife, Rita was also an associate member there and their children followed them into the club. In fact all the members of the Carr and McDonnell team, including Joe's right-hand man, Andy Doherty, would eventually become members of Donabate.

Recalling his close relationship with Andy, Joe said: "He started off as a sort of batman for me. He would come to the house and clean up for Dor. And at dawn during the summer months, he would come and knock on the window of Suncroft having set up all the balls for my morning practice session. But first, I would have a run so as to keep my legs strong.

"Then he was taken into Carr and McDonnell and later into the House of Carr where, as an outstanding worker, he became especially valuable to me."

All the while, Joe and Freddie were reinvesting all available profits back into the business. The upshot was that it was well into the 1950s before either of them began to reap the benefits of their endeavours. "I remember having a safe at home with up to £12,000 in it at any given time," said Joe. "Every now and again, Dor would dip into it for her priests and missionaries in various parts of the world.

"So, I had no money problems for a period of about 30 years, from the early fifties until the early 80s. I was worth a million, in terms of my holdings, and for much of that period I was earning about £100,000 a year. But I was spending about £95,000. So there was no question of a nest-egg. Still, this sort of financial independence allowed me to travel all over the place. And, of course, I was making business contacts everywhere I went.

"Through connections in the golf industry, I acquired the agencies for Titleist and MacGregor which I effectively gave away, for fear of being distracted from my clothing business. And I turned down the agencies for Ping and Taylor Made, on the grounds that I was making so much money in the rag trade, I wouldn't have had time for any other business venture."

Relationships were also established with the various golf writers of the time, outstanding craftsmen such as Bernard Darwin, Pat Ward-Thomas, Henry Longhurst, Leonard Crawley, Ronald Heager and Peter Ryde. As a former Walker Cup colleague, Crawley was invariably very supportive of Joe in his writings in The Daily Telegraph. In fact, Joe got on very well with them all, with the possible exception of Longhurst, who seemed to have a facility for antagonising Irish players, notably Harry Bradshaw, whom he referred to as having an agricultural swing.

Yet it would be wrong to think of Longhurst as being anti-Irish. For instance, he once wrote: "Some of the Irish links, I was about to write, stand comparison with the greatest courses in the world. They don't. They ARE the greatest golf courses in the world, not only in layout but in scenery and 'atmosphere' and that indefinable something which makes you re-live again and again the day you played there."

And after Ireland's marvellous triumph in the then Canada Cup in Mexico City in 1958, he wrote: "A year ago in Tokyo, he (Bradshaw) had to retire from this tournament through persistent nose-bleeding. I saw him standing cheerfully in the hotel entrance as we left. Only three or four people, of whom I was not one, knew that in the intervening days, he had been so near to death that a priest had been called to administer the Last Rites.

"My colleagues are due shortly to elect a Golfer of the Year who has 'done most for British golf.' Had they seen him in Mexico, they would look no further than Harry Bradshaw – and never mind what part of Ireland he comes from." Bradshaw was duly awarded the Association of Golf Writers' Trophy for 1958. So much for Longhurst's anti-Irish bias!

Joe also grew to admire Arthur McWeeney of the Irish Independent and his brother Paul, who later became golf correspondent of The Irish Times. Indeed Joe played a lot of bridge at the St Stephen's Green Club in Dublin with the McWeeney brothers (curiously, Paul insisted on spelling his surname with a 'Mac'), along with a mutual friend named Gerry Reid, who was an Irish bridge international.

"The McWeeneys, who were the salt of the earth as far as Irish amateur golf was concerned, would have been interprovincial standard but Gerry, who incidentally was a member of Rathfarnham, was obviously in a class above them," recalled Joe.

He went on: "There was something very special about the way the players and the press got on together. The press were certainly very kind to me and I was very grateful for the fact that nothing derogatory was ever written about me on a personal level. And in general terms, I can remember getting a bad press only once in my career and that was at Sandwich where I got it around in 68 only to be beaten on the last green. And the heading the following morning was: 'Carr collapses under squeeze.' I considered that to be distinctly unfair, given the quality of the golf I had played over a notoriously tough links."

And did he have a favourite? Indeed he did. Like myself, Joe rates Ward-Thomas of the then Manchester Guardian and Country Life magazine as having been the best of them all, by some distance. "I was closest to Pat, who was a great, great friend of mine and a supreme writer on golf," he said. "He got on well with Dor and his wife Jean and Dor also became very close. When they travelled to Dublin they would stay with me for weeks on end. Our relationship was special and I feel it had much to do with the closeness of our wives.

"He was an extraordinary man to play golf with – so hard on himself. I remember on the second at Sutton, after driving the ball out of bounds, he bit himself on the wrist and actually drew blood. He was a remarkable character. Though I wasn't always aware of it at the time, I realise now that he wrote like an angel - a wonderful gift for words. In a class of his own.

"I remember him telling me about his time as a prisoner of war and how he had worked out all the odds for cards, especially for poker and bridge. My understanding was that his figures later became accepted statistics for the game of bridge."

Joe's love of bridge also involved the most celebrated golfers of the time. In the build-up to the 1966 British

Open at Muirfield, where it wasn't permitted to play golf on a Sunday, he was invited by Arnold Palmer, Jack Nicklaus and Gary Player, the Big Three, to join them for a game at Carnoustie, where they were contracted to play a television match a few weeks later. So they flew to Dundee, where they were picked up by a limousine which took them the remainder of the journey to Carnoustie. And in a less than friendly fourball, Joe and Player threw the party.

Afterwards, Palmer and Nicklaus figured they could bank on the same success at bridge as they had experienced at golf. But the benefactors of Carnoustie got their money back, with interest.

All of these players enjoyed a close relationship with the media at a time when television had yet to become a factor in golf promotion. So, newspapers were very much the dominant medium and players made allowances for a little over-indulgence by scribes such as Longhurst and Crawley at the 19th. Indeed Joe recalled old Henry on a boat to America, winning the prize for nominating the mileage of the day, which was probably a few hundred pounds. And he felt obliged to stand drinks all round, whereupon those players who didn't drink – and Joe was among them at the time – made sure that they ordered large ones for those who did drink.

As for Crawley: In 1947, there was a round-robin to see who would lead the Walker Cup team at St Andrews that year, and Crawley beat Joe by 4 and 3, which meant that he led the side. The upshot was that The Daily Telegraph's man was hammered 5 and 3 by Harvie Ward, while Joe beat Stanley "Ted" Bishop by the same margin, at number two.

Then, in 1954, Crawley beat Joe again, in the British Amateur at Muirfield. And the Englishman beat him yet again, in the Home Internationals at Portmarnock in 1961. After that particular match, Joe got a wicked little note from Crawley saying: "St Andrews 4 and 3; Muirfield 4 and 3 and your own Portmarnock, 4 and 3."

So it was little wonder that colleagues should have decided to have a little fun at the Dubliner's expense, when they happened to meet at Porthcawl, where Joe was playing Gerald Micklem. In the event, when Crawley arrived on the scene and took his clubs out of his familiar, old Mercedes, he said to Joe: "I'm playing you", but Joe protested that he was playing Micklem. Still Crawley insisted that Joe would be his victim. Whereupon our hero handed him a ball and said: "Look, I'll play both of you." And the three of them had a good laugh.

In January 1971, when gross sales in the House of Carr topped £1.5 million, Joe made his first venture into racehorse ownership when he and Freddie took half-shares in a two-year-old colt at the Melitta Lodge stables of Paddy Prendergast on the Curragh. Named Karelle, which was a combination of both their surnames, it went on to win the Birdcatcher Stakes at The Curragh at 8/1, though by his own admission, Joe didn't have a penny on it.

By that stage, Freddie was no stranger to racing. In fact, he had a three-year-old gelding, Tulyroi, in training with Paddy Prendergast Jnr. And as it happened, Karelle ultimately became his sole property, as part of the settlement deal when their partnership split up.

The year 1971 was a time when the company was commissioning work from 26 factories which, at peak output, were producing 25,000 garments per week. Remember, this was a time when there was import duty of 25 per cent on clothing coming into this country from the UK, making it a protected market for Irish manufacturers. And Carr and McDonnell were one of the six biggest companies in the industry. It was only with Ireland's accession to what was then the European Economic Community that tariffs had to be reduced and ultimately removed altogether.

Meanwhile, since 1968, Joe was a director of the Munster and Leinster Bank, which later became part of Allied Irish Bank. He was also a director of Friends Provident and Century Life, as well as being part owner of the River Club, with Gerry McGuinness. And he was one of the principals in a £6 million property development in the centre of Dublin. This was a proposed shopping mall between Bachelor's Walk and Abbey St, which fizzled out some years before becoming a reality for other developers, in the form of the ILAC centre, nearby.

But in Joe's view, a major downside to all the travelling he had been doing, especially during the late 1960s, was that it was responsible, ultimately, for the break-up of his partnership with Freddie. As he reflected: "While I had taken my eye off the ball, as it were, the entire complexion of our key staff changed, with various members of Freddie's family moving into the business. And I gradually began to feel I was being squeezed. I had nobody from my family in the business at that time: my son Jody became involved later."

He went on: "I suppose things came to a head when Freddie's wife Rita came to me this day, explaining that Fred junior had come home from Spain and would there be a place in the business for him. And I regretfully had to tell her no. In my view, things had already gone too far.

"This family spleen culminated in a very bad year between Freddie and myself. People were sacked. And there was a period of nine months in which Freddie and I, while running a fairly big operation, never spoke to each other unless it was absolutely necessary. That was very sad. In fact I don't think I endured a worse nine months in my life. It got so that I hated getting up in the morning and I hated going into the office. I thought of buying him out but I couldn't, because the money was too big.

"But I became determined that Freddie and I would have to split, however it was done. So I approached him and suggested that either he bought me out or I would buy him. 'Put a price on it', I said. And we brought in Gerry Wheeler, who had worked with the Revenue Commissioners, and he organised the whole thing. I paid £180,000 cash and gave Freddie a house in Sutton and the two racehorses we had. I suppose the whole lot came to about £200,000 which was a lot of money in those days. There was a shortfall and Gerry Wheeler arranged that I would get a loan of the necessary money from the bank."

The split was completed by 1972, at which stage annual sales had gone up to £2 million. As Joe said: "Both Freddie and I had large families and the company wasn't big enough to provide both with a living.

"Arthur Ryan, who went on to become the head man in Penneys; Greg Tully and Vincent Courtney decided to open a knitwear operation, which was their forte, on a 50-50 basis in our basement in Upper Abbey St. That arrangement helped me to fund the company buy-out. It had been a family problem and when we went out on our own, Freddie went his way."

Within three years, Gay Girl Dresses, a company with a £150,000 turnover, had been acquired, as was a leasehold interest in premises in Moore Lane, and an office was opened in Glasgow. P C Warren was financial controller and director of the House of Carr; Vincent Courtney was administrative director, Greg Tully held the position of merchandiser, Ted Firth, a golfing colleague of Joe's at Sutton GC was a director, and Joe's eldest son, Jody, was export director. Joe added: "Sadly, the parting was accompanied by quite a deal of ill feeling, though not between Freddie and myself. Our friendship remained strong through it all, but it was such a touchy subject that we couldn't really talk about it. In fact it was only when I had him to lunch in 2001 – about 30 years after the event – that we talked about those times. And despite everything that had happened, the bond between us was as strong as ever right up until his death on September 25th of this year."

By the mid-1970s, the company, with more than 1,000 accounts scattered throughout Ireland, had a staff of 275 but an additional 400 others worked with the 12 or so companies which manufactured for the House of Carr. "It costs 60 pence to send a coat to Cork," its owner famously remarked. Meanwhile, he was nominated by the Bank to the board of Silvermines. And he later became a director of the B and I shipping company.

Dark clouds gathered on the horizon with Ireland's accession to the EEC. It prompted a dramatic change of strategy as characterised by Joe when he remarked: "There was a time when, if you didn't sell in your home town, you shouldn't be in business. Now, if you don't export, you shouldn't be in business." So it became the target to build exports up to 50 per cent of the total business. And the House of Carr found cause for celebration in December 1976. That was when a rather special lunch was organised at the exclusive Mirabeau Restaurant, to mark the 30th anniversary of the business.

The diarist in The Irish Times reported: "I had never seen a Methuselah of champagne in my life until last Monday when one was produced at the Mirabeau, Sean Kinsella's humble little eating-house on the Dun Laoghaire sea-front. A methuselah contains either 16 or 18 bottles of the liquefied gold, or four gallons of the stuff – so I was told by people who should know. The monster bottle appeared, along with a monster cake, as one of the tributes paid to Joe Carr when he and some friends celebrated the 30th anniversary of the House of Carr.

"I had known and admired Joe previously as one of our greatest amateur golfers, but never knew that the Champ from Sutton was also a sort of champ in the Rag Trade before. I learned on Monday all about how Joe served his time with Todd Burns and in 1946 set up on his own with Freddie McDonnell, expanding a business that now turns out an average of 20,000 garments per week.

"What's more, said garments are both good-looking and reasonable. I asked Joe if he'd ever thought of turning pro. His answer was that in his prime, the money wasn't anything like what the professional golfer makes today. He did add that he had probably sold more House of Carr products over a fourball than he'd ever sold over a counter ...."

The motif for the company was a seagull, borrowed from the story Jonathan Livingston Seagull by Richard Bach, with photographs by Russell Munson. In the book, Jonathan was a seagull and an individualist who discovered that if you wanted something badly enough and had the courage to pursue it, you usually succeeded. It was a story which influenced Joe greatly, as it would later the song-writing of Neil Diamond.

"By sunrise, there were nearly a thousand birds standing outside the circle of students ..... they listened, trying to understand Jonathan Seagull. He spoke of very simple things – that it is right for a gull to fly, that freedom is the very nature of his being, that whatever stands against that freedom must be set aside, be it ritual or superstition or limitation in any form. 'Set aside,' came a voice from the multitude, 'even if it be the Law of the Flock.' 'The only true law is that which leads to freedom,' Jonathan said. 'There is no other.'"

In January 1982, the sale of Suncroft was reported in the national media. It had been bought privately for £120,000 by, ironically, a non-golfer. Though this price for a spacious, eight-bedroom house may appear modest by current standards, the country was in the throes of a major recession at the time and house prices were, consequently, depressed.

Though it was a wrench for Joe to part with such a significant part of his, and his family's, life, Suncroft had simply become too big for his needs. In the event, he used the proceeds of the sale to try and help his ailing business. "Our mistake was that we didn't stop manufacturing," he admitted. "We simply couldn't compete with low-cost imports from Turkey and the Far East."

In the way of things, Murphy's Law took over and the company began experiencing serious union problems. As Joe put it, one employee would want a window open and another would want it closed. It seemed that there were rows all the time. It was a losing battle, despite the fact that his position as a director of AIB gave the company an "undoubted" rating, which is as good as it gets.

So it was that having earlier eased himself out of company affairs, Joe felt obliged to take the helm once more in 1984. That was when a financial columnist with The Irish Times informed us: "With Joe Carr back in the saddle down at the House of Carr, it's going to be like old times for the rag trade company; well almost like old times, the staff members have been pruned from 500 to 115. I gather that Foir Teo, which has baled out the company with a substantial (preference share capital) injection, insisted as part of the deal that Carr go back in as full-time chief executive.

"Foir Teo is, however, going to nominate its own director to the company to keep an eye on things. Patrick Dowling, part-time university lecturer and consultant, will be the man going in." The piece went on: "Dowling's appointment and Carr's return sets the seal on the Foir Teo rescue package for the company, a rescue that had more than its share of heated moments...."

But the end came when the company eventually went into receivership. On April 21st 1989, The Irish Times reported: "Three clothing companies controlled by the family interests of former amateur international golfer, Mr Joe Carr, have gone into receivership with the loss of 70 jobs in Dublin.

"Last Friday, the State rescue agency Foir Teoranta, appointed Mr Gerard Mangan of accountants Gerard Mangan & Company as receiver to the three companies, Carr and McDonnell, Gaye Girl Fashions and Carr Holdings, and all employees, bar a small number kept on to finish off some orders, were made redundant.

"Mr Mangan said that efforts would be made to sell the business of the companies as a going concern but added that he hoped to sell the leases on the factory premises in Dublin. Mr Mangan declined to reveal the extent of the deficiency of the three companies, nor would be reveal how much is due to Foir Teoranta."

Against this background, it is hardly surprising that Joe's own financial position was far from healthy at that time. By his own estimation: "I probably had about £50,000 in cash and that was it. Earlier, I had a pension which would have been worth £50,000 a year to me but when I had the heart attack I had to relinquish it. So, the business cost me everything, partly because of the cheap imports during the 1970s and partly because of bad management."

He went on: "I never had any ambitions to be a wealthy man. As far as I was concerned, money was there to be spent, not saved. And I spent it. Then there was the business of rearing six children and giving them a reasonable start in life. It wasn't easy, but people were kind to me."

Settled in a delightful home on Howth Head, Joe had come to terms with his reduced circumstances when, in November 1990, he received a letter from the Royal and Ancient Golf Club of St Andrews, where he had been a member since 1960. They were inviting him to be their captain; to claim the most prized office in golf.

On reading the letter again, he exclaimed: "Oh Jesus! I can't afford this." But his children thought differently.

Chapter Four
On Home Fronts

For the most part, serious, competitive golf had become the stuff of memory by the time the decade of the 1980s had arrived. Yet Joe still found himself reliving the thrill of battles past, when he had occasion to revisit a particularly favoured stomping ground. Like the Co Louth Links at Baltray.

Indeed the celebrated terrain beside the Boyne Estuary had lost none of its appeal when he travelled there for a Hilary Outing in which pleasure clearly took precedence over prizes. "Have you even played here before?" came the innocent enquiry from the chatty young man who was employed as Joe's caddie. "Yes," he was told, "many times."

Further along their journey, the questions became more precise. "Did you ever play in the East of Ireland?" "Yes I did – on numerous occasions." Which prompted: "And did you ever do any good in the East?" "Yes. As a matter of fact I did. I won it on 12 occasions."

"Oh, you must be Joe Carr," the young man

exclaimed, without a hint of apology. He then proceeded to digest the information over the ensuing holes until they reached the short 15th. There, facing a pitch over a bunker from a sandy lie to the right of the green, Joe thinned the ball into the trap. Whereupon the caddie looked him straight in the eye and declared: "It must have been fierce easy to win the East in those days, Mr Carr."

Baltray was the scene of Joe's first championship triumph. As a 19-year-old, his slim, angular frame was seen stepping down from the Dublin bus before he walked to the clubhouse with a modest set of clubs slung over his shoulder. His target was the inaugural, 72-hole East of Ireland Championship staged over the Whit Bank Holiday weekend. And with rounds of 78, 73, 74 and 76 for an aggregate of 301, he finished at the top of the leaderboard, four strokes clear of local favourite, Kevin Garvey. A year later, he met Nancy Giles.

"That was before she became Nancy Gannon," recalled Joe of a young woman, who would become the mother of a remarkable golfing brood, apart from filling the role of Lady Captain of the club in 1965 and Lady President in Millennium year. "She was working as a receptionist at the Golf Hotel, which was owned by the Gannon family before it later became the Co Louth clubhouse." Joe paused before adding with a quiet smile: "I suppose you say that we had a bit of a flirtation."

The mention of romance brought a similarly amused reaction from the woman herself. "I was Nancy Giles, from Navan," she said. "In fact, myself and Meath's All-Ireland footballer, Trevor Giles, are first cousins once removed." Having established this relationship with the pride of the Royal County, she went on to recall how she started work at the hotel on May 1st 1942 and came to meet Joe Carr for the first time when the East was played a month later.

"We went out together for a short time," she said. "I suppose you could say it was a bit of a romance, but it didn't last very long." (Almost 40 years later, Joe would be non-playing captain of Ireland teams which included Nancy's son, Mark, as one of the key players).

As it happened, the brief encounter with Joe was doomed from the time she found herself attracted to the owner's son, Jack, in August of that year. Whatever about the brevity of her relationship with the champion of '41, this was truly a whirlwind romance in that she got engaged to Jack Gannon later that month and the pair were married in September 1943. She went on: "I suppose Joe could take some consolation for the fact that Jack was actually responsible for arranging his first championship win. You see Jack started the East of Ireland."

Nancy explained: "He got a golf magazine from the United States which detailed how many of the amateur tournaments there were 72-holes strokeplay events. That was in 1939 and he felt we needed to have a proper strokeplay championship in this country. So he went to Josephine Connolly who was secretary of the men's section in the golf club.

"There wasn't much enthusiasm for it at the start, either in the club or from the Leinster Branch, but it took off in earnest in 1942 when Joe was defending the title which Kevin Garvey won.

"Meanwhile, I remained great friends with Joe and with his wife, Dor. I remember Jack telling me that when Joe played in the first East of Ireland Championship in 1941, he (Jack) went down to Drogheda to meet him and they both stood in the bus to Baltray. And, naturally, Joe stayed at the hotel, which, incidentally, was built in 1928."

It had 13 rooms at the time, numbered one to 14: there was no number 13, presumably for superstitious reasons. Jack's mother, Theresa Doherty (she was married a second time), was known as Daisy and she ran the hotel until the club bought it for £7,000 and converted it into their clubhouse which was officially opened on February 1st 1944.

"Naturally, there was always great excitement when the East of Ireland came around," Nancy went on. "And young golfers were no different then than they are now, which meant there was quite a bit of noise in the hotel.

Indeed I have to admit that I joined in the fun and I can remember an occasion during the East in 1942 when Cecil Ewing, who struck a very imposing figure in a beautiful red, silk dressing-gown, came out of his room, stood at the top of the stairs and shouted: 'Will the noise ever stop down there?'

"As for Joe: I have always thought of him as an exceptionally nice fellow, a gentleman, who was great fun and always had a ready smile. And I can recall the card games he had with Clarrie and Val Reddan. We remain great friends to this day. I remember when my lads were small, bringing them to boys events and meeting Dor there with her lads. She was a wonderful mother, most considerate. And I remember thinking that Joe was a very lucky man to have Dor behind him.

"An occasion that stands out was the Leinster Boys Championship at Edmondstown where Joe caddied for Roddy, who was only eight at the time, and Jack caddied for Mark, who was only six and a half."

Joe, who became a good friend of Jack Gannon's and a great admirer of the short game skills of his son Mark, remembers those early years with obvious affection, including a romance between Jimmy Bruen and Clarrie Tiernan, before she met her husband, Val Reddan. And he treasured his friendship with Jo Connolly, who later donated the Jo Carberry Cup for the best net aggregate in the East, not that it was ever his target.

"During the years of World War II, I remember walking from Bettystown to Baltray. The reason we went there was to get a decent feed of bacon, egg and sausages. You see, it was outside the Archdiocese of Dublin where the Lenten fast was far stricter than in other, more liberal areas of the country.

"I used to play down at Baltray with my pals Kevin Hogan and Billy McMullan. Billy was a good player who died tragically in a fire in Australia some years later.

"Though the course obviously suited me, it was very different from what you experience there today. To say that the terrain was fiery is putting it mildly and anything in the middle to high seventies was a bloody good score. You couldn't pitch on a green; you couldn't stay on a fairway. Everything bounced off.

"Making allowance for bounces and plenty of run, it was the sort of challenge which demanded creative golf. And with my length, I had an advantage at the par fives. Still, it bore no resemblance to the modern game." He went on: "In many ways, the family atmosphere at Baltray reminded me of my home club, Sutton. There were the Gannons, Garveys, Connollys, the Lyons and the Reddans, whose commitment, dedication and foresight have brought worldwide recognition to the club. And rightly so.

"One lasting memory of Baltray was in 1942 when I was six shots ahead with nine to play and lost eventually to Kevin Garvey, by a shot. One of the problems I encountered over the finishing holes was hitting the pin with a bunker recovery, which was a two-shot penalty in those days.

"Then there was the occasion in 1945 when John Burke and myself tied on 302. And, most unusually, it was two Sundays later before they held the 36-hole play-off which I won by 154 to 157. That was quite a feather in my cap against a player of Burke's reputation.

"I liked Baltray. As with Rosses Point, I found it to be a big, strong golf course which gave me a great chance. I couldn't play the tight, tricky layouts, no more than Tiger Woods could play Royal Lytham in the Open in 2001. Incidentally, I was convinced Tiger couldn't win there, because his tremendous advantage in length was effectively no use to him. Whereas he was a stone cold certainty at St Andrews the previous year."

Joe captured the last of his 12 East titles in 1969 and he could hardly have hoped for a better postscript than to hand over the trophy to his son, Roddy. He did it with a score of 286, one year to the day after Joe's swansong. And Roddy was 19 at the time, the same age Joe had been when gaining his championship breakthrough.

"I was very proud of him that day and could see that he was already a better player than me, technically," said

Joe. "In fact, by the start of the 1970s, it seemed that all the young players were great strikers of the ball."

ROSSES POINT

Though the West of Ireland Championship was well established at the time, Joe's first visit to the Co Sligo links at Rosses Point was for the Irish Close of 1939. He remembers how the leading challengers, Jimmy Bruen, who was aiming for a third successive Close triumph, Cecil Ewing, John Burke and Joe Brown were each bought in the sweep for £50, whereas Gerry Owens went for something like £2 10s while Brennie Scannell and himself were effectively open to offers.

Along with Owens and Scannell, Joe stayed in bed-and-breakfast accommodation at the Point and on the practice days, they would have a quick snack before heading out to the course, whereas the more distinguished challengers would be enjoying a slap-up meal in the Hotel. Anyway, the weeding-out process eventually delivered this quarter-final line-up: Owens v Bruen; Scannell v Burke; Carr v Ewing and Roy McConnell v Brown.

The results were not quite what the local cognoscenti had anticipated. Hitting three-wood shots where his opponent was hitting eight irons, Owens still managed to beat Bruen; Scannell beat Burke, Joe beat Ewing and McConnell beat Brown. And after McConnell had defeated Joe in the semi-finals, he was eventually hammered 6 and 5 by Owens in the 36-hole final.

For 15 years after that, Gerry Owens took great delight in ribbing Joe that a champion wasn't worthy of the name until he had won his native title. And this didn't happen for Joe until 1954, when the Close was held at Carlow. By that stage, he had won no fewer that six of his 12 West of Ireland titles.

His early memories of the West were of weekends of joviality and mayhem. It didn't take him long to recognise such local characters as Frankie Kelly as people who were, in the immortal words of Myles na gCopaleen, to be avoided like the pledge. And, of course, it seemed that Burke and Ewing were rarely if ever beaten.

Played on what became an extended Easter weekend, it offered competitors and spectators – some of whose interest in golf was highly questionable – the opportunity of drinking after the clock had struck midnight on Good Friday, when almost the entire country was dry. It was a custom which prompted the Kilkenny golfer, Jim Murphy, to observe famously some years later: "You went down there feeling like Jack Nicklaus and returned home like Matt Talbot."

As an ambitious young player, however, Joe was most impressed by the golf course which he viewed as such an admirable test that he reckoned the best player would always win. But the weather could upset calculations and he could remember one qualifying round when he was 11 over par after only five holes and was lucky to get in with an 89.

"The success of the likes of Ewing and Burke at Rosses Point (they won 14 Wests between them in a 16-year span from 1930 to 1945), stemmed from the fact that they were excellent wind players," said Joe. "But I had no fear of them. I was just happy to be there, competing against the country's top players on one of our finest links courses. There are some great holes on the course, particularly the fourth, eighth, ninth, 14th and 17th. In fact, Rosses Point can boast some of the finest holes in world golf."

In his early years travelling there, he would get a lift from somebody and stay in lodgings. Later, when finances were more healthy, he stayed at the Hotel and later still, when he and Ewing became close friends, he would be a guest in Ewing's house in Rosses Point while the hospitality was reciprocated in Dublin.

There was a special appeal about the atmosphere around the Hotel, which offered wonderful camaraderie, a lively game of cards and no shortage of drink, though Joe was teetotal at that time. And for the serious competitors, it was the first test of a new season after dark, winter days of diligent practice. Normally, performances in the West were an accurate guide to how a player was likely to fare throughout the season.

After World War II, the growing prestige of the event and its importance in the amateur golfing calendar could be gauged from visits by such leading British practitioners as Guy Wolstenholme, Gerald Micklem and Sandy Saddler. And the prince of golf writers, Pat Ward-Thomas, was a particularly welcome visitor in 1962. That was when he wrote:

"For a long time I had promised myself a visit to Rosses Point, that fastness of golf far away to the edge of the Atlantic where, every Easter, the West of Ireland Championship is played. I had heard tell of its beauty, of its savagery when great winds roared from the ocean and I knew, of course, that on the links a rare genius for golf was bred within the vast and enduring figure of Cecil Ewing. The very names of Rosses Point and Ewing were compelling and I need no persuasion at any time to visit Ireland.

"Rarely has a golfing journey been so worth while. From the moment that Gerald Micklem and I left the bitter English spring behind, the days were filled with enchantment. Within the hour, it seemed, we were playing at Portmarnock with the blessing of Bradshaw's incomparable rhythm to inspire us on an afternoon of sunlit stillness. That evening, as twilight drew down to darkness, Carr drove us across the quiet, flat countryside into a world of warmth and humour and a beauty that far surpassed the expectation.

"There is a spell about the land; the welcome and kindness of its people, the eternal entertainment of Irish stories told in voices swift and liquid as a mountain stream, the miracle of bars that fill, although doors remain firmly locked; the growing enthusiasm for golf and, above all, the setting. Mention must be made of an enchanting place that inspired so much of the poetry of Yeats.

"No wonder Yeats loved this country so. One evening, we drove along peaceful lanes, where only a rare gleam of catkin and blackthorn and gorse bespoke the coming of summer, to see the Lake Isle of Innishfree. The waters were still and lonely in the soft grey light; all around the browns and greens of the hills rose to darkening mountains and the sense of solitude and peace was complete."

The scribe's journey was made all the more worthwhile that year by what proved to be a third successive triumph for Joe, equalling his achievement from 1946 to 1948. "Carr's victory was well nigh inevitable," commented Ward-Thomas. "He remains far away in a class by himself in Ireland and was never really hunted."

This was Joe's 11th victory, a broken run which had started with an 11 and 9 thrashing of his old friend, Scannell, in wretched conditions in the 1946 final. "I took no pleasure out of doing that to Brennie, but the conditions were particularly difficult for a man wearing glasses," he said.

Meanwhile, the auction sweep to which he referred prior to the 1939 Irish Close had become an established part of golfing life at the Point, especially in the West. In fact, it was officially sanctioned at a Council Meeting of the Co Sligo club in March 1942.

Needless to remark, when player valuations were made, Joe was no longer "thrown in" as an also ran.

LAHINCH

It should have been a splendid omen for challenges to follow. Yet the hole-in-one which Joe enjoyed at The Dell, on his competitive debut at Lahinch in 1946, did not culminate in the success he enjoyed at leading venues in the other three provinces. In fact, in the year in question, Joe was beaten in the final of the South by the incomparable John Burke, who outsmarted him on the 39th hole.

It was a time when Burke was master of all he surveyed at Lahinch and further afield. And we are told that Joe, the younger man by 22 years and with a youthful Paddy Skerritt caddying for him, was smashing the ball as far as 30 yards beyond the local hero. Yet a typical piece of Burke roguery brought him victory at the third tie hole.

The crowd was one of the biggest ever to watch an amateur final in this country and according to Joe, Burke used the spectators to his advantage at the short third. "He hit towards the back of the green knowing they'd stop the ball, which they did," he recalled. "And I made the mistake of coming up short in the bunker."

Joe won only three South of Ireland titles, in 1948, 1966 and 1969. And the most memorable of them was unquestionably the last, if only for a fascinating exchange which he had with his son, Roddy.

As it happened, Roddy failed to get through the qualifying stage that year whereas Joe was exempted, by way of acknowledging his status in the game. So, he decided to ask Roddy to caddie for him instead of his regular caddie, Big Tom. Before teeing off in the final against Noel Fogarty, Joe turned to his son and said: "I'll show you how to win a championship. I'll illustrate how important it is to win from the front. You don't win from behind. Noel is a good player and only once in a blue moon will you get a good player from behind."

Robert Burns's immortal words – "The best laid schemes o' mice an' men gang aft a-gley" – took on a fresh relevance for father and son after five holes of a memorable final had been completed. Instead of winning from the front, Joe had lost the third, fourth and fifth holes to be three down at that stage. "I remember Roddy looking at me as if I had two fecking heads," recalled Joe. "All I could think of saying to him was 'Look Roddy, the one thing about this situation is that I can't get them all back to level the match at one hole. Get one and he'll give you one; that's how it's done.'"

Such confidence was the product of priceless, past experiences in the heat of championship battle. Like the time at Lahinch where, in a match against the brilliant Waterford player Joe Brown, our hero was one down with one to play. And with the wind howling from the right, he proceeded to smash a huge drive down the long 18th. And fearing the worst, Brown felt obliged to go for the green in two, only to witness the dispiriting sight of his fairway-wood shot sailing into the army camp on the far side of the Liscannor road, comfortably out of bounds. And predictably, Joe went on to beat him on the 19th.

Roddy took up the story: "My memory of that final against Noel Fogarty is of J B taking me under his wing and teaching me everything he knew. But it became a matter of 'Don't do as I do; do as I say'. In a way, his greatness was that he didn't think or know what he was doing. Man-to-man combat was entirely instinctive to him, just as it was to Seve Ballesteros, when he was at the peak of his powers.

"From my experience as Seve's manager for some years, I could see that he and J B shared the basic matchplay strategy of mentally breaking their opponent. If you analyse this, it's impossible to do while one is concentrating on playing golf. Yet it became possible for them because it was instinctive. They simply stood on the first tee, looked their opponent in the eyes and straightaway thought of ways of seeking out his weakness.

"For instance, J B always said to me that matches were won in the first three holes. And he always believed himself to be two up on the first tee. Always. So, by his own reasoning, he was stone cold dead when he stood three down after five to Noel in the 1969 final.

"Yet, totally unruffled, he turned to me and said 'If I don't lose another hole I'll win by 2 and 1'. To make a statement like that, in such a matter-of-fact way, staggered me. No need to panic. He wouldn't go chasing his opponent. He'd just hang around and wait his chance.

"He had never told me this before, so I was left totally confused. But this was clearly the way his mind was working. Anyway, he won the ninth to be two down at the turn. Then he won the 10th. And though he made a half at the 13th, he was clearly disgusted at having three-putted when he could have drawn level. That lone, flash of anger carried to the next tee where he snatched the driver from my hand and smashed two shots to the front edge of the green at the long 14th, to square the match with a birdie four.

"We were still level going to the short 16th. Now, he had trained me to work to yardages, something he never did himself. He always played totally by instinct. Anyway, he wanted to hit a raking eight iron from 178 yards but I insisted there was a one-club wind against him. This is the stuff he had taught me, but he wasn't in the mood to listen.

"So he hit this hook which plugged in the face of the bunker. He then lifted a lump out of the face out of the trap with the power of his recovery, and when the ball emerged from the debris, he was about three feet inside Fogarty.

"Still, I couldn't see any grand plan and when Noel putted up five feet past, the Angelus Bell rang. In the eerie silence after a quiet prayer, J B proceeded to sink a 30-foot raker which slammed against the back of the cup. And, of course, the shock to Fogo's system was such that he proceeded to miss the putt. Then, at the next, J B two-putted from off the front of the green for a winning par after Fogo had pitched short. Match over."

Speaking separately about the match, after the passage of 33 years, father and son had contrasting memories. Roddy talked of the drive back to Dublin and asking Joe: "How did you know, Pop?" And how the reply came: "Sure, he left the door open." The fact that Fogarty had charged his putt on the 16th five feet past the hole, seemed to convince Joe that his own effort was holeable, even from 30 feet.

For his part, the father recalled: "When it was over, I turned and said: 'Now Roddy. That's the way not to win a championship.'" And at the thought of it, he gave a quiet laugh.

So, the South had been added to the East. But 1969 also had its downside, as far as Joe was concerned. In fact, it was only a few weeks after his Lahinch triumph that he found himself facing the bitter reality of something which hits most leading players at some stage of their career. Yet after 30 years of championship golf, he had thought he was home free.

"I'm talking about disqualification," said Joe, "and it happened to me in the Carrolls International at Woodbrook in 1969. That was when, in the opening round of the tournament, I signed for a wrong score – the first time this had happened to me." The problem occurred on Thursday, August 11th at the par-three ninth, where he had a four but his marker, Graham Henning, put him down for a three. As it happened, his total score of 73 was correct, but he failed to spot the error on his card and Dick Fell, the PGA tournament chief, had no option other than to impose the ultimate sanction.

Obviously it wasn't the end of the world, but he felt angry with himself and a bit embarrassed at having been caught in such a basic error, so late in his career.

Given the increasing demands of an expanding business and aware that he was some way past his golfing prime, Joe could see his appetite for the game begin to wane over the next two years. In fact, he said in 1971: "I'm in my 50th year and there comes a time when you have to decide that you have had enough. I have lost my enthusiasm for practice. I still go out and hit a few shots in the mornings and will play competitive golf for a while yet, but business has taken over. You know the feeling, having been at the top and then knowing that from there on, you can only go downhill."

Still, golf remained a hugely important part of his life. And in the company of friends, he would recall some wonderful stories of Lahinch and the South of Ireland. Like the one about the colourful Ennistymon butcher, Mick O'Loughlin, known as Mickey the Meat (pronounced mate), a wonderful character and a very useful player who gained successive "South" triumphs in 1937 and 1938.

"This particular story concerned a good friend of mine, Joe O'Reilly, who was a Dublin bus conductor and a member of Newlands," he said. "At the time of his meeting with O'Loughlin in the South, Joe was a bloody good player, off scratch. Anyway, when they were playing the old 12th hole, O'Loughlin hooked his tee-shot onto the beach and with the green hidden from view, he walked up to have a look at its location before walking back along the sand to his ball. He then played a wonderful recovery onto the green and holed it for a three.

"There was consternation, however, when O'Reilly promptly claimed the hole on the grounds that O'Loughlin had employed an outside agency, by using his own footprints in the sand as a line for his second shot to the green. But O'Loughlin insisted he had done nothing wrong and with the argument raging between them, they were brought in before the championship committee.

"The committee carefully considered the situation. Remember Mick was a great favourite around Lahinch and they wanted to ensure that he wouldn't be the victim of an injustice. And when they gently asked him if he had played over his own footprints when executing his second shot to the 12th, O'Loughlin admitted that he had. In that case, they said, he would have to be disqualified.

"Whereupon the outraged butcher retorted: 'Does he (O'Reilly) expect me to stick some seagull feathers up my arse and fly back to my f...ing ball?' Needless to remark, after reconsidering the matter, the committee found in O'Loughlin's favour."

Joe went on: "We had some wonderful fun at Lahinch. I knocked around with my usual pals, Kevin Hogan, John Deegan, Billy McMullan and John Cullen, but as a teetotaller, there were no late nights and no hangovers for me. And I soon realised the tremendous edge this gave me. I would imagine how a fellow must have been feeling on the first tee after a rough night. I knew he certainly wouldn't be as alert as I was and if the weather was rough, he was going to suffer, especially over the finishing holes.

"I didn't play Lahinch as often as I did the West or East. In fact, my success rate of three wins in the South was quite good for the number of appearances I made there, probably no more than eight in all. I loved the course, with its high dunes and wide open space, where you could hit the ball almost anywhere."

He then continued: "Royal Portrush, a wonderful second-shot course, was a vastly different proposition. And I had cause to become very attached to it after winning my third (British) Amateur there in 1960. But I never played in the North of Ireland Championship, probably because it generally clashed with the (British) Open in which I always played.

"I can assure my many friends in Northern Ireland that there was certainly nothing political about my decision. Such thoughts never entered my head. In fact, I received a number of death-threats for playing Walker Cup golf under the red lion of the R and A. Rather unpleasant terms like 'turncoat rat' were used, but they were wasting their time. I was never politically minded. I'm proud to be Irish but the notion of being part of a so-called British Isles team was never a problem for me."

Joe always saw himself purely as a golfer to whom no strings should have been attached. And whether it was a charity event or a national undertaking, he was always ready to make himself available as a leading figure of the Irish game. Like for a golfing spectacular which would form the sporting highlight of this country's three-week An Tostal festival in 1953.

Cross-country matches have been a feature of golf since the early part of the 19th century. And their fascination, certainly in the early days, lay in the fact that, generally, the number of strokes required to negotiate a particular "course" was greatly overestimated.

By the early years of the last century, however, the more astute observers reasoned that if a player were permitted to tee up for each shot, a simple calculation of allowing at least 150 yards for every shot would provide a fairly accurate estimate of his total. Granted, such calculations could hardly have been applied to the effort of Floyd Rood, who took one year and 114 days to play golf from coast to coast across the United States.

The irrepressible Rood took 114,737 strokes, including 3,511 penalty shots for the 3,397-mile course. But in the main, it was further acknowledged that if the player had to play the ball where it lay, "a sporting element thereupon enters the match, for unusual lies will cause uncertainties in scoring".

On Saturday April 18th 1953, the Irish newspapers carried a decidedly curious item in their weekend sports diaries. Listed under the heading "Golf" was an event called the Curragh Grand National. This became known otherwise as the Golden Ball Tournament and was hailed as the most original event of An Tostal.

Among other details was a spectacular prize of £1 million – about £50 million at today's values – for a hole in one. Barring divine intervention, there wasn't the remotest chance of this jackpot being collected, given that the competition involved 128 players in a cross-country match from the first tee at Cill Dara GC to the 17th green at the Curragh GC – a distance of five miles (8,800 yards).

Players could use only three clubs of their own choice and out-of-bounds was reduced to the minimum, for simplicity sake. Among the hazards to be negotiated were the main Dublin-Cork road and railway-line, furze bushes, trees surrounding the Curragh camp, the Curragh racecourse, hoofprints left by thoroughbred racehorses out exercising from nearby stables, Army tank tracks and about 150 telephone lines.

The trophy, comprising a standard-size golf-ball in gold on a black marble pillar beside the silver figure of a golfer on a green base, was designed by Captain Maurice Cogan of the Army GHQ, Dublin. And it was won with the remarkable score of 52 strokes – an average of 169 yards per stroke – by not only the longest hitter, but the country's most accomplished amateur of the time.

April 1953 was a distinctly productive month for Joe. On Tuesday the seventh, he captured the West of Ireland Championship at Rosses Point, beating Sutton club-mate Ray McInnally on the final green. Just over two weeks later, on Wednesday the 22nd, he claimed the best-gross award in the Tostal Open 72-hole tournament at Royal Dublin.

The Golden Ball came in between. "I remember I carried a spoon (three wood), a four iron and a short iron, probably an eight or nine," he recalled. "The four iron was specially made for me by the John Letters company and was probably the heaviest of its type, anywhere in the world. As the country's biggest hitter at that time, I suppose I would have been expected to win."

He went on: "You didn't know what was going to crop up from one shot to another. Looking back on it now, it was probably wide open to cheating and while there were some very tricky lies along the way, I can't remember taking any penalty drops."

In their issue of May 1953, the magazine Irish Golf reported: "The course was five miles but Joe Carr must have covered double that distance because, with the outstanding player's characteristic thoroughness, he insisted on walking every shot over the unfamiliar ground before he took a club in his hand.

"He lost three shots in the spinney behind the Camp but to use his own words, most of the time he was 'really burning them up with my spoon.' He must have been – 30 of his 52 strokes were spoon shots!" Still, he didn't have things all his own way insofar as he was three strokes behind with only a quarter of the course remaining.

That was when the leader, in attempting to carry two copses and a road, got caught in the trees and took 15 strokes to get out. For years afterwards, he claimed that a motor-car horn had hooted as he was at the top of his backswing, causing him to snatch the shot. Other players blamed ball-striking errors on the bleating of sheep.

There was also the competitor who spent 15 minutes in a concrete trench over 12 feet deep before eventually extricating the ball at a cost of 30 strokes. Meanwhile, a Government Minister of State and a prominent local racehorse owner decided to have a private competition between themselves. Their particular course was about two miles shorter than the official one and ended with a putt to a hole made in the lawn of the racehorse owner's house.

We are also informed that a number of competitors did not finish the course. Among these were three who stopped for "refreshments" and never reappeared. And in fading light, two competitors who had started six hours earlier, were seen to hobble disconsolately up to the finish with their golf shoes tied across their shoulders.

"Carr's National" and "Carr best in Curragh Grand National", the newspapers proclaimed the following morning. And he won it again in 1955. His friend and rival, Noel Fogarty, was the champion in 1954 and 1956, and when the event was staged for the last time in its original format in 1957, victory went, appropriately, to a four-handicap Army officer, Lt P J Cotter.

We are told that when Fogarty triumphed in 1954, he sank a 40-foot putt with a four-iron on the final green to tie, and then won a play-off. And a year later, a ball lodged in a moving truck whereupon the driver sportingly stopped so as to allow the player climb on board and hit a perfect stroke back onto the course.

As in most things, however, none of the subsequent stagings quite measured up to the first. And with Joe at the heart of the action one tended to expect something special. So it was that while most of his fellow competitors were taking a well-earned rest, the Sutton man, after a 10.0am start, set off immediately for Dublin.

His exertions allowed The Irish Times of Monday, April 20th to report on "An entertaining golf exhibition" at Elm Park. On the afternoon of his Curragh triumph, Carr partnered Philomena Garvey against Harry Bradshaw and Kitty MacCann before "a very large gallery".

Noting that our hero had come straight from the Curragh, he was reported to have taken "a little time to adjust himself to the narrower confines of the golf course", which would have explained a 2 and 1 defeat for himself and Garvey. At the end of it all, however, he had been centre-stage for one of the most remarkable days in the history of Irish golf.

Being centre-stage was, of course, pretty normal for Joe, certainly in this country. But by his own reckoning, the only time he was "made to feel like a star" was when he played Al Geiberger in a "Shell Wonderful World of Golf" match at Killarney in August 1964.

It was staged on the Mahony's Point course and with a viewing audience of 18 million in the US alone, the exercise gave an incalculable boost to the Kerry club. Christy O'Connor, who had been professional at Killarney until his move to Royal Dublin five years previously, was the original choice to face the American but on informing the organisers that he would be unable to take part, he was replaced by Joe.

The substitution of a professional by an amateur caused quite a rumpus in the Irish Professional Golfers' Association at the time, but with typical diplomacy, Carr anounced on television that his share of the prize fund would be donated to the IPGA Benevolent Fund. As things turned out, this proved to be the substantial sum of $2,500.

Though he has his own videotape of the match, Joe was delighted that the public had the opportunity of viewing it two years ago, when it was screened by Sky Sports. "I think I showed I could play a bit back then," he said. "The match lasted two days but it was a great experience. They made a big fuss of Al and myself, taking us into make-up each time before the cameras started rolling."

Geiberger, then in his fifth year as a professional, was a month short of his 27th birthday and had won the Ontario Open in 1962 and the Almaden Open a year later. But the best was yet to come, notably his USPGA

Championship win in 1966 and a tour record 59 in the Memphis classic on June 10th 1977.

Power-hitting from Joe was very much in evidence at the long, 478-yard 13th where he produced the highlight of the match. Granted, the drive of 245 yards was decidedly moderate by his prodigious standards, but even Geiberger gasped at the majesty of the second shot. With another driver, Joe guided the ball between the approach bunkers and onto the green. And he then sank the 27-foot putt for an eagle three.

"That was one of the best shots of the day," enthused Gene Sarazen, the celebrity half of a commentary team with George Rogers. To which Joe replied at the time: "If you can't hit a drive off the fairways over here, you're dead."

Using the small ball, Joe's drives were sometimes over 270 yards and comfortably outside the American. So, it was ironic that he should have been deprived of victory by under-hitting at the celebrated, short 18th. For the 202-yard shot with a breeze gently brushing the hole from right to left, off the lake, Joe was short with an over-ambitious five iron. It meant Geiberger's par was sufficient to tie the match at 74 each – level par.

Still, everybody went away happy, including the now defunct IPGA.

Chapter Five
A Biennial Love-Affair

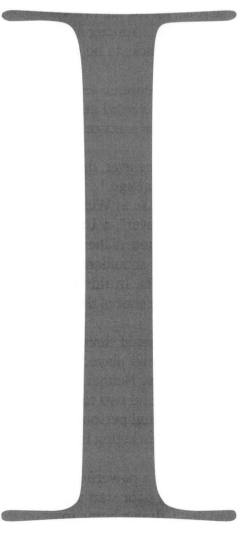

In a sense, Joe was a child of the Walker Cup in that it was launched in 1922, the year of his birth. He was only six months old when Bobby Jones was dominating the inaugural staging at The National GC on Long Island which, interestingly, would later become Joe's favourite course in the US. Perhaps destiny was already at work!

From the experience of 11 Walker Cup appearances – 10 as a player, with the additional honours of being captain in 1965 and playing-captain in 1967 – it is small wonder that Joe views it as the source of wonderful friendships. And he insisted: "I considered it to be the acme of achievement for an amateur player to make the Walker Cup team."

His was a time when the British and Irish players were essentially career amateurs. In fact, prior to 1960, Norman Drew was the only Walker Cup representative from this side of the Atlantic to turn professional, though greatly-enhanced financial rewards have since made it a common occurrence.

Joe's attachment to what grew into a wonderful, biennial celebration of the amateur game, is probably best reflected in his enduring affection for a black and white photograph of himself, driving off the first tee at St Andrews on the occasion of his Walker Cup debut in 1947. And he made it a memorable occasion by beating the reigning US Amateur champion, Ted Bishop, by the comfortable margin of 5 and 3 in the second day's singles.

Cecil Ewing, who partnered Joe to defeat in the top foursomes against Bishop and Robert "Skee" Riegel, was the only other Irishman on the team due to the withdrawal of the 1946 British Amateur champion, Jimmy Bruen, with a wrist injury which would plague the remainder of his career. But for the next staging at Winged Foot, in 1949, the Irish would be present in strength, with Joe, Bruen, Ewing and the newly-crowned Amateur champion, Max McCready, in the line-up.

By way of preparation, they spent about five days at Sunningdale where Brigadier Critchley, father of Sky Sports golf commentator and former Walker Cup player, Bruce, proved to be a genial host. And the quality of their play against professional opponents at Royal Mid Surrey, carried promise of a strong performance in the US. Then, in the week Joe's first-born son, Jody, came into the world, the team sailed for New York aboard the luxury liner, Queen Elizabeth.

"Jody's arrival and the fact that I was about to experience America for the first time as one of four Irishman in the team, obviously made it a marvellous occasion for me," Joe recalled. "Among my memories of the voyage across was the unbelievable humidity, which caused Max McCready's grey slacks to be stained with perspiration most of the time.

"But if conditions aboard ship were warm, they were as nothing compared with the heat-wave which confronted us on arrival in New York. We were told it was one of the worst on record and it lasted until three days before the match, during which time we were sweltering. Not surprisingly, our practice sessions were very limited during our first week at Winged Foot.

"By the time the Americans arrived for their three days' practice, however, there was a lovely, cool breeze. And while this raised our spirits, we were already at a considerable disadvantage."

As it happened, the British and Irish players stayed in the clubhouse at Winged Foot for what proved to be a decidedly ill-fated venture. "Carr is a brilliant rather than a sound player", a US scribe wrote after Joe had partnered Ronnie White to victory in the top foursomes over Ray Billows and Willie Turnesa.

The same writer went on: "Immense responsibility fell upon Carr's shoulders, since his partner was playing so magnificently that he alone could lose the match by destructive shots. In this match he played with measured steadiness and fine judgement and was responsible for perhaps the best shot of the morning, with a prodigious slice round the trees from the tee at the dog-leg eighth hole.

"Playing with great confidence, White and Carr forged ahead and stood three up at lunch. If they had been six up it would have been no injustice. In the afternoon Turnesa and Billows played much better but it was now that White showed his greatness and Carr his fine match-playing qualities. Neither winked an eyelid at the brilliant recoveries made by their opponents and they finally won by three up and two to play."

As a general observation, the writer concluded: "Carr's open and vital personality attracts crowds for the sheer excitement of watching him play. And whatever the circumstances, his engaging Irish manner, combined with a love of battle, endears him to spectators."

White was to become the only singles winner in a match in which a powerful American side coasted to a 10-2 victory: Joe effectively lost his singles through an uncharacteristically poor start which saw him cover the opening nine in 42 strokes. "The overall strength of the opposition was really driven home to us on that occasion," said Joe.

"To all intents and purposes, the Americans were full-time amateurs, either as college players or as independently wealthy businessmen such as Frank Stranahan, whereas we were all weekend golfers. The situation caused quite a deal of discussion between the USGA and the R and A as to whether the future of the competition might be in jeopardy, but essentially, we had little choice other than to accept it as a fact of golfing life."

He went on: "A considerable plus, however, was having Laddie Lucas as our captain. Though neutrals would have viewed him as a typical RAF type and terribly British, Laddie was a special guy in every respect."

As a keen follower of golf, Brigadier Critchley travelled to Winged Foot for the matches. And as his involvement with the White City greyhound stadium would suggest, he was not averse to the odd flutter. So it was that while at Winged Foot, he arranged a challenge match between the top British and Irish foursomes pairing and professionals Craig Wood and Tommy Armour.

Incidentally, before emigrating to the US, Armour was runner-up at Royal Portrush in the 1919 Irish Amateur Open, a title which Joe had already captured in 1946 and would win on three further occasions. But while the illustrious "Silver Scot" went on to win the US Open, USPGA and the British Open titles, he was 56 at the time of the challenge. Wood, his close friend, was 48 and the resident professional at Winged Foot, where he was succeeded by Claude Harmon. He also held the unwanted distinction of having been runner-up in the four "major" championships – the 1933 British Open, the 1934 USPGA Championship, US Masters of 1934 and 1935 and the 1939 US Open. But for the record, he broke through to win the US Masters in 1941.

"I gather the Brigadier had a considerable amount of money on Ronnie and myself and we delivered the goods, beating Armour and Wood by one hole in a tremendous match," recalled Joe. "I have to say that Ronnie White was one of the finest players we ever had. Afterwards, Armour invited the two of us to his golf-equipment factory in New York, where we could take our pick from what were then the leading irons in the world. Needless to say, we couldn't accept the offer which would have been a breach of our amateur status." As a footnote to that match, Armour and Wood both died in 1968.

One of the more interesting problems which Lucas faced on that occasion stemmed from an unexpected development in Canada the previous autumn. That was when the Taoiseach, John A Costello, took most people by surprise by declaring the Irish Free State to be a Republic, which effectively put an end to the country's membership of the British Commonwealth. Incidentally, R and A plans for the British Amateur at Portmarnock in May 1949, were already well advanced by that stage, which explains the only staging outside the UK of the world's premier amateur championship.

Anyway, the British and Irish skipper was clearly conscious of these political developments, especially with four Irishmen in his team. So he instructed them: "If the correspondents (media) ask you anything about Ireland and Britain, don't answer them. Have no discussion on the matter, good, bad, or indifferent." As it happened, there was no problem. In fact with a large Irish-American membership of Winged Foot, the hosts took an entirely positive view of the situation and local officials were delighted to have such a strong Irish presence in the visiting team.

Six years later, as guest speaker at a luncheon of the Dublin Rotary Club in the Royal Hibernian Hotel, Joe referred to his team captain's instruction in a presentation titled "The Game of Golf." He told his audience: "When myself and the other Irish members of the team were asked what we thought of the English members, we replied that they were extremely nice fellows. And when we were asked what we thought of partition, we said nothing."

As it happened, Lucas characterised the wonderful friendships which became a by-product of Walker Cup selection. "I have very fond memories of Laddie, who was a wonderful letter-writer," he said. "In fact, I got a lot of letters from him, right up to his death a few years ago."

Lucas was, in fact, born in the clubhouse of Prince's GC in Kent, where his father was the co-founder. This is the course which contributed an all-time classic phrase to golfing literature as a result of being used for bombing practice during World War II. So outraged was Lord Brabazon that he stormed: "My God! It's like throwing darts at a Rembrandt."

In the context of Prince's, it is also interesting to note that when Lucas was an RAF fighter pilot during World War II, he used local knowledge to admirable effect. Recalling a much-loved tale, Joe said: "When his Spitfire was hit during the Battle of Britain and he was searching desperately for a place to land, he told us he could see the window where he was born. He then headed for the first fairway at Prince's, which he missed, as usual. And he also missed the second and several others until eventually he ditched the plane in a marsh."

Lucas's own recollections described how images of childhood came flooding back in those critical moments. "....suddenly through the haze, away to the North, past Deal and St George's, I could see the faint outline of Prince's Clubhouse.

"It's prophetic, I thought. I'll try and stretch the glide, dead stick, and put down on the old, flat, first fairway, just past my nursery window. True to all known form, I missed the first fairway, the second, the sixth and the eighth and finished up, out of bounds, in the marsh at the back of the ninth green."

According to Joe, all of the players delighted in that story because their captain, a golfing left-hander, was known in the States as "the Southpaw Sprayer" due to a penchant for hitting his ball in all directions during the Walker Cup at Pine Valley in 1936. So inaccurate was he that when Henry Longhurst, who partnered him in practice, shouted to their caddies "Watch it! Watch it!", he received the immortal rejoinder: "Boy, you can't watch 'em. You just gotta listen for 'em."

The 1949 Walker Cup was also the occasion when the visiting players went on to Oak Hill to play in the US Amateur Championship ... and got involved in what became known as acorn diplomacy. And during practice for the event, the American, Skee Riegel, and Joe both holed in one on the short sixth on the same day. The following morning's headline in the local paper read: "Game's hotting up ... Here's a couple of aces."

As for the acorns: Dr John R Williams, the club president had the idea that the visitors should all take some home with them from one of the great oaks at Oak Hill. And the upshot was that they were sent through the British Embassy in Washington, the idea being that each British and Irish player would plant acorns at their home club.

Lucas remarked later: "This bloody great sackful of acorns turned up in my office and I had to put them around the UK. I sent handfuls to the clubs represented by the players – Cork (Bruen), Co Sligo (Ewing) and Sutton (Carr) in Eire and to Hendon, Hoylake, Parkstone, Royal Norwich, Sandy Lodge (his own club), Sunningdale and Wildernesse in England."

He later admitted: "I really don't know what went wrong but so far as I am aware, there are only two left (oak trees) in existence. We have one at my club, Sandy Lodge, and there is another at Wildernesse, where Gerald Micklem was a member."

Joe said: "I must admit that I have no recollection of the acorns which were supposed to be planted at Sutton, except that there's no evidence of them there today."

By 1951, Joe was widely regarded as a veteran of Walker Cup combat while his regular championship victories made him almost an automatic choice on the side. As it happened, all four Irish players from the Winged Foot side were retained for this latest challenge at Royal Birkdale.

In view of their success in 1949, it was no surprise that skipper Raymond Oppenheimer again paired Joe with White in the top foursomes. There, they halved with Stranahan and Bill Campbell before giving real hope to the home side by winning their singles matches at two and three in the order: McCready was at number one, wherein lay an interesting tale.

Joe recalled: "On the eve of that match, Frank (Stranahan) came over to me and said 'I'm at number two and I hope I get you tomorrow, Joe,'. And he went on to tell me that the Americans had Sam (Urzetta) at number one and Charlie (Coe) at number three. And he didn't stop there. In fact he went right down the list to number eight.

"Now, I must admit that I wasn't averse to a bit of skulduggery in those days. Anyway, upstairs in the team room I saw Raymond scribbling. 'Is the team not in yet, Raymond?' I asked him. And when he indicated that it wasn't, I proceeded to tell him that I knew the American order. Whereupon he exclaimed: 'What? Sit down there and write it out.' So we got a few changes done and I got Frank, while Ronnie White was pencilled in at number three against Charlie Coe. Funny old world, isn't it?"

Still, the US retained the trophy by a comfortable, 6-3 margin, with three matches halved.

When Americans come across somebody who is not especially bright upstairs, they like to suggest that he wouldn't be the sharpest tool in the shed. From Joe's experience, Stranahan would have fitted comfortably into that mould. "I always considered myself to be a very bad bunker player and when I had beaten Frank by 2 and 1, he was kind enough to give me a bunker lesson," said Joe. "And when I returned to Sutton after the Walker Cup, I practised what he had taught me for about a week. And my technique improved no end.

"As things turned out, the Amateur was played at Porthcawl that year and who did I meet in the fifth round, only Frank. And I got up and down eight times out of bunkers to beat him. Whereupon he stormed: 'I'll never do that again. That's the last time I'm ever gonna teach anybody anything.'"

Despite the uneven nature of these Walker Cup battles, Joe succeeded in being admirably optimistic before each new assignment.

He recalled: "The captain would normally write to his panel on January 1st and the gist of his instructions would be 'Now boys, I'm leaving it largely to you but, if I was in your part of the country, I might try doing such-and-such. But will you, in any case, write to me and let me know how you propose getting your game to high pitch by next August.'"

Dedication to practice was something Joe never needed to be reminded about. So it was that before departing what was then Collinstown Airport (Dublin) for London, en route to the US for the 1953 matches at the Kittansett Club, Marion, Massachusetts, he assured the Irish media: "Despite America's 10-2 win in the last Walker Cup competition over there, I expect we will win this time, because we have a much younger team than our opponents."

He added: "I also expect to do well in the US and Canadian individual championships." The only other Irish player in the team on that occasion was Norman Drew and this would be his first step towards gaining the unique distinction for a British or Irish player of becoming both a Walker Cup and a Ryder Cup representative. In the event, their first stop was the Canadian Amateur Championship in Montreal.

Before leaving this country, it was announced that while in the US, Joe would meet the Mayor of Boston and other civic leaders in that most Irish of American cities. And he would act as an "Irish ambassador" in a drive for funds for the Cerebral Palsy National Association of Ireland.

For the matches at Kittansett, which was located on an exposed piece of land extending into Buzzards Bay, Joe stayed with a family of Irish-Americans. Such arrangements were common at a time when the R and A welcomed any opportunity of economising on such potentially expensive trips. "So we stayed in people's houses – the Scots with Scottish descendants and the Irish with the Irish and so on," said Joe. "It was the most marvellous place, right on the 17th green, which meant we could practise at night-time. And it being located in Cape Cod, I remember going out on a boat and fishing for marlin and the like. Fish I'd never seen before.

"Tony Duncan, a Welshman, was the captain that year and he was something of a disciplinarian: bed by 10.30 and that sort of thing. And when he spoke, you stood to attention for fear of being sent home."

That was the famous or arguably infamous occasion when, in the third foursomes on the opening day, Jim Wilson and Roy MacGregor were opposed by the formidable American pairing of Jimmy Jackson and Gene Littler. Having lost the opening hole, Jackson was walking along the second fairway when he realised he was carrying 16 clubs. He had travelled from Missouri with an extra brassie and wedge which he had forgotten to take out of his bag.

Understandably disconsolate, Jackson honourably reported the transgression to the referee, expecting instant disqualification. Indeed the possibility of leniency never crossed his mind, given some well-known precedents in the US. The most notable of these occurred in 1938, shortly after the introduction of the 14-club rule there. It involved no less a figure than Stranahan who was promptly disqualified after his caddie volunteered the information that his master was carrying 16 clubs during the Dixie Amateur Tournament.

It was ironic that it should have been Duncan, a British army colonel and noted stickler for detail, who got the Americans off the hook. Having indicated to Jackson that there might be a way of avoiding disqualification, Duncan mustered the support of Wilson and MacGregor. He then made an impassioned plea to USGA official, Isaac Grainger, that Jackson and Littler be allowed play on.

According to Duncan, if Britain and Ireland were to win, it should be by the superiority of their golf. The upshot was that the tournament's executive committee were brought together from different parts of the course and having hastily discussed the issue, they decided to apply what is now Rule 33-7, which states: "A penalty of disqualification may in exceptional cases be waived, modified or imposed if the Committee considers such action warranted."

On being informed that his plea had been accepted, Duncan made the memorable comment: "Britannia waives the rules." So it was that despite the imposition of a two-hole penalty, Jackson and Littler went on to win their match by 3 and 2. And by way of revenge for his defeat in the final of the British Amateur at Hoylake earlier that year, Harvie Ward proceeded to beat Joe by 4 and 3 in the top singles. And while overall American dominance continued, by a margin of 9-3, Joe observed: "The fact that there wasn't a murmur of complaint from our guys about the decision to let Jackson off the hook, speaks volumes for the sportsmanship of the Walker Cup."

Long before he became the voice of American golf on the CBS Network, Ken Venturi played in that match and teamed up with Urzetta to beat Joe and White in the top foursomes. Coe, the 1949 US Amateur champion also played. And after winning a second US Amateur in 1958, he and Joe would have a stirring tussle in the Walker Cup at Muirfield a year later.

That was in the top singles in which Joe led by one hole with six to play, when eager spectators temporarily got a little out of control. "In those days, I had a very old, hickory-shafted putter," said Joe, "and in the stampede, the shaft was broken by a young schoolboy named Hogan, of all names. It meant I had to putt the remaining holes with a three iron and lo and behold, I proceeded to sink a 15-footer on the 35th green for the match!"

Joe added: "Whether it was out of a sense of guilt or something, the lad Hogan kept in touch with me afterwards. And he'd always say: 'Remember me, Joe? I'm the lad who broke your putter.'"

In the meantime, the 1957 matches had been played at Minikhada GC in Minneapolis. That was where Joe stayed with a man named Totton Heffelfinger, and where he got to know Michael Bonallack for the first time.

He recalled: "Gerald Micklem was captain that year and I considered it most unusual that he didn't pick Michael in the team, given the great regard he had for his game. But at 23, Michael was young and up and coming and I suppose Gerald thought it better to rely on established form away from home.

"Tot Heffelfinger, of course, was the head man in Minneapolis. As far as I can recall, he was in the mining business and was also president of the USGA in 1952-'53. And I recollect that the president of Coca-Cola was a member of the host club and he had a special house there for his children, down at the bottom of his garden.

"Reid Jack, who won the Amateur Championship at Formby that year, was in our side. So was Doug Sewell, who followed the lead given by Norman Drew and Guy Wolstenholme as British and Irish Walker Cup players to turn professional, which he did after winning the English Amateur title for a second time in 1960. Later in his career, incidentally, he was the club professional at Ferndown.

"After Formby, we had the Home Internationals at Royal Co Down where Gerry Owens was the Irish captain, and I remember ribbing Reid by saying that I didn't think much of Amateur champions. And I beat him 6 and 5. Then he beat Guy Wolstenholme and Wolstenholme proceeded to hammer me. So much for form in amateur golf. But Reid was a very fine player. In fact he was two strokes ahead of the eventual winner, Gary Player, after 54 holes of the Open Championship at Muirfield in 1959 before eventually finishing equal fifth. And a year later he was 16th in the Centenary Open."

By that stage, the British and Irish players noted the arrival of a formidable foe on the Walker Cup scene. Jack Nicklaus made his debut in the '59 matches in which he had a 5 and 4 win in the anchor singles. This was against Dickson Smith, the 41-year-old Scot who also had a marvellous finish of tied fifth in the 1957 British Open at St Andrews. These amateur achievements were not surpassed until 1998 when Justin Rose was tied fourth behind Mark O'Meara at Royal Birkdale. In the event, Joe admitted: "I didn't appreciate the full extent of Jack's talent until I played him in the Walker Cup two years later."

It was a tradition among captains that the first six or seven placings in the singles order were more or less automatic. But for the anchor position, a captain generally picked one of his own, a man he knew he could rely upon. In other words a Scot would pick a Scot, an Englishman would pick an Englishman and an Irish captain, if the opportunity arose, would probably put his faith in a compatriot.

Contrary to tradition, the word at Muirfield was that Smith would be great in a tight finish with an American, even though the skipper, Gerald Micklem, was English. But according to Joe, the captain's confidence wasn't shared by Oppenheimer, who was chairman of selectors. "The problem is," said the chairman caustically, "that he'll never get into a tight finish." And so it proved to be.

Deane Beman, who won the British Amateur that year, was also in the 1959 team and he and Nicklaus were there again for the matches at Seattle GC 1961. That was when Beman struck up a close friendship with Joe. "When Deane came on visits to Dublin, we'd take him out to Irish ballad sessions which he loved," he said. "And he developed a particular affection for the bodhran (a traditional Irish drum), so we sent him one when he went back to the States."

Later, when Beman was attempting to resurrect his golfing career, he came to play in the Irish Open in 1986 and '87 at Portmarnock. Recalling the 1986 tournament, Joe spoke of having dinner with him in the St Stephen's Green club where, to his astonishment, Beman enquired: "What price am I in the Irish Open?"

"I tried to tell him that he was no longer competitive and that he hadn't a snowball's chance in hell," said Joe. "I told him I'd bet my house, car, business, everything I owned, against him winning. That was a time when Seve Ballesteros, Bernhard Langer and Sandy Lyle were dominating European golf.

"Yet he remained utterly determined and I must admit I was surprised and delighted when he shot rounds of

74,79,77,80 to finish tied 68th in difficult conditions. It showed the guts of the man. And he returned to Portmarnock the next year but withdrew after an opening 76. I admired him greatly as commissioner of the US Tour, which he ruled with an iron fist."

Joe went on: "When the second Eisenhower Trophy was played at Merion in 1960, I had bets of a dollar a shot with three members of the American team, Bruce Dudley, Nicklaus and Beman. And I remember sitting down, utterly dejected when the whole thing was over. When Ben Hogan won the 1950 US Open at Merion, his lowest round was 69 and he shot an aggregate of 287. Now, only 10 years later, Jack beat it by something like 17 or 18 shots (it was 18), carding rounds of 66 like they were level par.

"The upshot of it was that I had to pay out for 99 shots, that's how far I was behind the three of them. By way of compensation, however, we played poker afterwards and let's just say they hadn't the same skills at poker as they had earlier displayed on the golf course!"

As things turned out, Joe was to receive serious grief from Nicklaus a year later. "After I had played the American champion, Ted Bishop, on my Walker Cup debut at St Andrews in 1947, I was either one or two in the singles order on four occasions," he said. "Eventually in 1961, I said to the captain, Charles Lawrie, 'Put me down a bit in the order and I'll teach one of these young fellows a lesson.' So he put me at number seven and I got hammered 6 and 4 by Nicklaus."

Meanwhile, there was a change to what was to become the current Walker Cup format, for the 1963 matches at Turnberry. The shorter matches worked to the advantage of the home side, albeit in a 14-10 defeat. And the gap disappeared completely, two years later in Baltimore, where Joe captained Britain and Ireland to the first tied match on either side of the Atlantic.

"In my view, Baltimore was a very significant milestone, despite the fact that we were well beaten at home, two years later," said Joe. "None of the golf writers bothered to travel there because the results had been so poor. But when we arrived home, they were all there to give us a staggering welcome. And we proved it was possible to compete with the Americans on equal terms."

He went on: "To be captain of a Walker Cup team requires experience, especially as a player at that level. This is necessary if you're to be an effective motivator, which is the most difficult thing to do. But I felt it was just as important that the players expressed their ideas, as it was for me to tell them what I thought. Finally, you've got to get players to stick together and play for each other, yet retain the individual pride that is going to deliver a singles win.

"The 1961 skipper, Charles Lawrie, was a fine captain and a great character. I was always joking him about his age, though in fact we were of similar vintage. And I had a bet of £100 that I would outlast him. And then thought no more about it. As it happened, when he died sometime in the mid 1970s, I got this cheque for £100 in the post. It was from the executor of his will. My immediate thought was: 'Thank God I didn't go first because I didn't think of making any such arrangement.'" In the event, Joe gave the money to charity.

"Charles happened to have the ear of the R and A at a time when, as I've indicated, they didn't like spending too much money, for the simple reason that they didn't have much of it to spend. And for Turnberry in 1963, he was the first to get the players over for squad training the previous week. It made a tremendous difference, especially in establishing the right foursomes partnerships."

Two years later, Joe was leading a line-up cast in the role of perennial whipping boys, having had a succession of defeats since their last victory at St Andrews in 1938, when Jimmy Bruen was in the team. As was the case in 1938, Joe instinctively put his faith in the youngsters, players like Peter Townsend, Ronnie Shade and Clive Clark.

And he had Gordon Clark, who won the British Amateur at Ganton the previous year. Then there was the experience of Michael Bonallack.

Following on the concession made to Lawrie for Turnberry, Joe was permitted to bring the players together for a week's practice before they left for Maryland. And looking at an American team which included such old hands as Bill Campbell, Billy Joe Patton and Dale Morey, he sensed his players had an edge. In fact, the Americans were an average of seven years a man older.

Typically, Joe breezed into their locker-room on one of the practice days and enquired: "Is there room for another senior in here? Can I play?" Which didn't go down too well. Before battle commenced, one of the British officials, G Alec Hill, announced grandly: "We shall strive to eat the cherry in two bites over the next two days. If we fail, we will pick up and try again in two years."

Joe's memories of the clash are that while "our lads obviously played really well to get a tied match, it was probably not a very good American side, certainly not by the standards of the fifties and early sixties. My representative career ended in 1969 and by that stage, several Americans weren't far behind me, as far as sell-by dates were concerned.

"As things worked out, we should have won. I remember Clive Clark playing the 17th in the last match out against Mark Hopkins, who had been two up with three to play. Clive holed a 15-foot putt to win the 16th and the match looked like going all square at the next, where the American shanked his drive into trees. But Hopkins made a three from nowhere to halve the hole, which meant he was still one up going down the last.

"The excitement was immense. I imagine it might have been different had we won. But it certainly gave me enormous satisfaction to see Clive sink a 35-foot putt for a birdie on the last to finish all square with Hopkins. So, the match was tied at 11-11 – the first time it had happened since the event was instituted in 1922."

He added: "Looking back on those heady days, I find myself remembering the wonderful hospitality we experienced in Baltimore. We were all given courtesy cars, big Buicks. Brigadier Brickman, secretary of the R and A, was there and our hotel was about 15 miles from the course. And you know the situation in the States whereby you can't seem to get off a turnpike once you're on it. Anyway, by the end of the trip, Brickman had been christened the Mad Brigadier, because of his cavalier attitude to the American rules of the road."

In 1967, Joe was actually playing-captain for his Walker Cup swansong. That was at Royal St George's, where Bill Campbell was the hero of the American side, beating Shade twice in the top singles. He also won both his foursomes matches to emerge with a 100 per cent record – four out of four. And as Joe bade farewell to the dominant experience of his golfing life, he mused: "Wouldn't it be marvellous if Roddy could follow in my footsteps."

So it was that the first step was taken towards a Carr family involvement in a 12th Walker Cup. Roddy went to South Africa to see Gary Player, who had always been a good friend of Joe's since they first met during the 1950s when Player was little more than a schoolboy on his first trip to Europe.

Ensuing correspondence between the two men had Joe asking Player to give Roddy all the help he could. By way of reply, Player assured his long-time friend that he would, before adding: "Where did Roddy get a swing like that?" In a further letter, Joe issued the terse instruction: "Don't try and teach him your swing. I want him to play in the Walker Cup, not the Curtis Cup."

Player clearly looked on helping Roddy as an opportunity to discharge a debt of gratitude which he hadn't forgotten. On the occasion of Joe's captaincy of the R and A, Player said: "Joe Carr is a gentleman of gentlemen. When I first arrived in Britain as a nobody, he was always very kind. And what a striker of the ball!

"A family man, Joe always had a keen sense of humour and made a wonderful contribution to the game we all love. He fully deserves his high position with the R and A."

Roddy also went to Jamaica around that time and he and his father later spent a month together at Sotogrande. This was Joe's first visit to the splendid parkland layout designed by Robert Trent Jones Snr at the western end of Spain's Costa del Sol, and it impressed him enormously. Father and son would rise at 9.0 every morning and after breakfast, would hit about 1,000 balls. They would then play in the afternoon.

With further assistance from John Jacobs, who had helped Joe modify his own method more than 10 years earlier, Roddy became a much-improved player. And after victories in the East of Ireland Strokeplay Championship of 1970 and the matchplay West of Ireland the following Easter, he earned selection as the only Irishman on the 1971 Walker Cup team at St Andrews. Incidentally, it is interesting to note that when the GUI issued their list of Irish scratch golfers for the 1971 season, father and son were on it, Joe and Roddy Carr, as one of the great family achievements in golf. But there was more to come.

"You can imagine what a wonderful thrill it was for me, especially to have him playing under the captaincy of Michael Bonallack," said Joe. "And that the matches should be on the Old Course where, as things turned out, history was repeated and the Walker Cup was won for a second time after a lapse of 33 years. We went absolutely wild."

He went on: "It was a great, great, great, great victory. At a stroke, on the 50th anniversary, it resurrected a wonderful competition that was in danger of going down the drain. And for me, it wiped out all the disappointments myself and my Walker Cup colleagues had suffered down the years, home and away. It was an occasion for reminiscing with old friends, a time for golfers to stand alongside their counterparts in rugby and other sports, as successful competitors internationally.

"I remember that in the moment of victory, the applause went on for about five or six minutes. The players were in tears. Actually now that I remember it, Michael (Bonallack) was in tears. He talked about his wonderful, wonderful team and how they had won despite him. Which, of course, wasn't true. He was a great captain who got the very best from his players. They looked up to him because of his marvellous record in the game. "

Then Joe added with a chuckle: "Of course there was a downside to it all. I remember when Roddy and I played in the Antlers (father and son foursomes at Royal Mid Surrey) in 1969 and won it, the captain in his presentation speech made a point of saying how wonderful it was to be giving the trophy to Joe Carr and his son. Later, after the 1971 Walker Cup, we won it again. And this time the captain talked about how nice it was to have Roddy Carr and his father back with them."

For Roddy, memories of 1971 had to do with how his father's thorough approach to golf "was reflected in the way he helped me." He went on: "I was extremely grateful for effectively having everything handed to me on a plate. There were times, before I won my two championships, when it was difficult to handle the baggage that went with being Joe Carr's son, but overall, the benefits far outweighed the negatives.

"Yet, during the Walker Cup I was anxious that he would keep out of the way, in case the sight of him would heighten the tension. The knowledge that he was actually present was enough for me." As things turned out, Roddy was dormie two against Jim Simons but lost the treacherous 17th only to recover brilliantly with a birdie at the last, where he holed a 30-foot putt. It was a wonderful effort, given that his approach had landed almost exactly where Doug Sanders had been a year previously when three putts, including one of less than three feet, effectively handed the British Open to Nicklaus.

"As I stood over that putt, I bowed my head, said a 'Hail Mary' and beseeched the Almighty to guide the ball into the hole," Roddy recalled. And when it dropped, he was rewarded with the biggest prize of all – a hug from his father.

"It was the first time in my life that I could remember him hugging me," he said. "Years later, when Sam Torrance secured the winning point for Europe in the 1985 Ryder Cup at The Belfry, his father, Bob, hugged him for the first time. And I was fascinated to discover that Sam felt the same way about it as I had done.

"Both men were from the same, conservative school which apparently ordained that you didn't show your emotions. As Sam said, the hug he got from Bob was better than the Ryder Cup win. And I felt the same way."

It meant that the achievement of setting a British and Irish record of three and a half Walker Cup points out of four, paled for Roddy in comparison with the demonstrative approval of his illustrious father. Which was why, on that occasion of unprecedented joy, he walked off the 18th green in tears.

Chapter Six
The Right Stuff

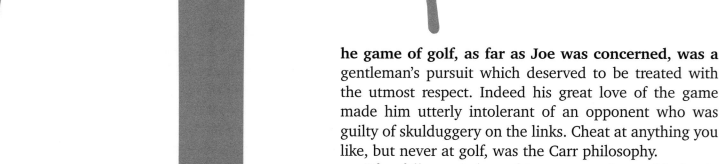

he game of golf, as far as Joe was concerned, was a gentleman's pursuit which deserved to be treated with the utmost respect. Indeed his great love of the game made him utterly intolerant of an opponent who was guilty of skulduggery on the links. Cheat at anything you like, but never at golf, was the Carr philosophy.

"If a fellow tried anything on me, it would simply make me all the more determined to do him," he said. "I'd give it all I'd got, without letting him get under my skin."

He went on: "In this regard, my upbringing at Portmarnock was a wonderful advantage. I never felt the game owed me anything, so I didn't harbour resentments. Later in life, this absence of any emotional baggage could be attributed to the fact that there was probably nothing I pursued which I didn't accomplish, at least to some degree.

"My experience has been that the breaks even themselves out in golf. Bad luck doesn't pile up, waiting to

crush you." Mind you, Joe would also concede that such a philosophy was facilitated greatly by unparalleled success, certainly in this part of the world.

In the event, it is interesting that the members of Portmarnock GC, who would have been the elite of Dublin society, helped him to become a wonderful mixer: the class divisions which one tends to associate with golf, didn't seem to exist as far as the Carrs were concerned. This was especially evident in the use of first names.

They treated Joe's parents like friends, while the six live-in girls on the club staff became part of an extended family. As caretaker, James Carr was known to be a kindly, understanding man who would hold dodgy cheques pending an assurance they would be cleared. And there were some decidedly sporting members who would go swimming at night off the old landing stage, about 50 yards from the first tee, where the boat used to come in.

They weren't always discreet, either about their swimming attire or the amount of alcohol they had consumed. But James Carr ensured that they came to no harm, while his wife, Kathleen, would always have a plentiful supply of dry, warm towels on hand.

By his own admission, Joe also applied himself to the business of getting on with people. And from early in his golfing career, he was aware of an innate toughness which made him a formidable competitor. "I was a fighter, who loved the man-to-man stuff," he said simply. But ironically, his love of matchplay was to militate against him in a battle to avert the biggest disappointment of his sporting career.

This came in the 1959 Dunlop Masters tournament at Portmarnock where, carrying a four-stroke lead into the final round, he was overhauled and beaten by Christy O'Connor Snr, who carded a course-record, closing 66. "The fact that Christy and I played in separate two-balls meant that I found myself fighting shadows," he explained. "While cheer after cheer swept across the links in response to what Christy was doing, I felt helpless to make a fight of it."

He added: "I didn't particularly like playing against the course." If so, how did he manage to win 12 East of Ireland strokeplay titles and countless scratch cups? "I really don't know," he replied. "The only explanation I can offer is that I was what you would call a great recoverer. Even playing badly, I could get it around in 71 or 72. That's the key to the game, though it wouldn't have saved me against Christy's 66."

Head-to-head was Joe's metier. Before every match, he would coldly assess his opponent. If he knew him, he would think about his record, what he'd done and what chance he had of winning, if Joe played well. "I would study the man's body-language as he walked onto the tee, looking for a weakness of some kind," he said. "Then, if I didn't get a good, firm handshake, I would take that as one up for me. And if he didn't look me straight in the eye, I knew I had him by the balls."

While Jimmy Bruen was heading for Royal Birkdale for what would prove to be an historic British Amateur triumph in 1946, Joe was at home, talking with Irish Times golf correspondent J P Rooney. Arising out of their conversation, Rooney wrote:

"Joseph Carr, who had contemplated making the trip to Birkdale, has assured me that he will be at St Andrews for the Open Championship. He has all the qualities of the first-class stroke player, even in such company as St Andrews will provide. I have no doubt he will get to the final stages of the world's premier event and finish well up in the aggregates."

Interestingly, Rooney spoke about a visit he had made around that time to Southport, where discussion centred on the possibility of the British Amateur being brought to the Irish Free State. And remarkably, it came to pass, in decidedly interesting circumstances at Portmarnock in 1949. As to his decision not to travel to Birkdale, Joe explained that he simply didn't have the resources to fund the trip.

His circumstances were very different, however, in 1953 when the Amateur was staged on the Royal Liverpool links at Hoylake, which Joe viewed as "a very big golf course and right down my alley." He went on: "The last five holes in particular, are long, tough holes. Yet having said that, I was one down playing the 18th on three occasions that week. And on each occasion I got a three at the 18th to take the match down the 19th, where I won."

Joe discovered that there were, in fact, other unplanned elements which could work to his advantage. Like on the morning of the final against Harvie Ward, the gifted American who had beaten him by 2 and 1 in the semi-finals at Prestwick the previous year. Joe knew he was lucky to be in the final, having gone to the 18th more often than would have been considered healthy. It had been a rough passage.

As he recalled: "On the morning of the final, I was thinking about meeting this bastard who'd beaten me the previous year. I was determined to be positive. And noticing that the weather was bitterly cold and the wind was up, I remember turning to my wife and saying: 'Things have changed, Dor. This is my day.' I decided that a rough, dirty day was just the situation to give me an edge. And I took it. That's the important bit. When you feel you have an edge, you must exploit it for everything you're worth."

In the opinion of certain observers, however, it wasn't the weather, but Joe's antics on the practice ground which gave him the edge that day. While Ward looked every inch the defending champion, rifling shots within arm's length of his distant caddie, Joe's man had to dash all over the place in order to retrieve wildly wayward balls. Obviously the lesson he had just received from a well-meaning Cecil Ewing didn't seem to be working too well. But Ward knew nothing of this.

The wind had risen appreciably and the temperature had dropped as the players headed for the first tee. And as things turned out, the American hit his second shot out of bounds on Hoylake's treacherous opening hole, whereas Joe drilled a two iron to within 10 feet of the pin. "I had him rattled," said the prospective champion.

After an approximate, morning round of 71, Joe was three up at the halfway stage of the final and could see that Ward was feeling the cold. This wasn't the sort of weather he was used to in his native North Carolina. Yet he battled back to square the match going down the home stretch, before Joe eventually took the 35th and 36th for a two-hole victory.

"That was marvellous," he reflected. "To me, it was the ultimate achievement; the realisation of my golfing dreams. Winning the British Amateur Championship was almost beyond belief and that victory remains the most important of my career."

At the time, he said: "I have been expecting to win this championship for the last five years and I thought I would have a good chance this year." And of the climactic moments, Dor said excitedly: "Joe was on the 18th green in two, putted and then Harvie conceded the next. Oh! I was so happy I couldn't believe it. And I think Joe felt the same way too...."

Dor, who had walked every hole of the championship with her husband, later revealed the worrying secret she had kept from him. Their two-year-old son, Roddy, had been threatened with mumps on the Friday night. So, anxious to reach their Sutton home as quickly as possible, the happy couple sailed on Saturday night from Liverpool, cutting short the arranged victory celebration at the Royal Liverpool club.

On his arrival home in Dublin on the Sunday, Joe handed over the trophy to his brother-in-law, Dr Desmond Hogan, the captain of Sutton GC. The newly-crowned champion, smiling but somewhat embarrassed by all the fuss, had been driven the short distance from his home on Dublin Road to the club in a car specially decorated for the occasion. Indeed the procession involved several cars, a pipe band and hundreds of well-wishers.

Earlier in the day, he and Dor had been met at the North Wall on Dublin Docks by a number of Sutton members, as they disembarked from the Liverpool boat. And Joe told the awaiting media: "I have played better golf before but have been beaten. I don't consider that I played well and I was lucky, because Ward did not play up to his form in the final."

On arrival at Sutton GC, he was welcomed by Tom Fitzpatrick, vice president of the club. And after handing over the trophy, a somewhat overwhelmed Joe remarked: "It was much easier to win the Amateur Championship than to face all this." Mr P Harrington, captain of Royal Dublin, expressed the delight of his members at Joe's success and Brother T N McDonagh, superior of the Christian Brothers, Baldoyle, joined in the congratulations, describing Joe as a model golfer and a model gentleman.

As a handsome dividend for his Hoylake triumph, Joe was voted "Golfer of the Year" for 1953, by the Association of Golf Writers of which, incidentally, he later became a vice-president, joining such elite company as Peter Thomson, Jack Nicklaus, Arnold Palmer and Charlie Yates. To date, the only other Irish winners of this prestigious award have been Harry Bradshaw (1958) and Christy O'Connor Snr (1977).

There were occasions, however, when he found it impossible to ascend the first tee with the sort of optimism with which he had faced Ward. "I felt really up against it when I played Jack Nicklaus," he admitted. "I figured that with a quick start, I might have a chance of getting him over 18 holes, but I found it impossible to convince myself that I could beat the best golfer in the world over 36 holes in the Walker Cup. His reputation was enough."

Generally, in man-to-man combat, the most important thing, as far as Joe was concerned, was to make sure that he stood where his opponent could see him, whatever the circumstances. He wanted the man to know he was there, that he wouldn't miraculously disappear, no matter how desirable that might be, especially if the match was going against him.

It was one of his quirks. And he saw nothing especially unusual about the shock results in the Accenture Matchplay Championship at La Costa, in spring 2002, when the virtually unknown Kevin Sutherland emerged victorious from a field that included Tiger Woods, David Duval, Phil Mickelson, Vijay Singh, in fact all of the top players.

"It's very easy to get caught over 18 holes," he said. "The match is over too quickly. I have always held the view, however, that against a better player, you'll never get out over 36 holes. Over 18 holes, a few missed putts and a few holed ones can turn a match. In my view that's why the Walker Cup matches are much closer these days than they once were, and why the British and Irish players seem to be doing far better than was the case in my day. It's down to the length of the matches and for that reason, I would hate to see a return to the 36-hole format."

He went on: "I never played well unless I was nervous. Normally after the morning round of a championship, I would come in, have a quick lunch and then get into the car and have a bit of a snooze. And before the next match, I would be out to have a few putts before heading for the first tee.

"But I remember an Amateur Championship when, as I arrived out for my afternoon match, my prospective opponent was still on the course, playing the sixth or seventh tie hole. It meant I was there for an hour waiting for him and the upshot was that when he eventually arrived, I was in absolute bits. I didn't know what was going on. All my carefully-laid plans had been scuppered. Yet I started with six threes in the first seven holes and demolished him 7 and 6, which I can attribute only to concentration and nervous energy.

"You've got to be keyed up to play competitive golf. As for having a fear of failure: I had escaped so many times that I always felt there was a way out, no matter how bad things might appear."

But a player can suffer from pure bad luck. For instance, one could acquire a reputation as a quitter, simply by being caught from behind on a few occasions, whereas it might have been totally beyond one's control. The converse became true of Joe. The more he got out of jail, the more his reputation grew as an indomitable fighter.

And this became hugely significant in that even when an opponent got a one or two-hole lead on Joe, it was obvious he wasn't comfortable. He was waiting for Joe to strike back. Which is what generally happened.

There were certain Irish opponents he knew he had to treat with the greatest respect, but for the most part he felt confident of handling anyone who came his way, provided his own game was in reasonable shape. And he retains a vivid recollection of a European Championship match against Michael Bonallack at Sandwich in 1967, when these two rivals had a remarkable dog-fight. And when Joe had broken 70 and still lost, he did some quick, mental arithmetic afterwards. "Do you know, you bastard, that you holed about 115 yards of putts against me," he said in mock anger. But he added: "The crucial thing was that I never gave Michael any inkling of how I felt out on the course. And that's not easy."

Just as he could recognise from an opponent's body-language that he was on the brink of defeat, it was imperative never to betray the same weakness. And he rejected the suggestion that he had a penchant for conceding long putts early in a match and then asking his opponent to hole everything, just to throw him off balance. "I don't believe I engaged in that sort of gamesmanship," he said. "I'd concede putts if I felt sure he wouldn't miss. But I wouldn't tolerate any fiddling about by an opponent.

"For instance, I remember playing Cecil Ewing in a final of the West of Ireland, when Gerald Micklem was referee. And as we were heading back to the second tee, before the caddies went up the fairway, I turned to Cecil and asked: 'Are you sure you haven't forgotten anything – tees, cigarettes, matches?' And Cecil assured me he had all his needs. But when we set about driving at the second, he discovered he didn't have a tee. And I wouldn't give him one. Which meant he had to hit it off the deck."

The renowned Carr equilibrium, even in moments of acute stress, was clearly a wonderful asset. And it was highlighted beautifully in a piece by Arthur McWeeney in the Irish Independent in June 1958.

It read: "A cool and sanguine spirit is one of the greatest assets of the top-class player at any game, and it is a quality which Joe Carr has always possessed in a good measure.

"Never was it more needed and better displayed than in a match which I saw him play in the Open Amateur Championship of 1954 at Muirfield. Joe was the holder of the title, having won it the previous year at Hoylake, and he had fought his way to the sixth round in which his opponent was a young man named Peter Toogood.

"Eighteen-year-old Toogood had just emerged as the 'dark horse' of the tournament. He was from Tasmania and was completely unknown on this side of the world; but his victory over the much-fancied South African champion, Arthur Jackson, in the fifth round, had suddenly focused attention on him as a live challenger for championship honours.

"With him, and always at his side, was his father, a short, terrier-like little man who clearly thought that his son was the greatest amateur player since Bobby Jones and did not hesitate to say so.

"A small, slightly-built youth, Toogood hardly looked strong enough to match a hitter of Carr's calibre, but his compact swing and good timing helped him to offset his physical disadvantage to a large extent.

"Not that he looked likely to worry the champion in the early stages of the match, for Joe started 4,3,4,3, and was two up. The Irishman failed to maintain the high standard he had thus set, however, and when he took two to get out of a bunker at the 13th, he found himself in arrears for the first time in the match.

"Both were in the same bunker at the 17th, and when Joe exploded out to within four feet of the pin to sink the putt and level the match, the odds were that his greater experience would now tell in his favour. The Irishman missed a great chance at the 18th, however, where Toogood was bunkered off his drive; for Carr played a bad second and had to be content with a half.

"And he had the narrowest of escapes at the 19th, for here Toogood had a four foot putt for the match – and missed it!

"Then came the incident which so well showed the calm, unruffled courage in a crisis, which I referred to in my opening paragraph.

"The second hole at Muirfield measures 383 yards and skirts the left hand side of the course, and our hearts sank as Carr hooked his tee-shot badly, ominously close to the stone wall which marks the boundary.

"When we arrived near the spot where the ball had been seen to pitch, it was discovered that it was heavy tussocky ground, with water oozing from it here and there. There was no sign of the ball, and we spread out to look for it with heavy hearts, for even if we could find it, there was little chance that it would be a playable lie.

"A ball was found, half-plugged in the mud, but it was not the Irishman's and the search went on until it must have been close to the time when Carr would have had to accept his ball as lost and go back to the tee to play another one.

"Then there was a sudden shout from a spectator. A fugitive gleam of white had caught his eye and soon we were taking turns to peer at a ball buried some inches below the surface, with only a little of its top visible.

"And now the question arose – how was Carr to know whether it was his ball? After much argument, a spectator was permitted to insert a finger into the hole and gingerly rotate the ball until the number (Dunlop 65 no 6) became visible. Thus it was identified as his.

"There was water in the hole and after careful inspection, the Irishman declared that he would like an official ruling as to whether this was casual water and whether he was entitled to lift without penalty. Clearly the ball was quite unplayable where it lay.

"A messenger was sent hot-foot to the clubhouse and for fully 20 minutes, everyone waited: and there was no man more cool and unperturbed – outwardly, at any rate – than Carr, who chatted away cheerfully and casually as if he had not a care in the world.

"Young Toogood, on the other hand, looked more and more nervous and unhappy; and Papa Toogood did not help by his loud and forcibly expressed opinion that this was all a waste of time and just a calculated attempt to bustle his cherished offspring.

"In due course, Championship Committee members, pillars of the Royal and Ancient, arrived and held solemn conclave. And an interesting fact emerged. There was a hidden spring at this spot which was known and mentioned in the local rules. Carr was entitled to lift and drop without penalty.

"Toogood had to play first, and in the circumstances hit a good shot, but it was too strong and the ball went through to the back of the green. Then Carr shaped up to an approach of some 120 yards and after all the worry and arguments, and the nerve-fraying hanging about, he slammed the ball to within three yards of the pin and then rolled in the putt for a birdie three and the match. That is what I call being a good match player!

"Incidentally, the importance of having a good caddie was well demonstrated in that match. Carr had a famous, travelling caddie with him called Cecil Timms and when finally all the fuss at the 20th hole had been resolved, Carr looked around for the caddie and saw Timms, for all that he was carrying a heavy bag, running in the direction of the green. He arrived there in time to hold the pin for Toogood's shot and to whip out the pin as the ball sped over the hole and well past it.

"If Timms had not taken the trouble to be there, the ball would almost certainly have hit the flag-stick; and might have come to rest right beside the hole. By such attention to detail are matches lost and won."

"Looking back over my life, I think how lucky I was to have been adopted by such wonderful people. And there were hidden benefits, like the fact that my background made me a loner, so giving me a burning desire to succeed. To prove myself, I became introverted, shutting the outside world off from what was going on in my mind."

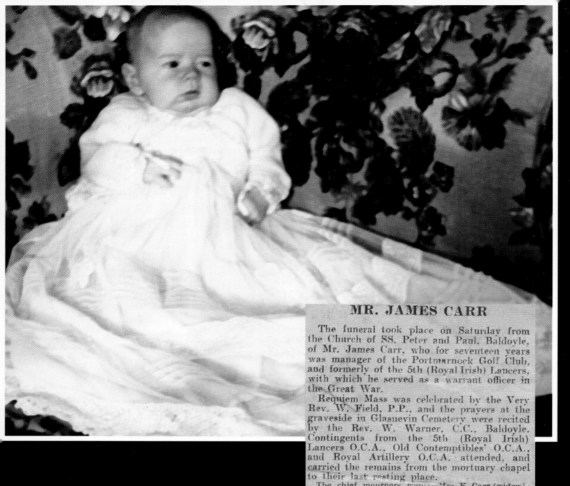

Top left: Joe in his christening robe 1922.

Top middle: At the age of 16 shortly before playing in the Lumsden Cup final in which he lost to Royal Dublin's Vincent Herlihy by 2 and 1. Royal Dublin members standing were Jack McLoughlin (left) and Billy Wynne.

Far right: The Carr finish in the mid-1930s.

Middle right: Winning the 100-yard final at the Leinster Colleges' Championships, 1937.

Middle: Holding (left) the O'Connell's Schools 1937 Junior Athlete of the Year trophy. Beside him is the Senior Athlete of the Year, Louis Magee who went on to represent Ireland in showjumping.

Right: Details of the funeral attendance of Mr James Carr who died in 1939.

MR. JAMES CARR

The funeral took place on Saturday from the Church of SS. Peter and Paul, Baldoyle, of Mr. James Carr, who for seventeen years was manager of the Portmarnock Golf Club, and formerly of the 5th (Royal Irish) Lancers, with which he served as a warrant officer in the Great War.

Requiem Mass was celebrated by the Very Rev. W. Field, P.P., and the prayers at the graveside in Glasnevin Cemetery were recited by the Rev. W. Warner, C.C., Baldoyle. Contingents from the 5th (Royal Irish) Lancers O.C.A., Old Contemptibles' O.C.A., and Royal Artillery O.C.A. attended, and carried the remains from the mortuary chapel to their last resting place.

The chief mourners were:—Mrs. K. Carr (widow); J. Carr (son); Mrs. Sloane (Belfast) and Mrs. Lowey (sisters); Mrs. and Miss McDonagh, Messrs. Michael, Joseph and Thomas McDonagh; Mr. and Mrs. McGovern.

Representing 5th (Royal Irish) Lancers' O.C.A.—Major J. D. Barry, M. J. Singleton, H. Reeves, E. Flower, P. Parker, T. Scully, C. Robinson.

Representing Old Contemptibles' Association—Mr. Bates.

Representing Royal Artillery O.C.A.—W. Hopkins.

Representing O'Connell School—S. C. Conway.

Among others present were:—The Captain of Portmarnock Golf Club (M. Hennigan), R. F. Browne, Surgeon A. L. Butler, Seumas O'Connor, William O'Brien, Dr. Cecil Robinson, Derek Robinson, L. J. Smyth, B. F. Smyth, W. C. K. Meeke, H. I. Robinson, Dr. J. Eustace, G. V. Ryan, M.D.; P. G. Ryan, M.D.; G. V. Ryan, jun., M.B.; E. C. Powell (Hon. Secretary, Portmarnock Golf Club), Dr. R. J. May, Walter Carroll, Vincent Carroll, Charles Carroll, Captain Lionel Hewson, George Collopy (captain, Sutton Golf Club), J. P. Spencer, J. A. Doyle (hon. secretary, Sutton Golf Club), J. P. Rooney, Victor Hamilton, W. J. Gill, Captain St. J. Pike, W. R. D. Bradshaw, P. Crinion, Thomas Fitzpatrick, Thomas Earls, W. J. Greenaway, J. A. Harbison, M.D.; J. J. Keane, Pierce McGrath, T. Walsh, J. J. Kelly, C. Stack, D. L. Kelly.

Dr. A. H. Davidson, M. J. Byrne, Kevin Duggan, N. Cuddy, C. J. McMullan, Miss May Hannon, Edgar and Mrs. Hogg, Eddie Hackett, S. C. Conway, Dermot Morris, J. Dolls, L. J. Redmond, C. French, C. S. Monks, Felix J. Hughes, J. L. Morgan, R. J. Butler, Captain C. W. Robertson, D. McGrath, John G. Aston, B. Thompson, A. W. Briscoe, J. C. Gregg, R. Callaghan, J. E. Greene, Dr. L. V. Ryan, E. P. Bourke, R. J. Quinn, W. F. Fitzsimmons, D. D. Moran, J. and Mrs. McAlister, the Misses M. and Nellie Murray, P. White, J. Henry, Miss Teresa Doyle, Miss N. Rickard, Miss N. King, W. S. Matterson, B. L. Plunkett, J. Fogarty and J. Fogarty, jun.; T. O'Malley, M. J. and K. M. Hogan, George and Michael Waters.

Wreaths were sent by:—Mrs. Carr and son; Captain, Committee, and members of Portmarnock Golf Club; 5th (Royal Irish) Lancers, the Old Contemptibles, and Mr. and Mrs. Edgar Hogg.

Mr. Michael J. Hogan
requests the pleasure of the company of

at the marriage of his daughter
Dorothy Mary
to
Mr. Joseph B. Carr,
at the Church of the Assumption, Howth,
on Tuesday, 5th October, 1948, at 11 a.m.,
and afterwards at the Gresham Hotel.

R.S.V.P.

Far left: Joe and Dor, who became teenage friends through their membership of Sutton Golf Club photographed at Milltown Golf Club. Inset is an invitation to their wedding which took place on Tuesday, 5th October, 1948. Dor Carr (née Hogan) was one of four children who lived at Stonyhurst, Sutton.

Above left: Joe and Dor.

Above right: Dor's father, Michael Hogan, warned Joe that he would get none of his money if he married his daughter. They went on to become firm friends.

Left: Socialising at the Gresham Hotel during the 1950s.

Bottom left: Dor celebrates Joe's British Amateur win at Hoylake in 1953.

Bottom right: Flanked by international golfers Bryan Malone (left) and Cecil Ewing.

The Carr swing. On first seeing Joe in action, Norman von Nida, the celebrated Australian professional, remarked colourfully: "He sets up for a fade, hits a draw and smashes the ball a f...ing mile." During a trip to America in 1949, when he competed in the US Amateur at Oak Hill after the Walker Cup at Winged Foot, distinguished professionals such as Tommy Armour and Craig Wood had advised Joe to change his method. He spent countless hours changing from a draw to a fade.

Right: Watched by (fom left) John Morgan, Alex Kyle and Cecil Ewing in 1951.

Above right: Receiving the 1953 British Amateur trophy from the captain of Royal Liverpool Golf Club, E.R. Orme. Joe beat Harvie Ward by two holes in the final, the first of three memorable victories in the championship.

Far right: Getting the shoulder-high treatment on his return to Dublin Port in 1953.

Bottom right: Shoulder-high treatment again as fellow Sutton members celebrate that 1953 win on home ground.

Right: All smiles with the Irish Open Amateur Championship in hand.

Above: With children Jody and Roddy and the British Amateur trophy.

Top left: The shooters take a break. Joe (centre) with friend Martin Winston (front left).

Top middle: Pictured with friend and mentor Harry Bradshaw.

Far right: Christy O'Connor ruffles the Carr signature tassel. It is one of Joe's great regrets that he failed to beat Christy in the 1959 Dunlop Masters at Portmarnock.

Middle: On the fairway with Dennis Hutchinson.

Right: Shaking hands with Dudley Wysong after the semi-final of the American amateur Championship in 1961 which Joe lost by one hole.

Above: With Arnold Palmer (left) and Billy Casper (right).

As a tribute to Joe's recovery skills, they later christened that area of the Muirfield course "Carr's Corner."

And as a further, fascinating footnote to the plugged-ball incident, Joe later explained that Willie Whitelaw (who would go on to become captain of the R and A in 1969 and a Conservative minister and peer in the Thatcher administration) was the referee and Alex Hill was the official observer. Both were prominent members of the R and A.

Said Joe: "I remember asking Willie if it was casual water. By way of response, however, he suddenly turned on his heel and was gone. That's why word had to be sent to the clubhouse for the Championship Committee. When I met Willie afterwards in the locker-room, I asked him why he didn't make a decision. To which he replied, hugely embarrassed: 'I couldn't Joe; I had you backed to win the Championship.'"

Much as he admired Muirfield, however, Joe's burning ambition was to win the Amateur Championship over the Old Course at St Andrews. By his own admission, the history and mystery of the place appealed to him enormously. This, and the knowledge that he had prepared wonderfully well, made him especially focused in 1958.

"With all the practice shots I hit by way of preparation for St Andrews, I almost wore through the blades of my eight and nine irons," he said. "I had worked out that the Old Course required two, basic shots and it still does. You have to drive the ball long and straight and you have to pitch accurately. It was all very clinical, I suppose, a bit unlike me in many ways, but I had never wanted to win more. And the work paid off."

He went on: "Looking back on it now, I can't believe the practice I did. Dor had a little notebook and when we totted up the figures, we discovered that I had hit 47,000 tee shots in preparation for that championship. I had to have two drivers because I'd wear the face off one. They were standard, persimmon Lambert Topping models, custom made in London, and my main concern was to have them exactly the same, so that they would be fully interchangeable.

"Most of that work was done on the practice ground at Portmarnock – before they asked me to leave because of the damage I was doing! I would go over there on a Saturday morning and leave a bare patch of ground behind me of about 10 square yards. When I was leaving for St Andrews, I said to Dor: 'Honey, I'll give you a ring between the two rounds of the final on Saturday. They can't beat me. I've done too much. There's no way I can lose.'"

Joe's second-youngest child, Gerald Andrew Carr, Gerry for short, was due that week but, with considerate timing, didn't arrive until after the champion had returned home. Gerald after Gerald Micklem and Andrew after the father's favourite venue. So Dor was now to be the mother of four boys and a girl and she kept in touch with Joe's progress through frequent phone calls to the course. Incidentally, when Gerry followed his brothers into golf, his seriously wayward hitting caused Joe to remark humorously of his game: "Air mail; no address." And the description has since stuck.

Among the many supporters who travelled to St Andrews by air and sea for the final against England's Alan Thirwell were Gerry Owens, who had been non-playing captain of the Irish international team the previous year; Joe's business-partner Freddie McDonnell, brother-in-law Des Hogan, and club captain, Gerry Connor, and honorary secretary, Hugh Quirke, from Sutton GC.

While Joe was achieving a memorable, 3 and 2 victory, his progress was being monitored in a decidedly curious manner by two other travellers from this country. They happened to be newspaper scribes who aroused quite a deal of interest by waving white handkerchiefs at their hero during the climactic stage of the match.

It was only when it was over and they were contributing handsomely to the celebrations, that Joe learned the truth of their apparent signals of surrender. It seems they had backed him and with a view to collecting their winnings before the local bookmakers closed, one of them ran ahead of the match and was waiting, strategically on Grannie Clark's Wynd when his accomplice raised the white handkerchief. The signal confirmed that there was, indeed, an Irish triumph and that the winnings could be collected post haste.

A few weeks after winning his second Amateur, Joe received a sharp reminder of the gap that still remained between an amateur at the peak of his powers and a top-flight professional. It came in the British Open at Royal Lytham. During qualifying at Lytham, he set a new amateur course record with a 67 while Peter Thomson, who would go on to win the title, set a record 63.

That evening, both cards were placed side by side on the wall in the clubhouse. On closer inspection, Joe discovered that had he been involved in matchplay with Thomson, he would have been thrashed by 9 and 7. Yet at that stage, he held the course records at Royal Dublin (65), St Andrews New (67), Carlow (68), Milltown (68), Royal Portrush (68) and, of course, Sutton, where his 61 equalled an earlier effort by Jimmy Carroll.

When he won the Amateur for a third time in 1960 at Royal Portrush, two of the most interested spectators were his sons Jody, who was almost 11 at the time and Roddy, who was nine. A neighbour drove the two lads from Dublin to Portrush, where they joined Dor, who was already there. So, mother and sons watched Joe crush the hapless American, Bob Cochran, by 8 and 7.

As far as Justice Murnaghan was concerned, however, Joe should have been elsewhere. In Dublin's High Court, to be precise. The story of how the prospective champion of 1960 had absented himself from jury duty, was told by Seamus Kelly in "An Irishman's Diary" in The Irish Times.

Kelly wrote: "In the words of the old anecdote, a titter ran around the court yesterday morning. The court was the High Court, Mr Justice Murnaghan presiding. When the jury was being empanelled, the name of J B Carr of 'Suncroft', Burrow Road, Sutton, was called but called in vain.

"Without further comment and with a face completely dead-pan (if one may use so frivolous an expression of a High Court judge), Mr Justice Murnaghan imposed a fine of £3 on the absent juror.

"The learned judge is, I understand, a pretty useful member of Portmarnock (where the said J B Carr was an honorary life member). Whether a challenge will shortly be issued to him to take on a well-known member of Sutton for stakes of £3 a side, remains to be seen. As to where the missing Mr Carr was yesterday – why your guess is as good as mine." Tickled on being reminded of an incident from more than 40 years ago, Joe mused: "I wonder if I ever paid the fine."

Cochran had been shown no mercy, but from tough competitor, Joe could also project the image of jovial sportsman, with equal conviction. And it was the latter persona which prompted Baltimore sports journalist and commentator, John F Steadman, to write a glowing assessment of him when he captained Britain and Ireland's Walker Cup team in 1965.

Steadman wrote: "Whether he's striding the fairway or retiring to an obscure corner of the locker room, the magnetism of Joe Carr draws the crowd. People are attracted to him. They listen, they learn, become fascinated and go away enlightened and delighted. Carr has remained an amateur golfer, but he could have handled himself with the pros without any fear or stigma of embarrassment.

"He laughs easily and is the epitome of masculine charm and good nature. He says his native Ireland has everything that makes for pleasant living and adds that he doesn't expect any argument. 'We have hunting, fishing, golf and good things to drink,' he says. 'If Ireland had weather, we would be over-populated in six months. When Bob Hope was in Ireland to play golf, he advised they should put an umbrella over the whole country.'

"There was another time when Joe was invited to play a round with President Dwight D Eisenhower (at Portmarnock). It was necessary that a golf cart be furnished for the President because of his heart condition. But Joe says that there wasn't a single golf cart in all of Ireland. 'Finally, a friend of mine arranged to borrow an open

Rolls Royce from nearby Sutton and we got on with the game,' said Joe in his delightful manner of speaking."

Involvement with the Eisenhower visit was, in fact, down to Matt McCloskey, the American ambassador of the time, who invited Joe to play with the former US president. McCloskey happened to be the father-in-law of Jimmy McHale, who got to know Joe as a player in the American Walker Cup teams of 1949 and 1951.

Steadman concluded: "The man is a sterling gentleman and golfer who is endowed with a wealth of Irish wit and wisdom."

Against that background, it is hardly surprising that two years later, Joe was presented with the Walter Hagen Award. Instituted by the American golf writers, it honoured the personality who, in their view, had done most to further Anglo-American golf. Sponsored by Dr S L Simpson, originator of the Daks Tournament, the award was especially precious to Joe, given that he had enjoyed the experience of playing with Hagen in California, albeit when the great man was some way past his prime.

On this point, Joe said: "As my career developed, I became aware that I was better known in parts of America than I was at home. I made a lot of friends in golf; people I stayed with. And whenever I returned home, I would never neglect to write a thank-you note. That was something which Dor drilled into the kids and I'm glad to say that they maintain it to this day.

"And we sent our own Christmas cards, carrying a photograph of the family, to our friends in America every year. I have kept copies of them all. Going back more than 40 years, we had them from the time there was only Jody and Roddy. Then Jody, Roddy and John. Until eventually the family was complete. They were sent each year to all the people we knew, all over the States. That was the way we kept in touch and ensured that friendships would be maintained.

"It's a custom that was copied by Jack Nicklaus who sends me a card every Christmas with a photograph of his family, including all the grandchildren."

Another aspect of Joe's character is his love of gambling. And he has always been that way, for as far back as he can remember, having five pounds or a tenner on a golf match, and generally winning.

Soon, it extended to horses, largely through the influence of a friend of his, a professional gambler who lived in a hotel in Dalkey. This particular character got the papers every morning and went through the various race-cards for the day. Bitten by the bug, Joe found himself joining his friend at race meetings, where he would attempt to match the professional's gambling expertise.

"Quite frankly, I loved to have a bet on a horse and on golf," said Joe. "In fact I loved to bet on anything – and still do. Though I had very little money of my own during World War II, I always seemed to associate with wealthy people and I remember my future father-in-law, Michael Hogan, had a room-full of tea, when it was impossible to get, even at a pound a bag.

"There was Billy McMullan, whose father owned the oil company of that name. Billy's job every Saturday morning was to count the petrol coupons. And another friend, John Deegan, whose father had a string of supermarkets in Scotland, finished up owning a racehorse and some greyhounds.

"Then there were the Cullens, a wealthy family from Temple Bar. And they all played golf with me. And they all thought they were better than I was. Needless to say, they became a steady source of income for me. Modest, mind you, but steady. John Cullen always thought he could outdrive me and I would have to be careful only to beat him by about 10 yards, so that there would be another bet. In truth, I could have outdriven him by 50 yards."

He went on: "I bet on every sport in which I was ever involved, and I suspect that my gambling instincts were a considerable help to my golfing career. In my view, there is a defining moment in every match when you know that it's now or never; when you have to produce something special if you're going to win. And in my experience, there's very few leading golfers who don't gamble.

"Nicklaus loves a bet, so do Arnold Palmer and Gary Player. And in his day, Sam Snead was acknowledged as the game's top gambler. I remember when my own career came to an end, Jack (Nicklaus) said to me with a grin: 'That's one source of income for me dried up: Barbara will be very disappointed.' Mind you, we'd never have more than £20 on a match."

Under the headline "After the golf.... the gambling", the William Hickey column in the Daily Express carried some fascinating gossip about events at St Andrews during the 1955 British Open. The scribe claimed that at the Home of Golf, he saw "gambling by golfers to match anything on the Riviera, or in Western thrillers. But the settings were different. And instead of music, there was merely the soft pianissimo of shuffling cards."

By way of explanation, the piece went on: "I observed the magnificent nonchalance of Irish amateur Joe Carr, rifling through a bundle of notes two and a half inches high, beside him on the table. Someone had asked him for change. 'Sorry, my boy,' said Joe. 'Nothing but fivers here.' He spoke like William Hill talking of a 2s 6d bet.

"None of the other players bothered to look up. No coins tinkled inside the tight huddle round the corner table. Silver was something for handing to waiters. Everybody spoke in undertones – even when the piled fivers and singles in the middle mounted to what must have been £150 or more, by the look of the 'kitty'. Players made bored £10 raises then threw their hands away."

(It may be worth very little these days, but £10 would have been an acceptable, working-man's weekly wage at that time.) The scribe added that the game went on night after night and that Arthur Lees, the Sunningdale professional, did rather well. "He is reputedly one of golf's best poker players," claimed the Express. "So is Joe Carr, who seems to do everything well."

Very little changed through the years. For instance, when playing in the Scratch Cup at Birr, Joe returned a round of 72, whereupon a local bookmaker claimed that nobody would ever break 70. What odds, he was asked by Joe: 8/1 he replied. So Joe proceeded to shoot a 67; got £90 back for his tenner and then gave the club the money to put towards their watering system.

The betting bug was still very much with him when the Millennium British Open was staged at St Andrews, where Joe simply couldn't see Tiger Woods losing. And he went on to back Woods to win the Masters for a second time the following April and a nice, each-way double also delivered in 2001 when Phil Mickelson won the Greater Hartford Open and Colin Montgomerie won the Irish Open on the same weekend.

"I used to play poker in the famous school in Room 104 in the Gresham Hotel," he went on. "There was the manager, Toddy O'Sullivan, Sean Lemass, who was then Minister for Industry and Commerce (and later became Taoiseach), the actor Denis O'Dea, who was married to Siobhain McKenna, and Cedric Cruess Callaghan. It was five-card draw and we'd assemble about 6.0 in the evening and play until about eight. Then dinner would be served in the room, after which poker would be resumed until 12.0. That was the deadline.

"I got skint. There were nights when I lost amounts varying from £400 to £600 which was an awful lot of money at a time when £20 a week was considered to be a very tidy salary. Though I could afford to lose, it hurt nonetheless. That was in the fifties and I remember being down in Longford, shooting snipe with Denis O'Dea and he warned me that I would be fleeced if I wasn't careful. He then spelled out the percentages which dominated his approach to poker and proceeded to ask if I knew the odds of improving on a pair, or two-pair, or of filling a run or a flush? And I hadn't a clue what he was talking about.

"'Then what the hell are you doing in there?' he asked, before going on to explain that if he thought he had the best hand going in, he would double the pot. And if he didn't have the best hand going in, he didn't bet. That was a golden rule in professional gambling. At that time, Denis was the best poker player in the country, by far, whereas I played cards with my heart, not my head. So I never went back to Room 104."

Greyhound racing provided another outlet for a flutter. It led to Joe and his brother-in-law Kevin Hogan buying a dog which Kevin had the temerity to bring home. And on being asked by his irate father what the idea was, Kevin replied: "Well dad, you always told me to be kind to dogs, so you should be pleased your words didn't fall on deaf ears." To which the father replied acidly: "I wasn't thinking about dogs with the number four on their back."

Joe also recalled going to Leopardstown Races, before he was married, with a great tip for a horse named Mister Fitz, which was owned by a certain Bill Fitzpatrick from Portmarnock. Though our hero wasn't especially flush, he figured he could scramble together £30 to have on the horse, only to discover that its odds had drifted out to 33/1. Obviously the connections didn't fancy him.

While he was searching for the owner, however, the horse's price began to tumble down to 20/1 and on down to 16/1. He recalled: "So I put my £30 on and it won by half the track. Then, nothing would do me only to go to the dogs that night – and come home skint. So, I had no option but to lie low and stay in bed for the weekend."

Losing the 1959 Dunlop Masters was made all the more painful for Joe by three, key factors. It happened at a time when he was at the peak of his formidable powers; it was the best chance he would ever have to beat a top-quality professional field, and it was at Portmarnock.

The celebrated North Dublin links had been his own backyard. And against a par of 74, nobody knew better than Joe the quality of the first three rounds he carded in the Masters that year: 69, 68, 69. Even with a final round of 74, his aggregate of 280 would have been considered unbeatable, in normal circumstances. Indeed 20 years on, Mark James won the Irish Open at Portmarnock with an aggregate of 282.

"To win the Masters from all the boys on what I considered to be my own home territory – wouldn't that have been the ultimate," mused Joe. "But in view of what Christy went and did, I would need to have scored a final round of 69, in fact four sub-70 rounds to win the title. That sort of scoring was unheard of around Portmarnock."

He went on: "I always had the ambition to 'peg' the pro boys just once. And it happened when I was 45, in the Southern Irish Professional Championship at Milltown in 1967. My aggregate of 270 equalled Jimmy Martin's score at the same venue in 1964 and was better than Paddy Skerritt's 273 in 1966 and Christy Greene's 276 in 1965.

"I also had a chance of taking the Martini at Hoylake where I needed 4, 4 to win, but I finished 5,6 and Neil Coles and Christy tied for the title. Another big disappointment was the Centenary Open at St Andrews, where I started 72, 73. I then broke the amateur record for the Old Course with a third round of 67 to be on 212, five strokes behind the surprise leader Kel Nagle. Roberto de Vicenzo (209) was second and Arnold Palmer (211) was third."

Joe made a marvellous 3, 3, 3 start – birdie, birdie, birdie – to the final round, to be tied for the lead with 15 holes to play. But as luck would have it, the round was abandoned because of horrific weather and by the following day, the momentum was gone. He started 4, 5, 5 and eventually had to settle for eighth place behind Nagle.

Meanwhile, in the timeless nature of great links terrain, Portmarnock looked pretty much the same in 1959, as we know it today. So, by turning our thoughts towards that narrow tongue of shallow duneland, with water on three sides, we can almost picture the climactic scene on September 20th, when O'Connor shot that stunning, course-record 66, to win the Dunlop Masters for a second time.

There was no disputing the honest simplicity of a layout which demanded length and a rare degree of control, especially if the wind blew. At 6,918 yards, it was only about 200 yards shorter than when Jose-Maria Olazabal won the last Irish Open to be staged there, in 1990. But, of course, the par was different. The 465-yard fourth and 461-

yard 17th were both par fives then in an overall 74, comprising equal halves of 37.

Though he had relinquished the British Amateur crown to American, Deane Beman, Joe's acknowledged status as Europe's finest amateur, gained him a special invitation into the select, 24-man field. And his remarkable scoring exploits included a holed second-shot of 100 yards for an eagle two at the third, in a 69 on the morning of the final day. All of which added up to an amazing 54-hole score of 206 – 16 under par – and four strokes clear of his closest challenger, O'Connor.

As tension built during lunchtime in anticipation of a thrilling climax, there were those who recalled how the wonderfully gifted Galwayman had come from no fewer than seven strokes back of Eric Brown, to win his first Masters at Prestwick, three years previously.

Brown was in contention again on this occasion, a stroke back from O'Connor, with John Panton, Rees and Bernard Hunt, while Drew was on 212 along with legendary British professionals Charlie Ward, Arthur Lees and Syd Scott. Paul MacWeeney, the then golf correspondent of The Irish Times, placed Joe's performance in perspective when he wrote: "Not since the days of Bobby Jones some 30 years ago, has an amateur made such a bid to beat professionals over 72 holes."

This was certainly true in a European context. But the amateur's hopes of an historic triumph became decidedly fragile when O'Connor turned on the heat with five birdies in an outward 32 to the final round. Remember, this was a time when the closing 36 holes were on the same day and there wasn't the sophisticated scoring system we now take for granted.

O'Connor was playing five two-balls ahead of Joe. As the Galwayman recalled: "I reckoned if I was to have any chance of catching him, I needed to get to work early and hope that the news filtering back down the grapevine would cause him to get worried."

The strategy worked to perfection. Relying on the bush telegraph and his own, keen golfing instincts, Joe knew that his fate was written on the wind. "From the almost constant stream of cheering, I realised Christy was burning it up," he recalled. Then there were self-inflicted wounds, like at the second, where a nervy chip ran past the target to cost him an unexpected bogey. But the most devastating blow to his hopes came at the long sixth, which then measured 576 yards.

Joe hit such a huge drive that he needed only a five iron for his second shot, but with two hacks from heavy rough off the green, he proceeded to take a dispiriting, bogey six where O'Connor had earlier sunk a 12-footer for a birdie.

Later, another bogey at the ninth brought Joe to the turn in 38, which meant that his third-round advantage had not only evaporated, he was two strokes behind the new leader. By that stage, nobody was in any doubt but that O'Connor was surging to victory.

His flawless progress included an eagle three at the long 17th, where a glorious fairway-wood second shot finished 10 feet from the hole. By the time he got to the 18th, the huge gallery had swollen to an estimated 15,000, milling around the green.

And when the final putt found the target for a course-record 66, the cheering could have been heard by Joe's club-mates across the narrow strip of water in Sutton GC.

O'Connor's figures were:

OUT .. 434,434,343 = 32
IN ...... 443,543,434 = 34

For his part, Joe also finished in style, even if it was for a level-par 74 to be four strokes behind the winner. Like the Royal Dublin man, his approach to the 18th kicked off the bank on the right, but he played a delightful chip and run shot to leave the ball within a few inches of the target for a tap-in par. And he had reason to be proud of sharing in what remains a unique achievement by Irish golfers, in that he was tied second with Norman Drew behind the irrepressible champion. As it happened, Drew had covered the eight holes from the fifth to the 12th in five under par. And given Joe's amateur status, the Ulsterman received the bonus of second prize-money of £500 on his own.

Reflecting on this marvellous triumph, more than 40 years on, O'Connor said: "I didn't know Joe especially well at that time and I remember thinking that four shots behind him going into the last round, my objective had to be to simply try and play as well as I could."

He went on: "Did I think I could win? Well I always took the view that there was no point in competing in anything unless you thought you could win. Even six or seven shots behind, I would still feel there was a chance. And I loved Portmarnock: what a great test! I always thought of it as my kind of course, though there was tremendous support for Joe at what was essentially his home track. It all changed at the ninth, where I chipped in. And I could go right now to exactly where the ball was, just off the right side of the green."

Did he feel sorry for Joe at the presentation ceremony? "Not at all," replied O'Connor, with typical candour. "Joe was a very wealthy man whereas I had only moved up from Killarney earlier that year to take over as pro at Royal Dublin. By comparison, I was a poor man rearing a young family."

Commenting on the tournament which he followed from a distance, Bernard Darwin, the celebrated former London Times correspondent, wrote some time later: "Every morning I looked in my paper expecting to read that Portmarnock had taken its revenge on those who had affronted it with 69s and 70s. But still the marvellous scoring went on and O'Connor's last round, with which he caught up and passed Joe Carr, was the most magical of all."

The incomparable Pat Ward-Thomas, who was there to witness the drama, was similarly moved by the occasion. And he ended a reflective article for the magazine Country Life, with the beautifully evocative lines:

"The following morning, Portmarnock was a wilderness of deserted tents and savage rain, and I thought of the transience of these things. All the tireless organisation and hard work, the really excellent scoreboards, the capable stewarding, the clamour, the excitement and the heroics, all gone.

"Then in the twilight, as the aircraft climbed over the city towards the dark sea, there was one last glimpse of that noble links, at peace once more on its lovely peninsula; of the little red clubhouse of Sutton across the estuary, a drive and a brassie from the house of Carr, and I knew that these were days which would not be forgotten."

Chapter Seven
A Fading Ambition

After the euphorea of his breakthrough to victory in the British Amateur of 1953 had eased somewhat, and the demands of a notoriously difficult game were taunting him once more, Joe made a remarkable admission. "I never got away with so much bad golf in my life as I did at Hoylake," he said. And he meant it.

Several matches had gone the full distance, by which stage he considered that he had been lucky to escape. It was typical of the cold pragmatism which had made him a champion, while it also reflected a determination to achieve many more triumphs, especially at the highest level.

On first seeing Joe in action, Norman von Nida, the celebrated Australian professional, remarked colourfully: "He sets up for a fade, hits a draw and smashes the ball a fucking mile." With a strong grip and his feet spread considerably more than shoulder-width apart, he employed a threequarter swing to work the ball both ways.

This was the hallmark of a consummate shot-maker, a by-product of being brought up in Portmarnock winds. Draw and fade were done instinctively, though the draw was very much his natural shot.

By his own estimation, Joe had gone through a poor run of form since capturing the Irish Amateur Open for a first time in 1946. Winning a fifth East of Ireland title in 1948, when he also won the West and the South, didn't seem to satisfy his lust for glory. And there had been further West of Ireland victories in 1947, 1951 and 1953, before he headed for Royal Liverpool and an assignment with Harvie Ward.

He could see flaws even in his Walker Cup performances, which included a 1947 win over the US Amateur champion, Ted Bishop. Much as he grew to love the Old Course, he knew deep down that it was a hooker's paradise and especially forgiving for a player who drove the ball as far as he did.

Indeed his power got him out of countless scrapes. As he recalled: "When I sprayed the ball, I would still hit it so far that I had only a wedge to the green anyway. So, even if the other fellow happened to be on the fairway, he was more than likely going to be hitting a mid-iron, which gave me a good chance of halving the hole in match-play."

He went on: "Prior to Hoylake, the only player in the country who was longer than me through the air, was Jimmy Bruen, who could pitch the ball further than I did. But the extra run that I achieved with a low, chasing hook, would get the ball out there beyond him. Essentially, I was playing block hooks, which is very difficult. But it was only after my Amateur breakthrough that I made a firm decision to change. The sweet smell of success had prompted me to set my sights very much higher."

In the three years prior to Hoylake, Joe's record in the Amateur was: 1950 – last eight; 1951 – last four; 1952 – last four (he lost to Ward in the semi-finals). "To me, those performances proved that I wasn't lasting the pace," he said several years later. "So I found myself saying bugger this, there's nothing for it but to change."

These developments were rendered all the more interesting by the nature of what became universally acknowledged as the "shot of the match", in his battle with Ward. It happened at the short, 200-yard 11th in the afternoon – the 29th. With the honour, though he was one down at that stage, the American came up short of the green. Newspaper reports described Joe's response as a "magnificent two-iron, finely drawn into the wind, which finished well into the green." So, while he may have considered his old method to be unreliable, it still proved to be most effective, even under the pressure of a major final.

Incidentally, after moving into Suncroft, Joe had a television mast erected so as to allow him view the BBC (Ireland didn't have its own television service until 1962). And as a keen admirer of the country's golfing hero, the supplier told him that if he won another Amateur title, the height of the mast would be raised 20 feet, free of charge. Which is what happened after St Andrews in 1958 and after his third triumph at Royal Portrush in 1960, by which stage Joe reckoned he had the tallest television mast in Ireland.

During a trip to America in 1949, when he competed in the US Amateur at Oak Hill after the Walker Cup at Winged Foot, distinguished professionals such as Tommy Armour and Craig Wood had advised Joe to change his method. And he was aware that the Walker Cup selectors preferred golfing orthodoxy. So, he embarked on a four-way approach to change – he studied film of Ben Hogan; he listened to Gerald Micklem and Raymond Oppenheimer; he played golf with Harry Bradshaw. And he visited Bill Cox.

Though it would be 1967 at Augusta National before he would see Hogan in the flesh, Joe, like every contemporary student of golf, was fascinated by stories of The Hawk playing out of his own divot marks. Hogan, of course, had become the first great exponent of the power fade and having set his heart on following suit, Joe had his own swing filmed. He then superimposed it on a film of Hogan's swing "to see where I left him." It proved to be a very enlightening process.

Cox, who was born in 1910, effectively retired from tournament golf after winning the Daily Telegraph Foursomes in 1951. Based at Fulford, near York, he proceeded to concentrate on teaching what became known as the Cox Method. Later, he was one of the early TV commentators, known for his confiding style and sense of humour, which contrasted with the fruity, earnest tones of Henry Longhurst. From an instructional standpoint, his approach appealed enormously to the enthusiastic student from Sutton.

"When they pointed out my numerous successes, I could see that people were baffled at what I was doing, but I wanted consistency," Joe recalled. "And I was aware that such a drastic change would be painful; that it couldn't be achieved overnight."

In certain respects, things got worse instead of better in that his performances in the next four Amateurs were: 1954 – last four; 1955 – last eight; 1956 – beaten in second round; 1957 – beaten in second round. But deep down, he knew this could be attributed to occasional lapses into his old ways. And there were times when he unwittingly got caught between the old and the new. Through dogged perseverence, however, he saw the first real chink of light during the Whit weekend of 1957, when he broke the Baltray course-record with a second-round of 68 in the East of Ireland Championship, which he went on to win by five strokes.

Meanwhile, there were also consultations, totalling three weeks, with John Jacobs who would later gain international renown as Dr Golf. Among other things, Jacobs impressed upon him the need to develop a safe shot, one he could depend on absolutely when pressure was applied in the heat of battle. He had to be able to put the ball on the fairway, even if it meant sacrificing possibly 30 yards in distance off the tee. Either way, length wasn't going to be a problem for the longest hitter in the amateur game on this side of the Atlantic.

A measure of his success was the observation, in 1956, of Walker Cup colleague and Daily Telegraph golf correspondent, Leonard Crawley. "From having been distinctly rough," wrote the abrasive Englishman, "Carr has made himself into a first-class stylist. As a hitter of the ball he is today as fine a model for young players as he is of the true amateur he has always been."

Hogan had provided emphatic proof that the power fade was a far safer shot than a hook. So, the instinctive Carr game which Joe decribed self-depracatingly as all heart and no head, was sacrificed. Now it would become a marriage of head and heart, delivering fluent shotmaking in the process.

The final touches to the Carr metamorphosis were applied by Henry Cotton during a visit to Dublin early in 1958. In the process, Cotton explained that a person who moved the clubhead through the ball as fast as Joe was doing, had to ensure that he had an immovable grip with both hands on the club. To achieve this, he suggested having all the grips of his clubs fitted with tacky leather, which Joe promptly did.

So, he was now a fully committed left-to-right hitter, which wasn't easy, though the transition was helped by weakening his traditionally strong grip. "I suppose it was a bit of a gamble, dismantling the method which had brought me victory at Hoylake, but I was convinced that it was only through a change of method that I could reach my full potential," he said. "Within a few years I had grooved it to the extent that it felt entirely natural, yet I could still draw the ball, when appropriate."

The importance of yardages was still some way down the road. In common with most players of the time, Joe didn't know precisely how far he could hit a nine iron, or any iron for that matter. "Nobody knew anything about yardage," he said, "and I didn't really take it on board until the 1960s, when Gardner Dickinson and Jack Nicklaus elevated it into an art form."

By way of explaining the technique of distance-control, Nicklaus would talk about going to the practice ground and hitting 50 balls with, say a nine iron. Then he would select the middle 15, which gave him the average length he was looking for.

As for Joe's modified technique: it came under the careful scrutiny of Irish Times writer Paul MacWeeney, in his coverage of a spectacular success in the Tostal 72-hole Strokeplay Tournament at Royal Dublin in 1954. MacWeeney wrote: "His swing has lengthened and become smoother and no longer does he take so much out of himself on the long game. At the same time, he is getting maximum distance with the woods and the long irons and it was his ability here that gave him the advantage over his rivals on the testing homeward nine (at Dollymount)."

So it was that as the 1958 golf season approached, Joe had the confidence to swing the club as he knew he should, especially under pressure. And he won the West, the East, the Cork Scratch Foursomes (with John Fitzgibbon) and was tied 11th in the Irish Hospitals Professional Tournament at Woodbrook. He then turned his sights towards St Andrews and the Amateur.

In conjunction with those swing changes, Joe was also fighting a battle in what had become known as the game within a game. He knew his putting left much to be desired.

As far back as 1946, one leading scribe observed: "On the greens, he has a weird stance with the feet splayed out and the knees almost touching, but putting is a matter of confidence rather than style, and Carr certainly gets results." Still, by 1950, Joe had decided to do something about his putting method. His solution? To putt the way the Americans did. This led to experimentation with American putting styles which he had observed in Walker Cup matches, where the arms only were used, so eliminating the damaging, flippy-wrist action. And it worked.

"Too many things can go wrong with your wrists when the pressure is on," he said at the time. "The arm action is entirely mechanical. You just do the same thing over and over." As a consequence of this change, he soon became recognised as one of the game's most reliable putters by most observers, with the notable exception of a certain Scottish critic.

In June 1955, as part of a build-up to the British Open at St Andrews that year, Joe played an exhibition match against the defending champion, Peter Thomson, in Glasgow. And as he stepped off the 18th green at Hardgate, he overheard the remark: "Ach, you're putting like a navvy. You're standing too loosely. You should have a more solid stance."

By way of response, Joe decided that the critic would be his caddie at St Andrews two weeks later. He turned out to be none other than Eddie Davies, a former greenkeeper who was then working in the Clydebank Shipyard. And his relationship with Joe went back to the time when the golfer was but a toddler at Portmarnock.

Davies happened to be the greenkeeper at Portmarnock back then, and would be followed around the course by Joe, scampering in his wake. Now, more than 25 years on, Joe remarked ruefully in Glasgow: "And to think that the best thing about my golf used to be my putting....."

The start of the 1954 season had seen him make the dramatic change of discarding his trusty blade in favour of a three iron. And a measure of his success could be gleaned from a sparkling second round of 65 at Royal Dublin, en route to victory in the Tostal Tournament in May of that year.

In a glowing assessment of that performance, MacWeeney wrote in The Irish Times: "Carr's second round of 65 takes its place among the greatest ever produced by an amateur in this country. Here was every stroke played to perfection – raking tee shots, approaches dead on the flag and putting of extreme accuracy with that number three iron. The use of this particular club on the greens has led many people to voice their opinions quite forcibly to Carr on the grounds that so freakish a method is bound to lead eventually to disaster.

But his answer to the critics is the best one possible – the putts go down with the number three iron, so there is no reason for making a change back to the more orthodox putter.

"Not only does Carr look comfortable and quite at ease when putting with this club, but he is hitting all his shots with more relaxation, and with more in reserve than at any previous time in his career."

As it happened, he didn't persist with the three-iron at that stage, but the switch became extremely fortuitous later in his career. By the 1959 Walker Cup matches at Muirfield, Joe had returned to orthodox putting with a highly-productive, rusty-headed blade which he had "borrowed" from his eldest son, Jody. Called a "Cleek Putter", its hickory shaft gave it a decidedly antiquated appearance.

But, as we noted earlier, this trusty, borrowed friend was to be wrenched from him in dramatic circumstances on the second day of the tournament when, at the top of the singles order, Joe was two up on US Amateur champion, Charlie Coe, after 28 holes. Then, while walking towards the 29th green trailing his putter behind him, a spectator inadvertently walked on it and smashed the hickory shaft.

There was nothing for it but to revert to the three iron which, in its own way, had served him well. As MacWeeney reported: "Joe spent years putting with a three iron and it was the club which brought him victory. On that 29th green, Coe had dealt him a fierce blow by holing a four-yarder for a birdie three but, whipping the three iron out of his bag, the Irishman dropped a six-footer for a half."

Joe then went three up with six to play, only for Coe to reduce the deficit to one hole with rallying birdies at the 32nd and 33rd. MacWeeney resumed the story: "Then the three iron got working again. Joe holed a crucial six-footer on the sloping 34th green for a win in three to become dormie two, and he clinched the match with a seven-footer for a birdie four at the 513-yard 35th."

Not surprisingly, for the second time in his career, the three iron became almost his "putter" of choice from then onwards. I say almost because, after having a new shaft fitted, he decided to use the Cleek Putter in defence of the British Amateur at Royal St George's, Sandwich, the following June. In an 11th hour change of mind, however, he opted for the three iron.

Indeed it was still the club of choice when, on June 30th, 1959, he set a new course record of 64 at Gullane No 1, wielding it to magical effect. As it happens, this is the only course-record which he still retains and he did it in the second round of qualifying for the British Open at Muirfield, beating the existing amateur record by four strokes and the professional target by three.

Using a three-iron on the greens, he was also two strokes inside the previous best amateur qualifying round for the Open, which was the famous 66 – 33 out, 33 back and 33 putts – set by Bobby Jones at Sunningdale in 1926. That was in qualifying for the Open at Royal Lytham, where Jones won the title.

All the while, Joe's lean frame seemed to leave him with no problems of stamina, at a time when the Amateur was fought over eight rounds of matchplay, often in the most hostile of weather. "I was fortunate in that I didn't have to look after myself physically until I was in my thirties," he said. "That was when I availed of the opportunity of training with Shamrock Rovers under Billy Lord, a man who smoked more Woodbines than even I, a committed smoker, ever thought possible. With Billy urging me on, I would run up and down the terracing at Milltown, just like Paddy Coad and the other great Shamrock Rovers players of that time, did."

He went on: "As I grew older, I became increasingly aware of the importance of fitness in championship golf. And I was fortunate in getting in touch with Commandant Joe O'Keeffe, whom we teased as the 'Body Beautiful'. I made a deal with Joe. Tipping the scales at 11st 7lbs at the time, I knew I was too light for my height. In fact by the time a championship was over, I was down to 11st 2lbs and worn out. I could eat like a horse but I would burn it off just as quickly. It was in my nature to be always on the go, doing everything quickly.

"So I told Joe, who happened to be playing off a 12 handicap at the time, that I needed to build some muscle. And the deal was that if he could build me up to 12st 7lbs, I would get him down to nine handicap. His solution was to put me through a course of lifting light weights. Quick repetitions. None of the heavy stuff. Meanwhile, with the help of the driving range we had in Sutton at that time – the first in this country, along the road from Suncroft – I got Joe down to eight. And I had established what was to become my fighting weight from then on."

Joe believed it was vital to keep pace with every form of physical and mental development. And as he continued with his strict, physical schedule, people would ask whether all the running, lifting weights and other forms of training were necessary to play good golf. They pointed to players like the great Walter Hagen and other overweight practitioners who had been successful without it.

His reply was that few golfers were fortunate in being as naturally endowed with stamina or talent as was Hagen. Certainly where Joe was concerned, physical preparation was something which had to be done if he was to get the best from himself in competition.

Even as late on in his career as the mid-1960s, this was Joe's winter schedule: Starting at the beginning of November, he did two nights each week of circuit training as well as play squash a couple of times a week. And he would hit a couple of hundred balls each day or at night, by floodlight.

This would be increased gradually to a peak period around mid-February, followed by a tapering off towards the middle of March. By then, he knew that he had done the necessary work to be ready for the fray. "The next major investment I made in my game was in 1957 when I did an unbelievable amount of work in the belief that it was the only way I could reach my full potential," he said.

Crucial to all of this was the support and dedication of Andy Doherty, Joe's Man Friday, who was with him from 1947 until 1973. This is Andy's story:

"I was living in Burrowfield Road in Baldoyle and went caddying at Sutton GC from the time I was about five or six. In fact I remember them having to tighten the strap of the bag a few notches, so that it wouldn't hit the ground. That's how I got into golf. Joe would have known me to see. And Dor too.

"When he let it be known that he was looking for somebody to collect balls for him, I went for interview to his house on Dublin Road, before he moved to Suncroft. I was about 18 at the time and I had just come back from England. I started work the next morning, which was absolutely magnificent for me at that time. Little did I imagine that I would be caddying for Joe when he won the British Amateur for a second time at St Andrews in 1958.

"I wasn't paid a regular wage as such. He would just give me money every so often, and if I was short I would say to him 'I could do with a few bob.' And Joe always came up trumps. I later went on salary when I joined his company which, among other things, meant that I ceased collecting golf balls for him.

"Early on, my duties had also involved being a sort of general handyman around the house. That would have been at the house on Dublin Road first of all and later at Suncroft, where all I had to do was hop over the wall to collect the balls, which was very easy.

"My memory of Joe at that time is that he hardly ever missed a morning's practice, except on the rare occasion when he might be called away on urgent business. I would arrive at his house at about 7.45am and he'd be ready to hit balls by 8.30. There were other occasions when he would be out on the course at 8.0 in the morning and would hit 200 balls, which took him about an hour.

"That was on the old fourth hole at Sutton, towards the clubhouse. And I remember he would always give the last few shots the full treatment, hitting them so hard that he sent them about 20 yards through the green.

Otherwise, he could hit them on the green with a three wood, a distance of about 270/280 yards.

"He hit the ball a colossal length and from all the practising, he became one of the straightest hitters in the business. You wouldn't believe how good he became. Anyway, after the balls were hit, he would go for a run up as far as Claremont Beach and back again, a distance of about three miles. Then, in the evening, from about 6.30 until 9.0, he would practise pitching and putting.

"We hit golf balls every morning without fail. Even in the winter. I remember I often went out with a kettle of boiling water to thaw the ground so that he wouldn't slip. There was a driving range at the back of the old second green and he would hit shots while my hands were numb with the cold. Sometimes, I would hit about 100 balls myself, just to keep warm.

"In those conditions, I would have to wait until 12.0 or 1.0 in the day to collect the balls when the sun came out and the ice and snow would have thawed. Prior to that, it would have been nearly impossible to find them against a white background.

"After his run, he would have his breakfast and then go into work. And when he had gone, it would take me about an hour and a half to collect the balls. I did that with him before I eventually took up golf seriously and joined Donabate. Prior to that, from 1956, I was a member of Ierne Pitch and Putt Club where I used to go and play the odd evening. I joined Irene in 1956, when the membership cost me £3 a year.

"I didn't tell him about the pitch and putt and he found out about it in amusing circumstances. That was in 1957 when I happened to win the National Pitch and Putt Championship and the committee had asked the great Joe Carr to come and play an exhibition match against their new champion.

"So, when he saw me there, he asked if I knew who the winner was. And I replied 'I do' and then started laughing when Joe told me about the exhibition match. 'It's not you, Andy, is it?' he asked, smiling. And I said 'It is.' And we played the match and finished all square after 18.

"Looking back on those times, I marvel at how unbelievably dedicated Joe was. I lived about half a mile away from Suncroft and when I got there, he had to get up. That was our understanding and he never tried to duck it.

"Knowing my way around golfing circles, I was convinced that nobody was working as hard on his game as Joe was at that time. Only the professionals would have been as dedicated. Sometimes we would go to Portmarnock to hit iron shots but mainly it was pitching and putting around the second green at Sutton.

"I went into the business in about 1959 and he was very helpful when I set about getting into Donabate Golf Club, which I joined in 1961. Joe's business partner, Freddie McDonnell, was on the committee there at the time and they were going to give me a five handicap, but I said no. In fact I told Freddie that I'd rather play off three and if it transpired that I couldn't, they could give me shots back. So, my first handicap was three, mainly because of my experience at pitch and putt and, of course, the tee-shots I hit each morning after Joe was gone. I then became a scratchman for about 20 years, but I'm afraid I've since eased out to seven.

"It was amazing how much I learned about golf, simply from being in Joe's company. For instance, when he would return after getting lessons from John Jacobs, he'd explain what he had been advised to do. Swing on the inside, things like that. And he became such a straight driver of the ball that it was unbelievable. And all the while, I was applying the same advice to my own game.

"During 16 years caddying for Joe, the British Amateur at St Andrews was obviously the high point. I also caddied for him later on, in the Shell Wonderful World of Golf match in which he tied with Al Geiberger at Killarney. But 1958 stands apart.

"By that stage, we had developed a wonderful relationship to the extent that there was nothing I wouldn't do for him. I always liked Joe. I admired his sincerity and the way he would look after me like one of his own. In fact it could be said that he treated me like a son, even to the extent of inviting me to eat with his family. Looking back, they were unquestionably the best years of my life. I couldn't have been happier.

"Sometimes when he'd practise at Portmarnock in the evening time, he'd stay and play bridge and give me the keys of the car to drive home and have my tea. And he'd stay playing bridge until 10.30 or 11.

"Among my warmest memories of Joe are of the time he won the Irish Amateur Open at Royal Dublin in 1954, when he beat Cecil Ewing in the final. And the famous Close final at Portmarnock in 1959, when he lost at the 38th to Tom Craddock. That was when Joe and I were faced with the long walk back from the second green. I remember Tom holed some great putts that day.

"Coming up to the British Amateur each year, Joe always did special practice for about six to eight weeks beforehand. He would play 18 holes on Saturday morning with Harry Bradshaw. And 36 on a Sunday. And he used to practise for about an hour and a half on a Saturday, on account of playing only 18 holes.

"In the final against Alan Thirwell at St Andrews, Joe birdied the short 11th and then drove the par-four 12th (316 yards) and holed the putt for an eagle two. So he had gone 2,2. He was later presented with a case of champagne for that.

"There was another famous match against Dr Jim Mahon in the final of the Irish Amateur Open at Portmarnock in 1956, when Joe holed a putt from across the 36th green. That was the old 18th, of course, which was then beside the clubhouse, not where it is now. Anyway, as the 25-footer was going into the hole for an eagle three – Dr Mahon had a birdie – many spectators were already on their way down the first, certain the match would go to tie holes. We had squared it with a birdie four on the 13th (31st) and both players shot pars from there, all the way in.

"In fact they had been all square after 18 and there was never more than a hole between them, all the way. When the end came, J D McCormack, a former Irish international, was standing beside me at the time and I remember him saying: 'I take my hat off to that man. You'll never see anything like that again.'

"Later, when I retired from Carr and McDonnell, I went to work with my wife Kay, who was in the clothing business herself.

"My time with Joe has given me many happy memories. We were great friends and we're still great friends. For years, Kay and myself went to his house for Christmas, just to visit. In all our time together, he never let me down and I would like to think that I never let him down. We were a team."

In his report of Joe's St Andrews triumph, Henry Longhurst wrote rather testily in The Sunday Times: "His driving is still a joy to behold and much straighter than it used to be, but the messing about and 'prospecting' which he now finds necessary in the short game, tend to make him tedious both to watch and to play against."

But John Stobbs, the golf writer of the Observer, saw fit to comment: "He has with considerable success remodelled his swing into something more orthodox. Nevertheless, towards the end of the week (of the Amateur), back came something of the old lurch and sway. Up heaved his right shoulder again and several times tremendous belts off the tee were met with the old delighted laughter among the spectators.

"Without the Irishness of it all, he might be more consistent but he never would be so enjoyed. He hits the ball between 50 and 70 yards farther than the average local tiger."

Joe resumes the story: "My expulsion from Portmarnock (because of the damage he was doing to the practice ground) meant that I was forced to go down to where the neighbouring Portmarnock Links now is. That was common land at that stage and there was a little shop down there.

"I used to have lunch at Royal Dublin every day – a cheese sandwich and a few cups of tea. Then I would go to the practice ground where I would spend an hour and a half. Every single day. And when I'd go home, I'd do another hour and a half practice-putting on the carpet. Then, when evening came, I would turn on the two, big 1,000-watt bulbs which were fixed on top of the roof at Suncroft and spend two hours playing bunker shots or chipping to the second green.

"By the time the 1958 season came around, I was convinced I was unbeatable. How could they beat me, I would ask myself, after all the work I'd done. Yet before heading to St Andrews for the Amateur, the notion of over-confidence never entered my head. I even told Dor that I'd give her a ring between the two rounds of the 36-hole final. And the justification for that confidence is reflected in the fact that I never saw the 17th or 18th greens that week until the first 18 holes of the semi-final, and the final against Alan Thirwell."

Observers marvel these days at the power-striking of such players as John Daly and Tiger Woods but, as with most things in golf, there is nothing new about long hitting. Indeed while playing in the Home Internationals at Troon in 1952, Joe drove the second green, a distance of 370 yards.

But his contemporaries must have wondered how much distance he had sacrificed by modifying his method. One man who never had any doubts on that issue, however, was the late John Nestor who, during one of many illuminating conversations I had with him, attempted to convey how seriously long a hitter Joe remained, when he reverted to the low hook which characterised his early method.

Nestor, a former amateur international, went so far as to suggest that Carr was as long, if not longer that most of his contemporaries in professional ranks. And as a passionate student of the game, he knew about such matters, especially having been on the receiving end of Joe's power, notably during mixed foursomes combat at his home club, Milltown.

So, he could have permitted himself a quiet smile on reading a report in 1961, about a long-driving competition held at Sundridge Park, Kent, on the eve of the Martini Tournament. With a huge effort of 311 yards, two feet and three inches, Joe scooped the pool.

Then aged 39 and at the peak of his formidable powers, Joe finished more than five feet clear of second-placed Tony Coope, a professional from Wigan who had a best hit of 306yds 6ins. Much more interesting, however, was the fact that broad-shouldered Welshman, Dave Thomas, who was noted as a prodigious hitter, was third on 305-1-10. A four-handicap amateur from London University was fourth.

So, our hero had left such established professionals as Harry Weetman, Peter Alliss, Bernard Hunt, Max Faulkner, Guy Wolstenholme and John Jacobs trailing in his wake.

Somebody should have warned them what to expect. The three Irish professionals in action that week – Christy O'Connor Snr, Harry Bradshaw and Norman Drew – certainly knew about Carr's formidable length. Which would explain why none of them bothered to take him on in the long-driving event.

The events of November 28th, 1974, would have a profound bearing on the remainder of Joe's life. By his own admission he had come through an extremely demanding week, which started with a trip to Cork where he was a guest at the wedding of a female buyer in Roches Stores. The trip involved all the wrong things, notably late nights of drinking and card-playing. Then, on his return to Dublin, there was a charity walk from Busaras to Howth Hill – a distance of about nine miles. And in another charity event, he swam against international Donnacha O'Dea at McKee Barracks in Islandbridge, Dublin. Apart from these physically-demanding distractions, there were the pressures of business in the aftermath of the break-up with his long-time partner, Freddie McDonnell.

As Joe was to discover later, the feature common to all heart attacks is fatigue. When he rose on the morning of the 28th, he went for a run from Suncroft up towards Howth and then back down the beach. "I remember that on returning to the house, I was coughing and spluttering," he said. "I had been smoking like a dog, sometimes as many as 50 or 60 a day. There were times when a fag was never out of my mouth."

He went on: "As I approached the house, I felt a bit of a dart while I was going over the second green, but thought nothing of it. Then I went into the office in Upper Abbey St, and at about lunchtime I got the most unbelievable pain in my chest." Aware by this stage that there was something seriously wrong, Joe told his eldest son, Jody, to get the car and drive him to the family GP in Sutton, though, ironically, he was only a few minutes' walk from Jervis St Hospital at the time. Dor was away in Spain.

When Dr David Chapman examined him, he said bluntly: "Joe, you've had a heart attack." He then contacted the distinguished cardiologist, Dr Risteard Mulcahy, who sent him directly to hospital. As Joe remembers it: "Jody, in his anxiety, was driving the car like he was competing in some rally and I pleaded with him not to get me killed on the way into hospital. And all the while, I was clutching my chest with the pain. Obviously I knew I was in trouble, but to be honest, I wasn't frightened.

"It was the first time in my life that my body had let me down, as it were. The only other medical problem I had encountered was having my appendix out. I had never missed a championship because of illness, nor had I ever to withdraw from a club team." Heart by-pass operations were still in their infancy at that time and there was clearly no question of surgery. But after meeting him on his arrival at St Vincent's Hospital, Dr Mulcahy left Joe in no doubt about the seriousness of his condition. "How bad is it?" Joe asked, after he had been examined. To which the good doctor replied: "Have you a will made?" "No," said Joe. "Well you'd better make one." Then came the words that Joe has never forgotten: "If you ever smoke again, you've got five years....."

After a two-week stay in hospital, Joe spent a further two weeks in a nursing home. And when he was well enough to return to Suncroft, he didn't work for about three months. All he did was walk the beach every day, though now the objective was actual physical survival rather than the winning of a major championship.

Gradually, his strength began to return and with it came confidence in the road ahead. But there was one crucial difference: he was now a committed non-smoker, with no intention of lapsing into the old ways when he would smoke two or three cigarettes a hole, "leaving them about, all over the place."

The body which had given him a wonderful, sporting career, would continue to allow him a full, active life. And as a further contribution to healthy living, his staple diet would become the fish collected each morning from the boats which arrived with their catch into Howth Harbour, down the road from his house.

But in golf, things would never be the same again.

❖

Chapter Eight
The Incomparable Bobby

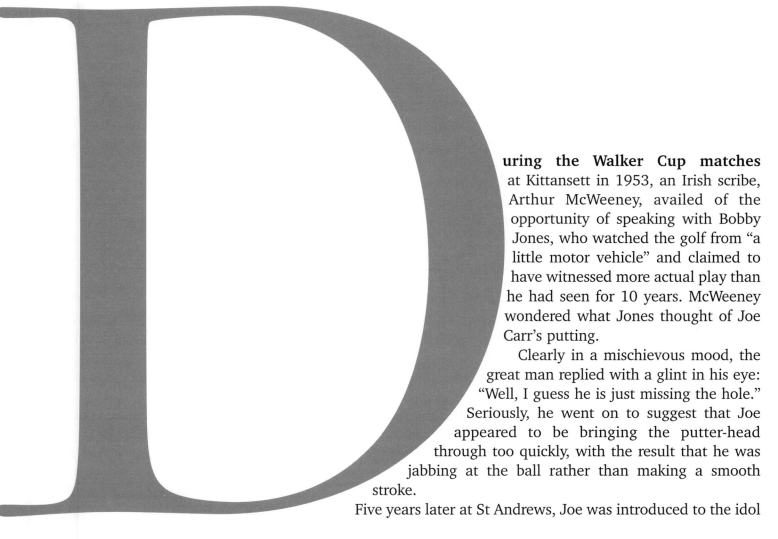

During the Walker Cup matches at Kittansett in 1953, an Irish scribe, Arthur McWeeney, availed of the opportunity of speaking with Bobby Jones, who watched the golf from "a little motor vehicle" and claimed to have witnessed more actual play than he had seen for 10 years. McWeeney wondered what Jones thought of Joe Carr's putting.

Clearly in a mischievous mood, the great man replied with a glint in his eye: "Well, I guess he is just missing the hole." Seriously, he went on to suggest that Joe appeared to be bringing the putter-head through too quickly, with the result that he was jabbing at the ball rather than making a smooth stroke.

Five years later at St Andrews, Joe was introduced to the idol of every amateur golfer as the reigning British Amateur champion. The occasion was the inaugural staging of the World Amateur Team Championship for the Eisenhower Trophy. And despite the merciless progression of syringomyelia through his crippled body, Jones had accepted an invitation to captain the US team.

In his small, modestly-appointed attorney's office in downtown Atlanta, he would sit behind his desk like, according to journalist John Ballantine, "an ancient emperor surrounded by trappings of former glory." There was a picture of the last putt of the Grand Slam going down at Merion in the US Amateur Championship of 1930 and another of the Royal and Ancient clubhouse at St Andrews, crafted by an admirer from inlaid woods which made a grey day come uncannily alive.

Now, in October 1958, he was visiting his beloved, golfing home for the last time. It was an occasion when he would become the first American since Benjamin Franklin in 1759 to be made a freeman of the Royal Burgh. And during a ceremony brimful of emotion, he famously said: "I could take out of my life everything except my experiences at St Andrews and I would still have had a rich and full life."

We are told that he then recalled a visit to the Old Course in 1936. And how, with a party of friends en route to the Olympic Games in Berlin, he stopped to play a round at the scene of his British Open triumph of 1927, when he retained the title by a six-stroke margin. When word of his arrival leaked out, a crowd of about 2,000 suddenly appeared on the first tee to catch a glimpse of him. And it had doubled in size by the time he had played three holes.

By that stage, Jones had been retired six years from serious competition and, by his own admission "had been playing dreadful golf." And fearful of disappointing all these admirers, he said to himself as he approached the first tee: "This is a terrible thing to do to my friends." But one of the Old Lady's most favoured sons, found the inspiration to par the first and birdie three of the next five holes in an outward journey of 33.

His play of the short, 178-yard eighth, was especially memorable. Taking a four iron from his bag, he hit a perfectly-flighted shot which saw the ball clear the front bunker and come to rest within six feet of the flag. While the crowd cheered their approval, Jones's caddie, who could have been no more than 20, looked admiringly at his "master". Both of them were near to tears. "Aye, you're a wonder sir," whispered the caddie. "A blooming wonder."

Twenty-two years later, the Auld Grey Toon bestowed upon him its highest honour. And Joe Carr was among those fortunate enough to be present in the Younger Graduation Hall, which was packed with more than 1,500 people. Observers later remarked on the wonderful dignity and warmth of Jones's acceptance speech. And how at the end, he left the presentation dais with the Provost and drove down the centre aisle in an electric golf cart, draped with the flag of the State of Georgia.

"Suddenly, people around me started singing 'Will ye no' come back again?' and I found myself joining them in full voice," recalled Joe, who had won prizes for singing during his schooldays. "It was an unforgettable moment."

In fact the emotion of the occasion was caught beautifully by the celebrated American golf writer, Herbert Warren Wind, who wrote later in Sports Illustrated: "So honestly heartfelt was this reunion of Bobby Jones and the people of St Andrews (and everyone else), that it was 10 minutes before many who attended were able to speak again with a tranquil voice."

As tears flowed freely on that October day, little did Joe imagine that he would have a rather special appointment with Bobby Jones only three years later.

Bob to his friends and Bobby to the public, Jones was very proud of having been born on St Patrick's Day (1902). In fact, he made special reference to it in a goodwill message to the organisers of the 1960 Canada Cup at Portmarnock. It read "....Since it was for a long time, years ago, my ambition to play the Portmarnock links, I envy those who will have this privilege. I might add that since I was born on St Patrick's Day, it is mandatory that I should pull for a victory for Ireland. With best wishes to all. Most sincerely, Robert T Jones Jr (signed)."

As the game's greatest amateur, he was beaten only once in 36-holes matchplay between 1923 and 1930, prompting Bernard Darwin to observe: "Like the man in the song, many of Mr Jones's opponents are tired of living but feared of dying. However, their fears are rarely unduly protracted since they usually die very soon after lunch."

The Bob Jones Award was initiated by the USGA in 1955 for "distinguished sportsmanship in golf". According to the USGA: "The award seeks to recognise a person who emulates Jones's spirit, his personal qualities and his attitude towards the game and its players." Francis Ouimet, the first American amateur to win the US Open, in 1913, was accorded the honour of being the inaugural recipient. The next five were: 1956 – William C Campbell; 1957 – Mildred D "Babe" Zaharias; 1958 – Margaret Curtis; 1959 – Findlay S Douglas; 1960 – Charles Evans Jnr.

Campbell was an outstanding American amateur who, among other things, qualified for the US Amateur Championship on a record 37 occasions and would later go on to become president of the USGA in 1982. The astonishing achievements of Zaharias need no embellishing; Curtis played a leading role in launching the Curtis Cup; Douglas was president of the USGA in 1929-30 and Evans was twice US Amateur champion. So Joe was, to all intents and purposes, the first "overseas" winner of the award, which was a truly remarkable achievement in that it meant the USGA were prepared to compare him to a much-loved, legendary figure of the American game.

The qualification stems from the fact that while Douglas viewed America as his adoptive country, he was, in fact, born in St Andrews in 1875. On emigrating to the US he soon became involved in the fledgling golf scene there and went on to win the US Amateur in 1908. Either way, Joe was certainly the first non-American citizen to receive the award.

Notification of the award came to Joe totally out of the blue and he remained tremendously proud of it, more than 40 years later. "It's probably the most prestigious award America can bestow on a golfer," he said. Then he added with a smile: "I must admit that I never saw myself as contributing distinguished sportsmanship to the game, but I'm glad the USGA thought so. At the time, I liked to think that being Irish might have had something to do with it. No, not the fact that Bob Jones happened to be born on St Patrick's Day, but the reputation we Irish have for our friendliness.

"In that context, I have always maintained that Ireland's greatest tourist asset is our people. Not the scenic beauty of the country, though that's obviously a considerable factor. No, the real drawing card is our marvellous people. I have always made a point of saying this in the various speeches I have made about my involvement in the game. Go into a pub at night and you'll be asked where your father hailed from and his father before him. And you can't help but believe that people are genuinely interested in you. And then there's the fund of stories which Irish people seem to have, especially in rural areas. I suppose that's what it's all about.

"As for sportsmanship: Henry Longhurst used to talk about having a respect for the game to the extent that you would voluntarily declare a penalty on yourself on a dark night with no man as a witness. And I agree with that. I'd cheat at most things but not golf. I remember saying to some colleagues while we were playing bridge, 'If I sneak a look at your hand, that doesn't mean that I approve of the idea of cheating. I absolutely abhor the thought of cheating at golf.'"

For the presentation of the award, Joe and Dor travelled to New York where the ceremony was performed at the Biltmore Hotel, as part of the annual general meeting of the USGA. "It was a very moving ceremony," he said. "Dor and I had a lovely time and when I came back, the whole business received great publicity. I accepted it as a gift to Ireland as much as a personal honour, the same as I was to feel about the captaincy of the R and A, 30 years later."

Unfortunately, the great man himself was not there to present it, but he sent a telegram expressing regret at his absence, and delight that the award, bearing his name, should have gone to such a fine sportsman.

There were other golfers, contemporaries of Joe's, who took similar delight in the honour. For instance, Leonard Crawley wrote in the Daily Telegraph: "After Carr had won the (Amateur) Championship for a second time in 1958, I wrote of him in these columns 'No championship of the last 30 years has been won so decisively from the tee and no championship has been won by a finer character. An amateur to the core, no riches, no help, no sponsor – just live, love, work and play when you can.'

"This remains as appropriate today and his thousands of friends all over the world will rejoice with me at the news of this latest and singular honour so richly deserved."

Throughout his competitive career, Joe always valued relationships in golf above all else. In this respect he could see himself and Jones as kindred spirits, though he never entertained serious thoughts of attempting to emulate the great American. As far as Joe was concerned, it was all very well to have the odd joust with professionals in challenge matches and regular tour events, but the idea of doing what Jones did and actually beating them in the British Open and the US Open was simply unthinkable.

On the occasion of that inaugural Eisenhower Trophy of 1958, the British and Irish quartet was: Joe Carr, Arthur Perowne (Royal Norwich), Guy Wolstenholme (Kirkby-Chuxloe) and Reid Jack (Dullatur). Gerald Micklem (Wildernesse) was non-playing captain.

Not surprisingly, the entire occasion was dominated by the presence of Jones. Indeed as things turned out, there was little reason for the local media to concentrate attention on the home players, insofar as they performed disappointingly. In the event, at a press conference prior to the tournament, Jones gave his impressions of the Old Course as it was then, compared with 30 years previously when he had been defying amateurs and professionals to magical effect.

He pointed out that advances in greenkeeping and general changes in the care of the course had made for lower scoring. There was an inescapable hint of criticism, however, in his observation that heavier growth had largely eliminated the running shot to the green, which he regarded as a more skilful shot than the high pitch which had gained universal popularity.

Another vital development, of course, was the introduction of steel shafts which had been legalised only shortly before he retired in 1930. He used them himself for the first time in 1931 and he pointed out that present-day experts (1958) could hit with full power all the time whereas with the hickory, much more discretion was required and low scores in all four rounds of a 72-hole event were rarely achieved, even by Jones himself.

In his view, steel gave players an advantage of one to two strokes per round. He also suggested that the development had been responsible for a levelling of standards at the top, thereby making it more difficult for any individual to dominate the game (as he had done).

Finally, he expressed regret at the apparent reluctance of American professionals to travel to the British Open, compared with the 1920s, when he was competing. In his view, weekly, big-money tournaments in the US were proving to be too great a counter-attraction. It seemed that money was more important than status. (Only two years later, however, the arrival of Arnold Palmer for the Centenary Open on the Old Course, was to change all that.)

Interestingly, in an interview at Augusta National 10 years later, Jones claimed that the biggest difference between the modern player and competitors of his day was putting. He said: "When I scored 66 at Sunningdale in the Open Qualifying of 1926, I holed only two putts of more than moderate length. Nowadays, players seem unhappy if they don't get down several long ones. Incidentally, that 'perfect round' was far from perfect; I was never completely satisfied with more than six shots in any round." The reference to that as the "perfect round" had to do with

BREAKING 80

JB

"My upbringing at Portmarnock was a wonderful advantage. I never felt the game owed me anything, so I didn't harbour resentments. Later in life, this absence of any emotional baggage could be attributed to the fact that there was probably nothing I pursued which I didn't accomplish, at least to some degree."

Rough stuff: Among other things, John Jacobs, known as Dr Golf, impressed upon Joe the need to develop a safe shot, one he could depend on absolutely when pressure was applied in the heat of battle. He had to be able to put the ball on the fairway, even if it meant sacrificing possibly 30 yards in distance off the tee. Here, at Pebble Beach in 1961, Joe clearly strayed off the straight and narrow onto a ledge above the Pacific, left of the famous 18th green during the semi-final of the American Amateur Championship against Dudley Wysong.

The troubles: Like Seve Ballesteros, Joe regularly found himself in the most bizarre of circumstances. Hedges, ditches, dykes, trees, fences and water were pretty much par for the course. In this sequence Joe's waywardness provides great entertainment for the gallery.

ROBERT TYRE JONES, JR.
75 POPLAR STREET, N. W.
ATLANTA 3, GEORGIA

February 1, 1967

Joseph B. Carr, Esq.
Suncroft
Sutton
Dublin, Ireland

Dear Joe:

To my great delight, I have just found
on my desk your letter to Cliff Roberts saying
that you will play in the Masters this year.

Please be assured that it will give us
all, especially me, much pleasure to welcome you.
I hope you will have your game in the best possible
condition and that we may be able to cause you to
have a good time.

With best regards,

Sincerely,

Robert T. Jones, Jr.

RTJ:jsm

cc: Mr. Clifford Roberts
Augusta National Golf Club

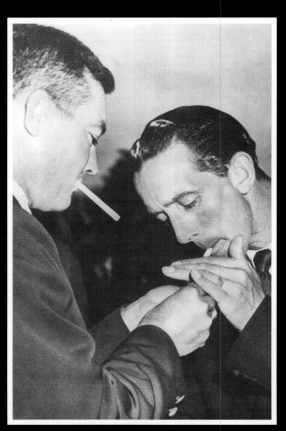

Augusta: Joe appeared in three US Masters at Augusta, becoming the first Irishman to play in the event in 1967. In that year he was paired with defending champion Jack Nicklaus for the opening two rounds. Nicklaus failed to make the cut while Joe went on to play the final 36. The following year Joe was paired with Arnold Palmer. He too failed to make the cut as Joe sailed into the final two days.

Far left: Bobby Jones expressing delight at Joe's acceptance to play in the 1967 US Masters.

Top left: On the road again.

Top right: The 1958 British and Irish team in the inaugural Eisenhower Trophy at St Andrews. Left to right: Joe Carr, Reid Jack, Gerald Micklem (captain), Arthur Perowne and Guy Wolstenholme.

Above: Holding the Walker Cup in Baltimore, USA, 1967. Joe captained that year's GB&I side to a memorable tied match.

Centre: Portrait from the 1950s.

Left: Joe lighting up with Billy Joe Patton some time prior to quitting the weed.

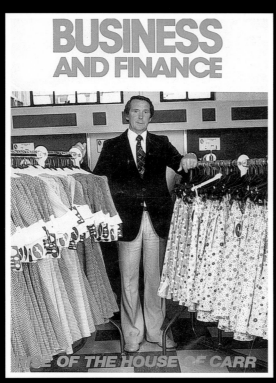

BUSINESS AND FINANCE

...SE OF THE HOUSE OF CARR

THE
BOB JONES
AWARD

IN RECOGNITION OF
DISTINGUISHED SPORTSMANSHIP IN GOLF
PRESENTED BY
THE UNITED STATES GOLF ASSOCIATION
TO COMMEMORATE THE VAST CONTRIBUTIONS
TO THE CAUSE OF FAIR PLAY MADE BY
ROBERT TYRE JONES, JR.

AWARDED TO
JOSEPH B. CARR
1961

Top left: Jack Nicklaus and Christy O'Connor enjoy a light moment at the opening of Mount Juliet Golf Club watched by Mount Juliet owner Dr Tim Mahony (second from left) and Joe.

Far left: With Sir Michael Bonnallack, former US Vice-President, Dan Quayle and Mrs Quayle.

Bottom left: With former President of Ireland, Mary Robinson.

Above left: On the cover of Business and Finance from July 1975.

Left: The Bob Jones Award which Joe received in 1961 for distinguished sportsmanship in golf.

Bottom left: Enjoying a moment with golf writer and broadcaster Henry Longhurst.

Above: Making a presentation to Jaime Ortiz Patino when the owner of the magnificent Valderrama Golf Club in Spain became an honorary member of Portmarnock Golf Club.

Top left: Joe, Jody, Roddy, Dor, Sibeal, John, Gerry and Marty. Sibeal turned out to be a one-shot-wonder driving the ball 200 yards at Sutton's second. She never picked up a club again opting for horses rather than clubs.

Top: Roddy photographed in Sutton Golf Club with the East of Ireland and the West of Ireland trophies which he won in 1970 and 1971 respectively.

Top right: Roddy and Patti's son, Jamie, and daughter, Sophie.

Above: Declan and Sibeal's family, Aisling, Shane, Sabina and Cian.

Left: Marty and Michelle's daughters, Sophie and Julia.

Next left: Jody and Margaret's son, Cameron.

Middle: John and Sandra's children, Darcey, Georgia and Joseph.

Far left: Gerry and Fidelma's sons, Jordan and Adam.

the fact that it contained two nines of 33 and 33 putts. "I knew Bob and his wife Mary quite well," said Joe. "By 1960, I had met him about six times – I always called him Bob, as his wife did – obviously the most memorable being at St Andrews in 1958. The other occasions were at the Walker Cup when any exchanges we had would have been a lot more formal."

Explaining his enthusiastic singing "with the best of them", at the Younger Hall ceremony, Joe said: "Even then, I had a good singing voice which had endured from the time when, as a teenager, I was highly commended in the Feis Ceoil as a boy soprano, the year that Terry Bent (later a well-known Dublin businessman) won the gold medal. I even sang Danny Boy on the Late Late Show during the 1960s."

(When I reacted somewhat sceptically to these revelations, Joe insisted on breaking into some Moore's Melodies which had been the set pieces for the competition, 65 years previously).

On February 1st 1967, two months before his US Masters debut, Joe received a typewritten letter, signed by "Bob Jones" with an address at 75 Poplar Street NW, Atlanta 3, Georgia. It read: "Dear Joe: To my great delight, I have just found on my desk your letter to Cliff Roberts saying that you will play in the Masters this year.

"Please be assured that it will give us all, especially me, much pleasure to welcome you. I hope you will have your game in the best possible condition and that we may be able to cause you to have a good time. With best regards ..."

Naturally, the invitation was promptly accepted, making Joe the first Irishman to compete in the Masters. Christy O'Connor Snr had previously turned down several invitations because he could not see the financial sense of travelling to the US simply for one tournament. Invitations to other events around the same time might have changed matters, but they never materialised.

On the other hand, Joe, as a successful businessman, had no such concerns. On his first time in Augusta National, he stayed in the Crow's Nest, at the top of the clubhouse, just as another Irish winner of the British Amateur, Garth McGimpsey, would do almost 20 years later, and Michael Hoey for this year's Masters. For his next two visits, however, he was accommodated in the Eisenhower Cabin as a guest of the club.

"I learned when I first got there that I was the recipient of a special invitation from Cliff Roberts (the notoriously autocratic club chairman)," said Joe. "In fact I became a member of Augusta National in 1967 and I retained my membership for about five years. But the annual subscription was about $7,500 which I found difficult to justify, even though I could afford it at the time. It was a lot of money in those days for what was only an annual visit.

"On the first occasion, they gave me the honour of playing the opening round with the defending champion, Jack Nicklaus. This was a great thing. As we're going around with close on 5,000 people watching us, they're shouting 'Go get him Jack. Go, go Jack.' And, of course whoever played with him was supported as well. So they shouted 'And you too, Irish'. But it transpires that I shoot 76, 74 against Jack's 72, 79 which means that I qualify and he doesn't.

"Then the next year they paired me with Arnold Palmer. And Arnie's Army are doing their thing and shouting 'Go get him Arnie.' And again I'm getting the consolation murmurs of 'And you too, Irish.' And I shoot 75, 73 as against 72,79 from Arnold, with the result that I make the cut and Arnold doesn't.

"When we sat down to eat on the Friday night of the tournament, Cliff Roberts said: 'Well, now. We're thinking of inviting Carr back next year but who in the name of God will play with him?' So they gave me Sam Snead in 1969 and neither of us qualified."

Snead was the butt of regular taunts about his reputed meanness. Joe admitted, for instance, that he and others would try to get at him by saying things like: "Come on Sam, you can't take it with you." To which he'd reply with a sly grin: "Don't matter. I'm not going." And he'd be similarly dismissive of accusations that he was the only man to use the ball-washer on the first tee at Augusta.

Accusations of parsimony were also levelled against Longhurst, the much-admired correspondent of The Sunday Times and television commentator for the BBC. As we say in Ireland, Henry enjoyed the odd sup, which prompted Joe to refer to him as "Longthirst". Whether this was responsible for the odd caustic comment in Longhurst's writings about Joe, is, of course, a matter of mischievous conjecture.

In the event, a friend of Joe's from Portmarnock GC bet him £10 that he would get Henry to buy a drink in the Augusta Clubhouse during the Masters. After half an hour of serious hinting at the bar, however, there wasn't a budge out of the bould Henry, as Joe suspected would be the case. Instead, he had the effrontery to turn to the Portmarnock member and ask for a few cents to make a phone call to a friend. Whereupon he received the exasperated retort: "Here's 10 cents; ring them all."

Joe recalled another occasion when he and Henry were staying at the home of an oil millionaire in Oklahoma. "Press a button and the wall went back to reveal a wardrobe containing 50 or 60 suits," he said. "I remember when we headed for the plane home, Henry had an extra bag containing at least four suits which were gifts from our host."

But memories of Bobby Jones at Augusta prompted kinder thoughts. "I would go regularly to visit himself and Mary during the Masters," he said. "By then, he was desperately crippled by his illness." Syringomyelia, a fluid-filled cavity in the spinal cord, causes pain first of all, then loss of feeling and muscle wastage. Like the more common amyotrophic lateral sclerosis, it leads to progressive paralysis, though it leaves the brain unaffected which means that the victim is always aware of his diminishing capabilities.

"He bore it all with astonishing grace," remarked Joe. "In fact he was a perfect advertisement for his own award." This point was emphasised in an exchange which Jones had with Pat Ward-Thomas. "How are you, Bob?" asked Ward-Thomas on a particular visit to Augusta National. Jones replied cheerfully: "Well, Pat, I have my heart, my lungs and my so-called brain. We play it as it lies."

Joe went on: "He would sit there in a wheelchair, smoking a cigarette with one of those long holders. And I'll always remember after I had carded an 84 in the final round in 1967, I went into Bob's cabin and Mary asked me: 'How did you do, Joe?' And before I had a chance to answer, Bob said: 'Mary, if Joe had done well, he would have told you long ago.'

"It was obvious that Mary loved him intensely and she cared for him with remarkable tenderness during his long illness. He was a great, great character who was also the golfing idol of my generation – the finest golfer the world had seen up to that stage. I think he did more for the game than a lot of people realise. You could say that he put golf on the map. From the time he started to make a serious impact on the major competitions, it became a spectator sport in which enthusiasts of all ages could take an interest. Before that, it was a fuddy-duddy, old people's game.

"I don't think even Jack Nicklaus could dispute Bob's astonishing charisma. Golf has produced a number of great men, but in my view, nobody has had the aura of greatness that we associate with Bob Jones. And, of course he did the Grand Slam. I must say that I was amazed to see Tiger Woods take possession of all four trophies at the same time but even he has acknowledged that the ultimate achievement is to win the four professional majors in the same season."

As it happened, 1967, the year of Joe's Augusta debut, was also the year of Ben Hogan's Masters swansong. And it was a memorable one. In the third round, the entire course was electrified as The Hawk recaptured much of his old magic when covering the back nine in 30 strokes for a marvellous 66. "I've never seen anything like the excitement," said Joe. "Everybody, including myself, went out on the course when we heard what he was doing.

"We were suddenly aware that the man who was reputed to have played out of his own divot-marks, was doing it again, as a 54-year-old. Though I had studied him on film, this was the first time I had seen him in the flesh. His reputation was immense. And what I saw at Augusta that day was a swing which was mechanical perfection. It seemed to me that nothing could go wrong. I will always remember standing on the back of the 18th green as the entire attendance erupted into sustained cheering. He had to hole an awkward one for his 30, but he managed to get it in. It was one of the most spectacular scenes I have ever witnessed in golf."

Hogan, who had won the Masters twice but lost a play-off to Snead in 1954, shared 10th place with his old adversary behind Gay Brewer that weekend. And along with prize money of $2,720 he came away with a crystal vase as his reward for the lowest round of day three.

On the question of greatness, I remember a small press conference which a few of us were fortunate to get with Nicklaus on one of the practice days before the US Masters in the mid-1990s. The Bear was in such a forthcoming mood that it seemed only a matter of time before the question would be asked. And so it was.

Who was the greatest player in the history of the game? "(Ben) Hogan is the best player I have ever seen," replied Nicklaus. "I never saw Jones, so I can't comment on him. As for myself, that's for others to judge."

As for Joe's Masters appearances: given that he was a 45-year-old with a decidedly streaky putting method and whose best displays were behind him, it would be universally acknowledged that he performed admirably on his Augusta debut, carding rounds of 76, 74, 79, 84 for an aggregate of 315.

Among those who failed to make the cut on that occasion were such luminaries as Nicklaus, Jimmy Demaret, Jerry Barber, Peter Alliss and the emerging Raymond Floyd. A year later, when Bob Goalby won the title in controversial circumstances after Roberto de Vicenzo had missed a play-off by signing for a wrong score on the 71st, Joe had rounds of 75, 73, 80, 78 for 306. The halfway casualties on that occasion included Palmer, Cary Middlecoff, Al Balding and Ryder Cup representative Peter Butler.

By 1969, however, the relentless strain on nerve-ends had taken its toll. With rounds of 79 and 76, Joe missed the cut in the company of 1967 champion Brewer, Snead, Hubert Green, Peter Thomson and Michael Bonallack. In fact, the casualties also included Tony Jacklin, who would capture the British Open crown at Royal Lytham a few months later.

"I would love to have played the Masters in my heyday, instead of in my mid-forties, but I didn't get the chance," he said. "So I feel I'm entitled to be proud of the fact that I could go over there and play all four rounds on such a difficult course at my first two attempts, especially when so many of the great names failed."

Meanwhile, his appearances produced stories which have since become part of golfing folklore. Stories about a time when Palmer had a red jet called AP I and Nicklaus had a blue jet, GB I (for Golden Bear). And how they used to fly over Augusta National and dip their wings to let the boys know they had arrived.

Recalled Joe: "I was practising one year for the Masters in the company of Julius Boros, Kenny Venturi and Tom Weiskopf, when the red one swooped over. Julius, who always liked to show that he was on top of things, looked up and proclaimed solemnly: 'The king's arrived: long live the king.' And then, about 20 minutes later, a blue one comes along, gives the mandatory dip of the wings and he says: 'Ah, there goes the crown prince: now the tournament can begin.'

"Later on, we're coming off the 18th green and this small propeller job flies overhead. Whereupon Julius remarks: 'Well now, wouldn't you think those fellows would have their caddies here before them.'"

Joe retains a great affection for Augusta National which he describes as a magnificent place. "Spread over 365 acres, I always saw it as a man-sized course where I could use my length to full advantage, especially at the par fives," he said. "And, of course, Cliff Roberts ran it as a sort of benign dictatorship, just like men such as John Arthur Brown did at Pine Valley where, I must say I am very proud to be an honorary member, and Dick Tufts at Pinehurst. Indeed I found that all the great courses in America, including Seminole and The National (on Long Island), had a strong man in charge. I liked that. I've always felt that a golf club is no place for democracy. You finish up with too many committees."

By way of acknowledging Joe's involvement with Augusta National, the then club chairman, Jackson T Stephens, wrote of him in 1992: "Joe played in the Masters Tournament in 1967, 1968 and 1969 and we were honoured by his presence at the 1992s Masters as captain of the Royal and Ancient Golf Club of St Andrews. We appreciate Joe's contribution to golf."

And Tony Jacklin recalled "fond memories of playing golf around the par-3 course at Augusta National in the late 60s with Joe, and also some happy times spent with him at Sotogrande in Southern Spain." The 1969 British Open and 1970 US Open champion went on: "For me, Joe is one of the greatest Irishmen alive and he always played the game in a true, sportsmanlike spirit. He has done a great job for golf and for Ireland. I wish him well and 'May the wind be always at his back.' Indeed I suspect that he would prefer it that way himself these days."

When Bobby Jones completed the Grand Slam by beating Gene Homans on the 11th green of the 36-hole final of the 1930 US Amateur Championship at Merion, he needed an escort of 50 marines to guide him safely to the clubhouse 600 yards away. The walk was described by The New York Times as: "The most triumphant journey any man ever travelled in sport."

After enjoying more than his share of adulation, Joe found he had gained a greater understanding of that famous journey during precious times with Bobby Jones at the course he had lovingly created in the heart of Georgia.

Chapter Nine
Friends and Rivals

Jack Nicklaus was only 21 when Joe had the misfortune to meet him in the Walker Cup singles in Seattle in 1961. And by his own admission, our hero could hardly credit that a player of such tender years could beat him so comprehensively, even over 36 holes.

So he had mixed feelings when, in the subsequent US Amateur at Pebble Beach, he lost to Dudley Wysong in the semi-finals. Naturally, his heart saw it as a missed opportunity of becoming the only Irish winner of the blue riband of American amateur golf, but his head told him that a meeting with Nicklaus in the final was not a prospect to be relished.

Still, there were seasoned observers who would have killed to see such a match. Among them was Henry Longhurst who, in his report of the semi-finals, informed his readers: "I can imagine the suspense with which the progress of this match (Carr v Wysong) was followed not only in Eire, but also in Britain. Joe Carr is 'one of ours', wherever he may play abroad and, in particular, in the

United States. He has a quality of endearing himself to galleries which is unique in my experience. Not a soul here bore any ill-will to Wysong, but everyone seemed to want Joe to win. A final between him and Nicklaus would have been a natural."

A morning round of 81 from Joe, however, effectively scuppered such a mouth-watering clash in that he went into lunch five down. Except that he didn't have lunch. Having ordered a meal to be sent to his room in the Lodge, it never arrived. So he had to make do with a hurried sandwich at a lunch counter in a drugstore near the first tee.

"If only I could cut him down to two at the turn, I think I could win," Joe said before venturing forth in the afternoon. As things turned out, he brought the match to the final hole but at this famous, 540-yard par five, Joe pulled his third shot onto a rocky ledge above Pacific breakers: four yards to the right and he would have been putting to save the match.

As Longhurst reported: "Nicklaus meanwhile, had slaughtered a luckless opponent by 9 and 8 (in the other semifinal). No one could really suggest that Joe or anyone else would beat him in the final, but what a final it would have been! If only I were staying overnight to see it."

Naturally, the embryonic Bear, who was a cumulative 15 under par in getting to the final, duly captured the title. It was another slaughter, with Wysong going under by 8 and 6. "I remember thinking at the time 'This boy is incredible,'" recalled Joe. "And on my return from that trip to the US, I wrote an article for the Irish Independent in which I stated that in the Walker Cup, I had played a guy who would become the world's greatest golfer."

This is the piece:

"A golfing visit to America is always a worthwhile experience. Four times I have played on Walker Cup sides on the East Coast of the States and recently I had the opportunity of going to the West Coast to play with the Walker Cup side in Seattle and in the American Amateur Championship at Pebble Beach, California.

"Our first stop was Vancouver, where we spent three days becoming acclimatised on the Capilano course, which is situated on the Guinness Estate – yes, the same Guinness family – overlooking the city of Vancouver. It was a typical American course – tree-lined and in perfect condition – and it gave us some idea of what faced us in Seattle.

"As everybody now knows, the Americans trounced us in the Walker Cup and that great player, Jack Nicklaus, won the American Amateur Championship. How it is that the Americans always have the edge over British and Irish golfers is a question I have been asked countless times since my return, and to my mind the chief reason is physical.

"They are tremendously hospitable people out there, so much so in fact that it is difficult enough to conserve your energy for golf. While the main thing is to try to win the Walker Cup, the goodwill achieved by attending various lavish functions cannot be minimised.

"The Americans really took this year's British and Irish team to their hearts – and I would say it was the most popular side ever to hit the States, despite our big defeat.

"I have little doubt that if I had been fully fit, I would have reached the final of the (US) Amateur Championship. Not for a moment, however, do I think I would have conquered Nicklaus who, to my mind, is among the four best players in the world today, the other three being Arnold Palmer, Gary Player and Sam Snead.

"If the American Open Championship was run on a two-year basis, Nicklaus would now be their champion – he finished second last year and fourth this year – and I am prepared to bet my bottom dollar that he captures it within the next couple of years. They say in America that Nicklaus weighs more and hits harder than the Brown Bomber, Joe Louis, did in his prime.

"I struck up quite a friendship with Nicklaus during my stay in the States and asked him about his programme during the present season. He told me: 'I have already played in 11 tournaments, three with amateurs and eight with professionals, and the lowest I finished was 16th, being first, second or third most of the time.'

"What a feeling of superiority he must have had when he faced an ordinary mortal like myself!

"The betting on the final of the US Amateur Championship took the same form as that of a one-sided boxing pairing – not who would win but in what round the KO would occur. You could get fair odds that Nicklaus would win by 8 and 7 or more. I have met many fine American golfers – Harvie Ward and Charlie Coe to mention two – but Nicklaus combines the best of what they all possess. He has physique, touch and power and at 21 years of age must bid to become the most fantastic golfer of all time.

"To give you an instance of the great respect I and everybody else have for Nicklaus, I will tell you a little story about an outing I had with him on the Monday of the American Championship. Jack and myself had a bye into the second round and along with another American, Bob Barton, who was also free on the opening day, we went along to the nearby Cypress Point course to have a round.

"We decided to play the second nine holes and Jack suggested that we toss and the odd man out play the other two over three holes and then we'd switch around.

"Jack and I beat Barton by two holes over the first three; the other two then beat me by one hole over the second three and Barton and I faced Nicklaus over the 16th, 17th and 18th.

"The 16th at Cypress Point is probably the most difficult short hole in the world – a full drive over an elbow of the Pacific to a green surrounded by ice plant.

"Nicklaus planted his drive 10 feet from the pin and rolled in the putt for a two; had another birdie at the 17th and with victory secure then asked: 'What about a bye?' 'No thank you,' replied Barton and myself almost simultaneously, realising that to win a hole against Nicklaus was no ordinary task.

"Will Nicklaus turn professional? A public relations officer in one of the biggest trouser manufacturing firms in the States, he is comfortably situated (Nicklaus was actually earning $16,000 per year at the time). He has plenty of money and plenty of time, but working on the lines of 'Do the thing you like best and get paid for it', I believe he may yet join paid ranks, as did Frank Stranahan, who was probably the wealthiest amateur to turn professional."

Joe was remarkably accurate when predicting in 1961 that Nicklaus would win the US Open within "the next couple of years." As things turned out, it took him only a year. In June 1962, Nicklaus captured his first professional title which happened to be the US Open at Oakmont, where he beat Arnold Palmer by 71-74 in an 18-hole play-off.

Top prize was $17,500 and as an interesting aside, on the final day of the championship, Nicklaus wore iridescent, olive pants which, several years later, his wife Barbara described as "army refugee pants." Still, the player was so superstitious that he insisted on wearing the same pants in the play-off the following day.

In conversation with the great man 40 years on, he reflected wistfully to me on those memorable times, saying: "It would have been a bit special if Joe and I could have met in the final of the US Amateur at Pebble Beach. Later on, I always looked forward to playing with him, especially in practice rounds for the British Open. I used to kid him that I had to finance my trip somehow.

"I'm aware that Joe has claimed that he won money off me playing poker, which was probably once or twice, whereas we played golf a whole bunch of times. So he's not getting away with that one. The truth is that when Joe told me he was retiring from competitive golf, I kidded him that Barbara would be very disappointed because he had always financed her annual trip to the Pringle tent.

"I remember the Walker Cup at Seattle in 1961 when I got Joe at number five in the singles order and beat him

6 and 4. The longer, 36 hole matches probably helped to enhance American superiority back then, which is clearly not the case over 18 holes these days.

"Two years previously, the Walker Cup was at Muirfield, and it remains one of the most interesting and exciting events I've ever played, because it was my first trip to Scotland and my first trip to Britain, period. It was also the first time I had seen a links and I really enjoyed it. I had fun with it.

"That was where I met Joe for the first time and though we didn't play against each other at that stage, we became good friends. Even with an age difference of 18 years between us, I certainly enjoyed his company and I would like to think that he enjoyed mine.

"Later, on the few occasions each year that we would get together to play practice rounds or compete, as we did in the Masters in 1967, it was always fun, kidding each other and having a bit of a needle. And we would have dinner occasionally.

"When I think of Joe, I picture a fun-loving guy who could play golf really well. I would characterise his game as being indisciplined discipline, if you can make sense of that. Though his swing looked like a slash, Joe was not a slasher. He knew exactly what he was doing with that swing, though it was not a taught swing, as I perceived it. It was a swing that looked as if it had been developed over time, and it worked for him.

"He knew how to hit that fade and keep the ball under control, and he used those big hands of his very, very well. He was also very effective around the greens.

"It is important to stress that self-discipline was a major factor in making him a very, very good player. To me, Joe Carr was a golfer who, in some ways, probably got more than 100 per cent out of what he had, yet in other ways, only realised half of his potential. By this I mean that if he had, say, turned professional early in his career and devoted himself exclusively to golf, his talents were such that he could have gone much, much further in the game. I have no doubt he could have competed at a much higher level, but he was obviously content to do what he did.

"For my part, I didn't grow up in wind and I had to learn how to play in it. And I know I learned a lot from watching Joe play links golf. I saw him play an awful lot of two, three or four irons off the tee and I came to realise that this was a pretty good way to play those courses. It was the only way you could be certain of avoiding the bunkers."

That was when I put a leading question to him: "Was Joe long?" "He was very long. Yeah," Nicklaus replied. "Even by your standards?" "Yeah. I said Joe was very long." There was a finality about that second reply which, from experience of the Bear, I recognised as a cold statement of fact on which he saw no need to elaborate.

He then laughed heartily at the memory of the Eisenhower Trophy at Merion in 1960 when, as Michael Bonallack recounts graphically in the Foreword, Joe had the effrontery to have a two dollars a shot bet with the Bear. That was the occasion when Nicklaus had an aggregate of 269 to shatter Ben Hogan's US Open total of 1950 at the same course by no fewer than 18 strokes.

"That was great; I liked that," he said. Then he laughed heartily again before repeating: "I really liked that." And one sensed he was thinking that Joe hadn't chosen the ideal tournament to have a bet of that nature. He then added: "As I've said, Joe and I always had this friendly bet, but to be fair to him, I never forget the things I've won and I suppose I was starting to come into the best part of my game at that point."

He went on: "I had a house on Great Harbour Key in the Bahamas and I remember Joe going over there with me and we had some fun, fishing and playing golf. And we had quite a few bets there, too.

"With all the good times we had together, I was delighted to be able to pay a visit to Sutton Golf Club in 1990, when he was the centenary captain of the club. Tim Mahony set it up that I would drop in by chopper on a trip back to Dublin from Mount Juliet. It turned out to be a nice way of honouring an outstanding golfer and a great sportsman.

"Looking further back and thinking about players like Joe, you realise that you don't remember as much about those amateur days as you'd wish to. But I like to think that it helped all of us in our education towards becoming better golfers."

Nicklaus concluded: "When I talked to Joe on the phone recently, he was chatting away as if we hadn't missed a beat for years. At first I didn't recognise him, though I knew it wasn't Christy O'Connor. And as he chatted on, it was as if those matches at Merion, Seattle and the British Open were only yesterday. Which, I suppose, is how it should be."

Meanwhile, an enduring affection for Joe is evident in the book "My Story" on which Nicklaus collaborated with Ken Bowden. In it, the Bear makes reference to the 1961 Walker Cup matches, recalling: "On the first day of September in Seattle, Deane Beman and I easily won our Walker Cup foursome, and the following day I was proud to have maintained a 100-percent record over my two matches following an enjoyable scrap with the legendary Irishman, Joe Carr."

And later on, in a reference to his ill-fated British Open debut at Troon in 1962, Nicklaus observes: "To really top things off, when the pairings came out I found myself teeing off in the opening round at 3:45 in the afternoon, and not with another contestant but with a marker. Boy, did that raise a head of steam! Thankfully, my good friend Joe Carr, the great amateur, bless his Irish heart, went to the organizing Royal and Ancient and told them it wasn't right to do that to the U.S. Open champion, so they moved me into a threesome."

Though it didn't save the great man from the indignity of carding an opening round of 80, Joe's gesture clearly meant a lot to him at the time. And it is worth pointing out that he was more than pleased to be associated with this book, on being approached earlier this year.

Noel Fogarty gained the distinction among Irish golfers of getting within an ace of slaying the Bear. A Dubliner, he was born in December 1924 and remembers Joe being taught by the nuns in primary school at Santa Sabina in Sutton. Indeed mischievously, he couldn't resist pointing out that it was, in fact, a girls school.

Fogarty, or Fogo as Joe affectionately called him, was to become one of Dublin's leading bookmakers. And as a latecomer to golf, he represented St Anne's as a 14-handicapper in the Barton Cup in 1950 before joining neighbouring Royal Dublin.

He recalled: "Joe was an established player when I got seriously into golf in 1954. That was when I was picked on a Leinster team to play a French selection at Golf-du-Lys, outside Paris, where Joe was also in the side. From then on, he and I became regular golfing partners and friends and were team-mates at provincial and international levels. We won the Killarney Scratch Foursomes together on three occasions, in 1961, 1962 and 1966 and we were to play each other head-to-head on three occasions, but I'll tell you more about that, later.

"On attaining scratch status, I began to make regular appearances in the British Amateur and played in the British Open in 1956, 1957 and 1958. And I was at St Andrews in 1958 when Joe won the Amateur for a second time. I remember sharing a room with him at Rusack's Hotel and getting special permission from the R and A so that, after I was knocked out, I could walk the fairways with Joe at his request, following his matches. To be honest, the only time he looked to be in any trouble in that Amateur was in the semi-finals against an up-and-coming Michael Bonallack.

"Joe and I had travelled together from Dublin Airport to Edinburgh and when we arrived at St Andrews, he said to me: 'Now Fogo, you'll be joining me in a few serious (fourball) matches in practice and if we play well and you get to bed at night, we could make our week's exes.' So, for once in my life I did what I was told and, sure enough, we had a very productive build-up to the championship, playing two matches a day.

"That was when I discovered what a press was in golf. And that it had nothing to do with newspapers. When opponents went two down, they would press, and keep pressing. All of which turned out very nicely for us. We won all our matches and with everybody wanting to play with the great Joe Carr, we had no shortage of victims. I never knew the extent of the money involved except that when it was all over, Joe paid my expenses, in full. Needless to say, with Joe winning the title, it became a very good week in every respect.

"At that time, Joe was very, very long off the tee. In fact I saw him do some amazing things during that championship, including his famous eagle at the 12th, where he drove through the green. Apart from his tremendous strength, he had extraordinary will-power and I looked on him as one of the game's great players which, naturally, made me value his friendship all the more.

"In 1959, Joe, Michael Fitzpatrick and myself entered the Amateur at Royal St George's. And I remember when Joe cast his expert eye over my section of the draw, he remarked: 'I'll tell you what Fogo, you're in the thick of the fray, very early.' Obviously he had noted the name of J W Nicklaus. But I didn't pass much heed, because I always tried to take each match in the Amateur as it came."

As it happened, Joe's prediction became a reality when Noel had a fourth-round meeting with Nicklaus, who would go on to capture his first US Amateur crown later that summer. In his report of the match, Paul MacWeeney of The Irish Times wrote: "Nicklaus was much the sounder and straighter in the long game, but while he took the fourth and fifth, he could not draw further away, and Fogarty, after a perfect approach to the ninth, dropped a six-foot putt for a win in three to reduce the deficit to one hole.

"Then he really began to hunt the American. At the 10th, he lipped the hole with a putt for a win; squared it at the 11th by chipping stone dead from the rough and saved the 12th in a similar manner. He lost his touch at the next two holes, showing that fatal tendency to hurry the downswing with the driver, and pushing out his tee shot.

"In fact, he put his second out of bounds at the 14th but back he came to win the 15th where both were in the rough, but the Irish chip was much closer. It was squared at the 16th, Nicklaus leaving the first putt four feet short and missing the next, but whereas Fogarty hit a fine drive at the 17th, he hooked the approach and this time could not save himself with the chip. So he was one down with one to play.

"The strain of all this, however, was taking toll of Nicklaus and the American made a surprising and horrible mess of the 18th. Both were in rough on the left off the tee but Nicklaus socketed across the fairway, was still short in three and could not chip close enough to equal Fogarty's five.

"Now the odds swung towards Ireland, with Fogarty's drive down the middle and Nicklaus's in the rough. After the American had found the bunker in front of the green, however, Fogarty lost a great chance by pulling into a neighbouring trap. The Irish recovery was good, but not good enough. Nicklaus came out stone dead and Fogarty's seven-foot putt to keep it alive just slid past."

MacWeeney concluded: "It was a great, fighting display by Fogarty – the best he had yet given in the top class of golf."

The hero of this memorable battle reflected: "The only time Joe and I ever discussed that match was after Joe had played in the 1961 Walker Cup in Seattle, where Nicklaus beat him by 6 and 4. When he returned to Dublin, I made a point of talking to him about the match and more or less by way of sympathy, I pointed out that Joe had lost to a truly great player. And I recalled the marvellous match I had had against Nicklaus two years previously at Royal St George's. Whereupon Joe turned to me and said: 'I'll promise you this Fogo, he has improved a helluva lot since you played him.' And I smiled quietly to myself."

Fogarty went on: "I was fortunate to play a few times in the 1950s and '60s with Jimmy Bruen, who would have been past his best at the time. We became good friends. And I was in Killarney in 1963 when Joe beat Jimmy in the semi-finals of the Irish Close. As things worked out, Eric O'Brien beat me in the other semi-final and he was then beaten by Joe in the final.

"In his hey-day, it was reckoned that Bruen was the better player, but the records show that Joe stood up much longer to the pressures of championship golf. There was a time when Tom Craddock – Lord have mercy of him – had a bit of a jinx on him, but I would have no hesitation in agreeing with those who rated Joe as the best British or Irish golfer of the post-war period."

Then, old competitive instincts came to the fore when Fogarty added: "Joe and I met three times in matchplay golf and Joe won just the once, in the final of the 1969 South of Ireland Championship. No doubt he told you all about that particular match, when his son Roddy caddied for him. But he wouldn't want to tell you about two years previously, when I beat him on the way to the title.

"Indeed after I'd beaten him, I can still picture Joe saying to me 'Fogo, I've invested a lot of money in this championship and I've only one runner left. That's you. Now get out there and win it.' Which I did, beating Scott MacDonald, a former British Universities' champion from St Andrews, in the final. He also promised that if I won, he would wine and dine me like I'd never be wined and dined in my life. That was 35 years ago and I'm still waiting for the meal.

"Later on, when I'd mention that promise to him, he'd appear outraged and say 'Fogo! You never feckin' beat me.' Then I'd give him chapter and verse of Lahinch 1967 before adding, for good measure, my Senior Cup win over him when Royal Dublin met Sutton in the Leinster semi-finals at Portmarnock. That was a wonderful match in which I eventually got him on the 22nd.

"But apart from those three meetings, we were as thick as thieves."

It was interesting that Jack Nicklaus should have mentioned Himself, who had a long association with Joe. Indeed as we have noted, O'Connor was responsible for the greatest disappointment of Joe's career, by beating him in the 1959 Dunlop Masters at Portmarnock, when Joe seemed to have the coveted title within his grasp.

O'Connor recalled: "I played an awful lot of golf with Joe. I played with him and against him, sometimes seriously, other times in silly matches and as far as I can recall, we were never beaten as a partnership. And that was often against two top-class professionals. For money."

"Joe didn't like putting on a bet, I don't think," Himself continued with an ironic smile. "You could see his eyes light up when a fella would mention having an interest on a match. He thought of it as money from America, which was small wonder, because he was a hard man to beat.

"I remember Joe as a great player who would have done very, very well had he ever turned professional. When

I first saw him, he had a three-quarter swing and hit the ball with a draw, and being such a big man, you could almost see the driver bending with the power that he got into it.

"He had a great pair of hands which, of course, is very important in golf. Long fingers. But I think he made a mistake in changing to an out-to-in swing. I always wanted him to get back to drawing the ball which, in my view, was when he played to his best.

"And he was long. I remember one time playing a game at Hillside, before a British Open at Birkdale (1965). Nicklaus was there and Joe asked me if I would like to join them. I was only too happy to tag along and we had a flutter.

"Anyhow, Nicklaus was very long at that time. Very long. But I felt I was driving the ball very well and with the honour at this par five, I hit a really good one. Whereupon I stood back and expanded my chest about two inches with pride. But I knew if Joe hit his with draw, he would definitely be outside me. Even my best." "You mean he was longer than you!," I suggested in mock surprise. To which Christy replied with a sly grin: "Well maybe not. But there wouldn't be much in it."

He went on: "Anyhow, he got it outside me on this occasion and my chest returned to normal. Then Nicklaus let fly, and his drive pitched where Joe's ball had come to rest. I hit a three iron to the green for my second shot, Joe hit a four iron and Nicklaus hit a nine iron. Joe was a very good iron player and whatever you may have heard about his putting, he was very good at that too. Don't mind those people who claimed he was a bad putter. You couldn't win the matches he won, putting badly.

"I played with him and against him for money, at St Andrews and other great courses around Britain, where he would have been invited to professional tournaments. Joe loved St Andrews and I remember him having a great chance of winning the Centenary Open in 1960 before the rain killed him.

"Then there were matches at Royal Dublin, naturally, but we had most of our battles at The Island and Baltray. And there were head-to-heads. I enjoyed playing against Joe; I always enjoyed his company but I'm not going to say how these matches turned out. That's for others to say. (By his own admission, Joe could never get the better of Christy, head-to-head).

"There would be matches in which Noel Fogarty would partner me against Joe and Nicky Lynch, who was a very good player. Nicklaus we used to call him for fun. A gentleman. My partner, Fogo, was also a fine player. In fact, I always thought he was good enough to play at Walker Cup level. And while there would be a good few bob on these fourballs, we didn't do it just to take money off each other, though it was serious money. The competition was important and Joe hated losing. So did I. Which meant that for all the world it was like playing in a tournament.

"There were also the annual matches in which the professionals played the amateurs: Ryder Cup teams against Walker Cup teams. And I played against Joe in those and since it's down there on the record, I have to say that I did him every time we met in singles. Admittedly, that was only two or three times but I have to say that I always enjoyed putting my hand in Joe's pocket.

"Another match which comes to mind was a foursomes I played with Henry Cotton against Joe and a Welshman called John Morgan. And we had to give them a three-hole start. We had a great match and Cotton and myself won, but there were other times when the amateurs killed us.

"Some of those Walker Cup men were great players. How could you give a guy like Michael Bonallack a three-hole start when he was liable to hole everything in sight? Reid Jack (British Amateur champion in 1957) was a great striker of the ball. So was Ronnie White (five-time Walker Cup player). They were great players who would have made very successful professionals.

"As for Joe: had be turned pro, I believe he would have attained Ryder Cup standard. I know people said that he might as well have been a professional, given all the time he spent at the game and the amount of practising he did. But he missed the regular competition that a professional has at the highest level. That's the key. It was a level that would have forced him to tighten up his game and not waste shots which he could afford to do as an amateur, especially in matchplay against weak opponents."

O'Connor concluded: "I suppose what made Joe different was his competitive toughness. That's what impressed me most about him. He wanted to beat everybody. And he would do it with a smile."

The essential difference between Joe and Jimmy Bruen was highlighted, ironically, not by an Irish observer but by Sam McKinlay in the Glasgow Herald. He wrote: "His (Bruen's) record is not as good as that of his great fellow countryman, Joe Carr, partly because he did not have Carr's tremendous competitive compulsion. But when Bruen's imagination was alight and when the 'loop' was working and when he was not breaking steel shafts like matchsticks, he was the most thrilling, accomplished golfer in the world."

Joe wouldn't argue with those sentiments. "I have no hesitation is acknowledging Jimmy as the best Irish amateur I ever saw," he said. "No doubt about that. I played him three times but I thank God it wasn't in his hey-day. I was lucky enough to beat him in the semi-finals of the Irish Close at Killarney in 1963. And I beat him in a match between Leinster and Munster at Little Island and later when Sutton played Cork GC down there.

"Though Jimmy could knock it around in 61 or 62, I never liked Little Island and on the first occasion we met there, I was at the top of the tree and he was some way past his best. For the interprovincial friendly, the crowds came from everywhere and I remember it being a fairly tight match until close to the finish.

"But when I was a youngster at Portmarnock, in the years just before World War II, I played a lot with Jimmy. He had started in the insurance business in Dublin and used to keep his game in shape at Portmarnock, where he was accorded the facilities of the course. He would give myself and Billy McMullan four up and beat our better ball for money.

"Of course he was already a Walker Cup player by then and was way ahead of us and certainly a long way ahead of me. He was long, considerably longer in the air than I was. He played a lot at Portmarnock at that time and he drove the second and fifth greens and I saw him go through the back of the third with another huge drive. Still, I could chase a ball which would run further than Jimmy's best.

"People talk about John Burke but he didn't have the shot-making talent of Jimmy who, from 1938 until about 1942, was among the six best players in the world, amateur or professional, in my view. Remember, had the 1939 Open at St Andrews been played over six rounds, he would have won it. There was nobody in this country in the same class as him at that stage, myself included.

"I had been abroad only to the Boys' Championships by the time of Jimmy's Amateur win in 1946. Then later, when I was on the way up, he was on the way down, so there was no real meeting place for us. I remember talking to Henry Cotton about the Birkdale Amateur and he told me that Jimmy was all over the place and that he played some astonishing recoveries. Of course Cotton and his wife Toots idolised him.

"Though I never felt I had to emerge from his shadow, I have no hesitation in saying that in his hey-day, Jimmy was better than me. And as a holer-out, he was probably better than me, even at my best. But I would like to think I had a better career, though I certainly wouldn't have relished playing him at the peak of his powers."

JOE ON TOM CRADDOCK

Joe always reckoned if he could get three up on a player he was dead as a dodo. In fact he considered it unthinkable that anybody could get four holes off him. In the case of Tom Craddock, however, he was forced to make an exception, for the simple reason that the unthinkable happened during a Senior Cup match between Sutton and Malahide at Royal Dublin.

"I remember him saying something to me like 'Don't be too hard', recalled Joe. "And he got me. I never forgot that. From that point onwards, I had great respect for him."

He went on: "He had scuppered a conviction which had served me well in my career up to then. And in the final of the Irish Close at Portmarnock in 1959, he got me again, on the 38th, after I had missed a putt for the match on the 35th.

"Make no mistake about it, Tom was a bloody good player. He would have been number two to me in these islands at that time. And we should have won a Walker Cup match together at Sandwich in 1967, when we lost by 3 and 1 to the American pair Robert Dickson and James Grant.

"I suppose what I admired most about Tom was his lovely, smooth action. They say that hitters linger and swingers last. I was a hitter and Tom was a swinger who lasted, despite all the physical problems he had later in his career. And he was a helluva nice fellow who came through difficult times with the help of his wife, Nola, who was the power behind the throne. One of nature's gentlemen."

...ON HARRY BRADSHAW

Arthur Lees and Gerald Micklem used to come over to Portmarnock on alternate years to play against Joe and the resident professional, Harry Bradshaw, affectionately known as The Brad. As the arrangement would suggest, there were return matches at Sunningdale, where, of course, Lees was the local professional and Micklem was the club's leading light.

"When we were there, we would stay in Gerald's house and on their Irish trips, they would stay with me," said Joe. "And if you wanted proof about home advantage, we never beat them at Sunningdale and they never beat us at Portmarnock." The latter part was entirely understandable, given the magic the Brad was capable of producing on his home patch where he could generally play to order and had an eclectic score of 41, including aces at all three par-threes.

Joe went on: "I played a lot of golf with The Brad and we won the Hermitage Foursomes eight times together. And when I won it with Christy Kane, we beat Harry in the final. In fact, our partnership eventually disintegrated because there was no contest.

"Of course the most famous, or infamous thing ever written about Harry was Henry Longhurst's reference to him having an agricultural swing. And in my view, Henry was right. The grip he had, with three fingers overlapping, seemed totally alien to the game of golf. But from 100 yards in, he was the best in the world.

"His extraordinary popularity at Portmarnock owed much, in my view, to the fact that he went there in 1950 when golf was going through major changes, especially in the treatment of professionals. Henry Cotton had won his third Open two years previously and the barriers were being broken down, even in the most exclusive establishments. And Eddie Hackett, who was always a gentleman, had done much to pave the way during his time there.

"Then there was the force of the Brad's own personality. He had an extraordinary way with people. The Americans adored him. To them, he was the classic, warm-hearted Irishman. He transcended all social strata. And the older he got, the more comfortable he became with people of all classes.

"When we were together, I always felt we were impossible to beat, though he didn't like the way I would put him into rough. He found the heather at Gleneagles especially difficult to handle, and wasn't slow in telling me so. 'Don't be putting me in that stuff,' he'd admonish me.

"The Brad always considered it a great advantage in our part of the world to be able to get the ball onto the green at the earliest possible moment. After that, the ball did its own job in trickling towards the hole. There was no question of putting stop on it. That was the golden rule. And whatever club could deliver that result was the one you used.

"He told me to play the shot as if your life depended on throwing the ball between your legs. That's all the height you needed. We had an unbelievable run of foursomes and from a financial standpoint, Gleneagles was a particularly productive venue for Harry."

...ON MICHAEL BONALLACK

"I played Michael probably 10 or 12 times over the years and on each occasion, win or lose, I always ended up saying the same thing: 'If I could putt like you, you'd never get near me.' We had some great, great matches and the dominant element in them all, as far as I was concerned, was Michael's wonderful putting stroke.

"The first time I beat Michael was in the semi-finals of the Amateur when I went on to win the title at St Andrews in 1958. Michael was three-up after nine and I remember saying to my caddie, Andy Doherty, at the time: 'Andy, an important thing to remember about the amateur game as against the pro game is that a fellow like Mike here can get it out in 33 but take 39 to come home.' And sure enough, that's what he did (In the Foreword, Bonallack reveals a rather different memory of that match).

"We became great, great pals almost straight away, and have remained so ever since. We kept in touch with each other all through the years and I value his friendship most dearly.

"I was especially pleased to be competing in the Home Internationals at Killarney in September 1969, when Michael was honoured as the first Englishman to play 100 matches for his country. I remember that by way of celebrating the occasion, he never lost a hole when beating Scotland's Andrew Brooks by 4 and 3 in the top singles and later that day, was presented with Waterford Crystal by Dr John Todd, president of the English Golf Union. As things turned out, that was my international swansong, so I was delighted that it happened to coincide with Michael's big day.

"I managed to keep Michael at bay for several years before he eventually got me and I think it's only reasonable to point out that I was 46 when he beat me in the final of the Amateur at Troon in 1968.

"When Keith McKenzie retired and they went looking for a replacement as secretary of the Royal and Ancient, I think they found gold dust in Michael. He did an absolutely marvellous job, especially in raising the profile of our events internationally. In fact I would go so far as to say that the R and A owes more to Michael than he could ever owe to the R and A. And that's saying something.

"I remember asking him in 1990, when he planned to retire. And typically, he asked me: 'When are you retiring from all your various commitments in golf?' To which I replied: 'Whenever they kick me out.'

"Michael has the wonderful facility for doing things thoroughly, without creating any fuss. And I know that he had tremendous respect from his R and A staff. All the secretaries treated him like a god, which was no more than he deserved."

...ON GERALD MICKLEM

"Gerald's father was very wealthy but he left Gerald with such a tax debt that it nearly broke him. We used to stay with him over in Sunningdale where he would put an entire team up. I think he had about 20 bedrooms in the house. He was a marvellous character and a very fine player in his own right.

"Golf dominated his life to the extent that he did very little else. He certainly never worked, not that I was aware. And he was very, very good for the game, especially in his encouragement of young players coming through. He would collect them in his old Rolls Royce and have his batman take care of them in what became a home from home.

"When you went into a bedroom in Gerald's house, your case was unpacked and your clothes were all laid out. Then, at 7.30 in the morning, tea arrived in the room. Downstairs, breakfast was self-service, something that hotels have only caught up with in recent times.

"In those days, not long after World War II, there were pancakes, bacon, sausages, eggs, tomatoes, the lot. Every day felt like your birthday."

...ON HENRY COTTON

"I had tremendous time for Henry and Toots, both of whom treated Roddy very well, like a son, when he was attempting to bring his game to another level in the late 1960s. And I must say Henry taught him very well, with the result that Roddy returned to Ireland and made the Walker Cup team. And Toots was like a mother to him.

"When I sent another of my sons, John, to him, it wasn't long after he came back that he, too, made the Irish international team. So, Henry's talents as a teacher speak for themselves, as far as my family is concerned.

"We used to have dinner with Henry and Toots and, of course, Henry would put a hand on a lady's knee if he got a chance. Anyway Toots had this big glass table that we all sat around. And she also put a mirror on the ceiling. And she'd admonish him: 'Henry! Henry! Henry!' She had him caught literally from every angle.

"Otherwise it was a marvellous table with the best of food. Which was in keeping with Henry's status as an aristocrat of the game."

...ON BILL CAMPBELL

"Many friendships are made in golf and the best friends of all are made when you play in the Walker Cup. There is something about Walker Cup players: they become friends for life. People like Jack Nicklaus. Normally it would cost well in excess of $50,000 to get Nicklaus to make a public appearance, but he came to Sutton in 1990 for nothing.

"Then there's Bill Campbell, a former R and A captain and president of the USGA. Bill and I have been great pals for a long, long time and I'll tell you why. We played against each other about four times with honours more or less even, though he beat me in the Walker Cup in 1957.

"I remember in 1958, when Bill was noted as a very slow player, we met at St Andrews in the last eight of the Amateur. We were last off, at about 3.30 or so and it was 8.0 by the time we were playing the 17th. And typical of the Irish way of doing things, Dor was at home expecting a baby (Gerry) and she got on the telephone. And the telephone exchange kept the line open all the way through the 18th and 19th until I won the match on the 20th.

"We do those sort of things in Ireland."

...ON FRANK STRANAHAN

"I always think of Frank as the first golfing millionaire, though nowadays they're two a penny. His father owned the

Champion Sparkplug company in Toledo, Ohio, so there was no shortage of silver spoons when Frank came into the world.

"Anyway, when Frank arrived in these parts for the Walker Cup at Royal Birkdale in 1951, he was acknowledged as a very fine player. Among other things, he had been tied second with Byron Nelson behind Jimmy Demaret in the US Masters at Augusta National.

"Still, Frank behaved like an innocent abroad, in a US team captained by Willie Turnesa, who was a kind of father-confessor to the players.

"Typically gullible, Frank's first inclination when he saw somebody hitting a good shot was to think that the answer lay with the club you were using. And he'd want to take the club out of your hand to see what difference it would make to his game.

"Anyway, we were sitting in the clubhouse at Birkdale when Frank came in and said to his captain: 'Gee Willie, I can't seem to get the ball into the hole.' To which Willie replied soothingly: 'Well you know Frank, putting is all about movement.' And Frank nodded: 'Well yes, but ...' 'By the way, Frank, do you breathe while you putt?' 'Sure I do.' 'Then that could be the problem.'

"So, off Frank went, sure he had found the answer, only to return in about half an hour, his face red as a beetroot from holding his breath. 'It doesn't seem to make any difference, Willie,' he moaned, despairingly. Then Willie, the personifaction of patience, suggested: 'What you have to do Frank is to make the stroke between heartbeats.' It took some time, but Frank eventually realised he was being had. And in common with the rest of us, he accepted that there was no magic cure for putting problems.

"Those familiar with St Andrews will be aware of a charming little Catholic Church, overlooking the sea, just down from the Scores Hotel. And those of us of the Catholic faith would make a point of getting mass there if it happened to be a Sunday.

"Anyway, back in 1950, when the Amateur Championship was at St Andrews, they didn't play golf on a Sunday. So those of us staying at the Russell Hotel had no excuse for missing mass. Willie Turnesa, a year prior to his Walker Cup captaincy, Henry and Toots Cotton and myself were coming down the stairs on our way to mass when we happened to run into the bould Frank.

"Afraid he might be missing something, Frank enquired: 'Where are you off to, Willie?' Which brought the reply: 'I'm going to mass, Frank. Are you coming?' 'Naw,' said Stranahan. 'I don't go for all that jazz.' Knowing his man, Willie piped up: 'Well then, you won't win any championship.' Whereupon Frank immediately said: 'Hold on Willie, I'll be with you.'

"Then, when we were all seated in the church, Willie turned to Frank and said: 'See Henry Cotton. He won three Open Championships and he always put a five-pound note on the plate at mass.' Naturally, Frank followed suit. And he even went so far as to tell the parish priest how much he had enjoyed the service.

"That was on the Sunday prior to the Amateur. And lo and behold, Frank went on to win the Championship, beating Dick Chapman by 8 and 6 in the final. But what really tickled our fancy was that for about a year afterwards, Frank went to mass before every tournament. Atheist and all that he was. Like every aspiring champion, he took confidence out of the belief that he had an edge. And for him, mass was it.

"They were wonderful times, made all the more enjoyable by the quirky behaviour of characters like Frank Stranahan."

❖

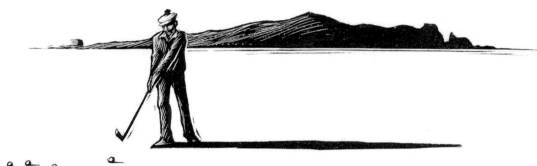

Chapter Ten
The Sutton Connection

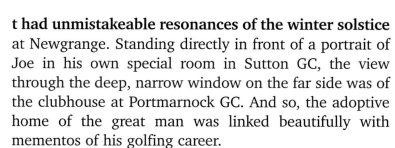

t had unmistakeable resonances of the winter solstice at Newgrange. Standing directly in front of a portrait of Joe in his own special room in Sutton GC, the view through the deep, narrow window on the far side was of the clubhouse at Portmarnock GC. And so, the adoptive home of the great man was linked beautifully with mementos of his golfing career.

"Normally, this sort of thing doesn't happen until you're six-feet under," said the club's most celebrated member, at the official opening of Sutton's new £2 million clubhouse in September 2001. "Even Bob Jones had to die before they named a room after him, so I feel truly honoured that Sutton have done this wonderful thing. I'm thrilled to bits."

It was interesting to note the unanimous acknowledgement of Brian Wallace, the club's 1999 captain, as the prime mover behind the project. And to ensure that no detail would be overlooked, Wallace visited the Bobby Jones room at Atlanta Athletic Club for pointers. The result is a magnificent tribute to a player rated by Peter Alliss as the dominant amateur on this side of the Atlantic for almost 20 years after World War II.

Taoiseach, Bertie Ahern, a politician noted for his love of sport, was suitably impressed by the new building. "I was wondering where you got the money to pay for this," he remarked with a mischievous grin to the assembled members. He also expressed the hope that Wallace "got well paid for his efforts." Clearly, Ahern's time as Minister for Finance had left its mark.

Silversmiths Larry Gunning (a past captain of Royal Dublin) and Bill Fleming did a marvellous job of re-creating the Irish Close and Irish Amateur Open trophies, as replacements for those which Joe had given away. And engravers Tony Lee and Tony Reddan had reason to be proud of a stunning silver salver into which every element of the player's career – titles, course-records, awards – was painstakingly etched.

Of course there were other trophies which were given away – to such institutions as the GUI and the Dublin Chamber of Commerce. And there were three Portmarnock Scratch Cup trophies which were donated to the club on the occasion of their centenary.

Over the formidable span of 68 years as a member, Joe has known three clubhouses at Sutton GC, to which he brought international fame. And on this splendid occasion, by way of acknowledgement, the club had done him proud.

❖

Joe's first handicap at Sutton was what might be described as a domestic plus six, which is what he played off when competing in a juvenile event. He was the backmarker with the limit set at scratch and any chance he might have entertained of winning had all but disappeared when he took a nine at the first. But he improved as the round progressed and eventually returned a highly creditable 82 gross. And even with the six handicap strokes added for a net 88, it was still good enough to give him the top prize. He was on his way.

By the age of 15, he made his first appearance in the British Boys' Championship at Brunsfield, near Edinburgh, where a future rival, Jimmy Bruen, was down to defend the title. And Joe can recall sighs of relief all round when it was announced that Bruen had been forced to withdraw. He had sent a telegram to the organisers explaining that: "Only the honour of playing for my country prevents me from defending my title."

In the event, Joe reached the last 16 and in the same championship a year later, he was beaten at the same stage at Moor Park. Then in 1939, he went with Mick Fitzpatrick, Kevin Hogan and Brian Smyth to the Boys' Championship at Carnoustie where he reached the semi-finals before losing to Sandy Williamston. "I had been three up after seven but never recovered from a shank on the short eighth," he recalled. "Still, I treasured the bronze medal."

It was seven years before he got revenge on Williamston, in the quarter-finals of the Irish Amateur Open at Royal Portrush in 1946. And as it happened, he went on to capture the title for the first time.

On March 19th, 1954 – not an ideal time of year for hot scoring, even on links terrain – Joe equalled the course-record of 61 at Sutton, which had been set by Jimmy Carroll three years previously.

And he was furious with himself for not improving on Carroll's target, given that a par at the last would have meant a magical round of 60. From the edge of the green, however, he left his first putt five feet short and then missed the next. The score was done in a Hilary Society Outing which he won, despite playing off plus-two.

His figures were:

OUT.... 3, 3, 3, 3, 4, 3, 3, 3, 4 = 29
IN ....4, 2, 3, 4, 4, 3, 3, 4, 5 = 32

Among the features of the round was that he drove the green at the 283-yard 11th (second) and holed the putt for an eagle two.

At the mention of Sutton GC, Joe will always make a point of expressing his deep gratitude to the club for the enormous support they gave him throughout his career. And a measure of that support was his selection as club captain in 1948, 1949 and for the centenary year in 1990. He joined Sutton in 1932 at a time when only the cream of society had any chance of getting into Portmarnock: it happened to be relatively near where his adoptive parents lived. There was also the not inconsiderable fact that Sutton were willing to have him. Had they turned him down, it is a matter of conjecture as to where, among the north Dublin golfing fraternity, he would have ended up.

Among the members was his future brother-in-law Kevin Hogan who would become his closest friend. "From my earliest days, I remember Sutton as a friendly, sociable club where the members backed me 100 per cent in anything I did," Joe recalled. "I think you'll find this to be true more of the small clubs than the big ones. I remember as many as 70 members travelling to the Amateur Championships in which I competed. As my friend Bobby Cuddy recalled: 'The opening order was 69 gin and tonics please' (Joe didn't drink alcohol at the time) – at 7.0 in the morning."

He went on: "As for the course: I soon discovered that I had to become a chipper and putter of the highest quality to score around there. It was said that if you stood on the first tee at Sutton and shouted 'fore', the entire course dropped to its knees, but the fact remained that it placed a priceless premium on a productive short game. My good friend Pat Ward-Thomas used to point out that there was out of bounds on both sides off the first tee, to the right into the sea and to the left, over the ninth, though it would be stretching things a bit to reach trouble that far out.

"When I started there, we had a wooden clubhouse. And when I stayed overnight at Hogan's (a few hundred yards away on the Dublin Road), the old man took me under his wing and would drive me over to Sutton early in the morning. He was very keen on golf and we would wait in his big car at the railway gates for the sun to come up. That was when I was working in Todd Burns, before Freddie McDonnell and myself went into business together.

"Later, when old man Hogan and myself developed what might be described as a strained relationship over my marrying Dor, he tried to withdraw the £500 guarantee which he had stood for me in the Munster and Leinster Bank. But when he went to his accountant Ernie Dawson, rugby international Ronnie Dawson's father, to withdraw the guarantee, he was told: 'He (Joe) doesn't need it now.' I must admit to having experienced a particularly warm glow when this was revealed to me later on, though old man Hogan and myself got on quite good terms again when I won my next championship."

Fame on the golf course opened many other doors for Joe. For instance, life turned full circle for him when he became an honorary life member of Portmarnock, the scene of his first, tentative strokes at a game with which his name would become synonymous. And in 1961 he was made an honorary member of Pine Valley, widely regarded as the best course in the world. Royal Lytham, South Herts and the Medici club in New York were among the total of 60 establishments which would confer the same honour on him.

Casting his mind back once more to Sutton, he continued: "When I think of those early days, I think of old man Fitzpatrick and Mrs Fitzpatrick and Michael and Tommy (their sons). I became very close to Michael and to Jimmy Carroll and Ray McInally. And, of course, we had remarkable success in the Senior Cup which we won three times in a row from 1948 to 1950, and the Barton Shield in 1946, 1949 and 1950. They were the glory years: we had a bloody great team.

"We were favourites all the way and any team that was drawn against us must have felt a bit like opponents of Manchester United or Arsenal would feel these days. I remember a Senior Cup match at Royal Dublin which I lost. And I said to my opponent some time later: 'I wouldn't have won the Amateur (at Hoylake) only for you.' He had shaken me up to such an extent that I felt obliged to go back to the drawingboard."

But there was another, more famous loss at Royal Dublin, where Tom Craddock beat him in the Leinster final of the 1959 Senior Cup. So highly regarded was Joe at the time, that nobody would have considered it brash of him when he made the casual remark to Harry Bradshaw: "Name the golfer who could give me three holes in nine."

Bradshaw, a great admirer of Carr's, especially after their remarkable foursomes successes at Hermitage, was not about to offer any argument. The Brad might have been more forthcoming, however, after the dramatic events of Friday, May 8th, 1959. That was when Sutton met Malahide in an eagerly awaited clash.

Predictably, the top match was between Joe and Tom Craddock and a big crowd was amply rewarded by the most astonishing finish imaginable. For the Malahide supporters, it didn't seem to matter that the other four matches were going, inexorably, Sutton's way. This is how Paul MacWeeney described the match in his report in The Irish Times the following morning:

"Carr has carried all before him so far this season and has been playing some of the finest golf of his career. But, as has happened so often to great players before now, he lost his grip of a match in which he looked to have complete control.

"He had all the better of the outward journey, barely missing birdies at the first two holes and, with wins at the third, fifth and ninth, where he holed a 12 footer for a two, he turned three up, having gone out in 34. Meanwhile, Craddock was shaping rather like a man whose fate was inevitable, and when he cut his second shot out of bounds at the 11th, with Carr at the back of the green with two mighty blows, the lead changed to four and it looked to be all over."

Joe recalls of that moment: "I remember Tom turning to me with a quiet smile and asking me not to go too hard on him. And of course I knew that it was his way of telling me he had no intention of lying down. And I admired him for that. In fact, that particular moment shaped my opinion of Tom for the remainder of his career."

MacWeeney went on: "Then came an incredible swing, for Craddock holed a 10 footer for a two at the short 12th, which set the spark alight. He got another back at the 13th where they both left long putts well short, but whereas Carr missed from six feet, Craddock holed his five-footer. At the 14th, Carr cut his second into a horrible, bare lie but played a masterly pitch with sufficient stop to give him the chance of a four. His putt stopped on the lip, however, and Craddock, on in two, holed a five-footer confidently for his third successive win.

"The 15th was halved in fours, Craddock again holing from the nasty, five-foot distance after leaving his first one short. The match was squared at the 16th where Carr, bunkered on the left, could not equal his rival's birdie three. And Craddock took the lead at the 17th, Carr hooking his drive into an impossible lie.

"The match was sealed up by Craddock's second at the 18th where, from the middle of the fairway, he played a superb two-iron past the pin and while Carr hit a huge drive up near the corner of the garden, his approach was well short of the pin. He never looked like saving his neck with the putt.

"Craddock won five of the last seven holes and had covered that journey in three under fours, which was wonderful golf over such a testing finish and under the big-match strain."

So was born a great rivalry which, for the best part of a decade, would captivate the media like nothing else in

BREAKING 80

"Golf changed my life, introducing me to a world that I might otherwise not have entered. It is a bit like having a second passport: the official one gets you into different countries but for me, the golf passport gets you through a door marked friendship, camaraderie and enjoyment."

Far left: Paul Dillon's
2001 to celebrate his
Left: Joe's drive-in
Andrews, 8.00am, Sep
after the big cannon
Bottom left: Who's
endary Portmarnock
Left: Joe in full flight
speeches he was to
(left) is Prince Andrew
Below: Flanked by
many engagements o
Bottom: Receiving h
law at Trinity College

Legends: With Sutton's lady captain, Toonie Murray, greeting Jack Nicklaus during the club's Centenary Year, 1990. The Golden Bear's flying visit to Sutton, where he had lunch with some members, was arranged by Dr Tim Mahony for whom Nicklaus was working on the design of Mount Juliet. "Jack and I have been friends since our Walker Cup days. Indeed prior to the US Masters, Dor and myself used to spend quite a bit of time with himself and Barbara at Great Harbour Key in the Bahamas, where Jack had a rondette (a house built on stilts). We'd play golf in the morning and fish in the afternoon."

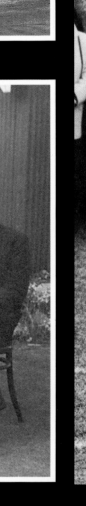

Right: The old Sutton clubhouse.

Far right: Joe's Centenary Year drive-in at Sutton Golf Club, 1990. Behind him and to the right were lady captain, Toonie Murray, captain of Portmarnock Golf Club, Tom Cuddihy, Hugh Quirke, former President of Ireland, Patrick Hillery and Bill Thompson.

Right: Surrounded by by his fellow team mates from Sutton with the Senior Cup. Left to right: Tommy Fitzpatrick, Ray McInally, JB Carr, Michael Fitzpatrick and Jimmy Carroll.

Below: Sitting inside the room dedicated to him at Sutton Golf Club.

Below middle: With Taoiseach Bertie Ahern and Sutton captain Michael Coyne, at the opening of the Joe Carr room, September 24th, 2001.

Below right: Joined by former President of Ireland Patrick Hillery and his wife Maeve at the opening.

Far right: Dr Willie Grant, Joe and Michael Coyne at the opening.

Extreme right: With Sutton's Brian Wallace at the opening.

Old Head: The uniquely spectacular Old Head Course at Kinsale, which Joe and owners John and Patrick O'Connor have transformed into a "must-play" venue for visitors to Ireland. "I had never designed a golf course and from my experience in the game I could see that it was a very specialised skill. Sure, I could recognise a good golf hole from an unfair one and a layout which was sympathetic with its surroundings, as against one which was simply imposed on the terrain. But even people like Jack Nicklaus had to learn the craft from other, experienced hands. In Jack's case, it happened to be Pete Dye, but I had no experience at all."

Far left: At ease in front of Sutton Golf Club's 9th green, August 2002.

Top: With Tiger Woods at Portmarnock Golf Club.

Left: Joe, wife Mary and Tiger at a dinner with friends.

Above: With Padraig Harrington at Mount Juliet in 2001 following Padraig's Volvo Masters win.

Portrait by Alan O'Connor taken August, 2002.

Irish golf. Indeed, it was only a month after the Royal Dublin clash that Craddock beat Joe again, this time at the 38th in the final of the Irish Close at Portmarnock. But revenge came Joe's way the following Easter when he beat Tom in the final of the West of Ireland Championship.

When I spoke with Craddock and his wife Nola later in Tom's career, they invariably referred to Joe in the most kindly terms, with obvious affection for a one-time rival. Indeed an enduring friendship – and, perhaps, not a small degree of mischief – was reflected in Joe's decision to call on the Malahide man when "packing" a Sutton team for a match against Yorkshire. "We explained that Tom was an honorary life member of our club," said Joe with a wicked grin.

This episode was recalled by the late, distinguished scribe, Peter Dobereiner, in a piece he wrote when Joe was honoured by the Legends of Golf Society at St Margaret's GC, Dublin, in August 1992. Dobereiner, who himself delighted in innocent mischief, wrote:

"To date, the medical profession has failed to come up with an effective form of treatment, let alone a cure, for the distressing, inherited condition of having been born in Yorkshire (Michael Parkinson please note). The symptoms of White Rose Syndrome, as it is officially designated in the psychiatric textbooks, are well known.

"The tykes, as these unfortunates like to style themselves, talk the way Freddie Trueman used to bowl, often giving added stress to the high speed stream of vernacular balderdash with a stabbing finger in the midriff of the helpless victim.

"Bluff ... blunt .... salt of t'earth.... Tetley's bitter... Harry Ramsden's finest fish and chips in t'world .... Speak our mind, mind .... Mushy peas ... nowt so daft as folks .... your's while the stars lose their glow.

"When subjected to a typically vainglorious diatribe extolling the matchless virtues of Yorkshire and her sons, most people simply allow their eyes to glaze over and wait for the tempest to blow itself out.

"Joe Carr, you will be happy to learn, is made of sterner stuff. He was once pinned in a corner by the late Reg Alvin, secretary of the Yorkshire Union of Golf Clubs. The general theme of Reg's discourse was the clear superiority of Yorkshire and everyone in it, in particular the unprecedented strength of amateur golf in the county.

"Reg expressed the firm conviction that Yorkshire could field a team under the incomparable Rodney Foster which would slaughter the national side of any country in Europe. In the millisecond of silence which interrupted the verbal fusilade for the essential purpose of drawing breath, Joe interjected sharply: 'Behave yourself, Reg.'

"Reg was rocked back on his heels, momentarily lost for words. Joe pressed home his advantage. 'I could put together a team which would stuff your Yorkshire out of sight.' 'Oo aye?' replied Reg, in a tone of scornful incredulity.

"'Not from a whole country,' said Joe. 'Nae, what then?' 'Not from an entire city.' 'Nae' (This time with heavy sarcasm). 'But from one golf club.' 'Ay oop, lad'. 'A small golf club.' 'Think on.' 'With only a nine-hole course.' 'Happen you'll put your brass where your mouth is,' said Reg. 'Of course' said Joe. 'Champion is that, reet gradely,' said Reg, or some such Yorkshire gibberish.

"And so it came about that a team of Yorkshire's finest amateurs, led by the legendary Rodney Foster, flew to Dublin to play Sutton Golf Club.

"If you had to characterise the Carr family in one word, the word you would have to choose would be 'hospitable.' How else could you explain the circumstance of John O'Leary going to spend a weekend with the Carrs and staying two years? Joe was the perfect host. On the eve of the match, he entertained the Yorkshire team to a sumptuous party in the trophy room of his house at Sutton.

"It so happened that Richard Dodd, a sports writer from the Yorkshire Post, had accompanied the team and he was privy to a dastardly plan. Rodney Foster had explained to his men that the Irish were terrible men for the drink and Joe Carr was no exception. They must all make a concerted effort to keep Joe's glass topped up. If J B could be nobbled, then the Sutton team would collapse in disarray.

"Everything seemed to go to plan. Joe was plied with innumerable gin-and-tonics. Even with the notorious, hollow-legged capacity of the Irish, no human being could consume so much alcohol without suffering dire consequences in the morning.

"Of course, the Yorkshire lads had to down the odd jar themselves but, as they say in boxing, you have to take a few in order to land a knock-out punch.

"Strange to relate, on the morrow, the Sutton team (with Malahide's Tom Craddock, a teetotaller, as a guest) annihilated the hung-over pride of Yorkshire. And that famous victory was inspired by a bright-eyed and bushy-tailed Joe Carr.

"How could this have happened? Could this have been a reverse of the Miracle at Cana, with gin mysteriously being turned into water? Actually, such a fanciful notion is not far from the truth.

"That self same sports writer from the Yorkshire Post had overheard a whispered exchange between Joe and the barman he had hired for the previous evening's reception. It went something like this: 'I know these guys. They will keep pestering you to ask me what I want to drink. I will say a gin-and-tonic, a large one. And you will give me straight tonic.'"

When an eagerly-awaited return match was played in Yorkshire, it fell to Jimmy Carroll to provide the gory details, which he did with some relish. Indeed he attributed to a certain colleague, the distinction of producing "the best golf I have ever seen played" over a crucial stretch of 11 holes.

The performance came from none other than Teddy Firth who, as things turned out, was unable to leave Dublin with the remainder of the team and had to fly out on the Saturday. Since he happened to be in a hurry, the flight was delayed, naturally. Light refreshments led to further light refreshments with the result that Firth was decidedly tired and emotional by the time he reached Leeds.

Unfortunately for him, the condition had not improved to any significant degree by the time he had gone into battle the following morning. So it was that while experiencing extreme difficulty in actually seeing the ball, Firth's first four holes included the only socket with a three wood that Carroll had ever witnessed. And he was four down. Worse still, he proceeded to go five down after five.

Gradually, however, the mist began to clear and the hammering by the little men in Firth's head became less enthusiastic. And with a two-iron to six inches at the sixth, he gained a badly-needed win. Ten holes of magnificent golf later, Carroll was enthusing – "Great man that Teddy Firth" – as his colleague went to the 17th two up. But the malaise returned, having moved from his head down to the digestive system.

The impact was such that even with the putter firmly gripped by knees as well as hands, Firth missed an 18-inch effort on the 17th. Though even greater torment beckoned on the final green, salvation was at hand. Surrounded by a large crowd who had come out from the clubhouse to witness the climactic moments of a torrid battle, Firth stood over a five-foot putt to halve the hole and win the match. But just as he was attempting to get the blade into position, he almost collapsed with relief when his opponent conceded the putt.

Jimmy Carroll had never seen the like.

Matches with Yorkshire continued for some years until the cost of travelling became too prohibitive. A reunion match was planned for August 1990 during Sutton's Centenary Year, but Yorkshire were prevented from travelling, this time by the collapse of Capital Airlines. But in that particular year, Sutton, as they say, would have considerably bigger fish to fry.

In 1961, after the Americans had achieved a crushing 11-1 Walker Cup victory, Joe and Dor travelled south for the US Amateur at Pebble Beach, where Joe lost to Dudley Wysong in the semi-finals and Jack Nicklaus captured the title. While there, they stayed with a family named Sheehan, whose background, predictably, was Irish. They lived with their two small children, just beside the Lodge.

Joined by John, Joe decided to pay them a return visit in 1990. After Dor's death, he had still kept in touch with the Sheehans, sending pictures of his own children and news items of family matters: the sort of things that parents do. "I wondered if they would still be around," he said. "As luck would have it, there was only one J Sheehan in the book, so John and I called to the house, which had changed somewhat in the intervening years. When we knocked, a lovely, white-haired lady called down 'Hello' from an upstairs window. 'I think I stayed with you in 1961,' I ventured. 'Where are you from?' she asked. 'Ireland', I replied. To which she said: 'Do you know Joe Carr.' Wasn't that amazing?"

He went on: "So we went in and they showed us some family keepsakes. And lo and behold, didn't the items include a little R and A tie-pin I had given them in 1961, which was a bit rusty by that stage. We shared wonderful memories. These are the things you never forget. After the passage of 30 years, both parents were alive but their kids had grown up and married and they had something like seven grandchildren."

Pebble beckoned once more in 1992 when, in his capacity as captain of the R and A, Joe returned there as an official guest at the US Open, which was won by Tom Kite. Though Ireland's two challengers, David Feherty and Ronan Rafferty, failed to survive the cut, Feherty had already made his mark elsewhere.

On the Thursday night of US Open week, a party was thrown by the Fisher family at Sea Drift, which was built on three acres of prime real-estate on the legendary 17-mile Drive. And, as one of the guests, Feherty was in splendid voice, trotting out a few Puccini arias before rounding off an impressive performance with a rendition of the old favourite, Danny Boy.

Nick Faldo was also there, suitably impressed at being back among the Irish, as he put it, after his second successive Irish Open victory at Killarney, two weeks previously. Naturally, his guru of that time, David Leadbetter, was also there, along with Ian Woosnam and Nick Price.

When called upon to make a speech, Joe enthralled his audience, especially the hosts, Bob and Marylin Fisher. And by way of a thank you for their hospitality by the Pacific shore, they were Joe's guests when the British Open was staged at Muirfield a month later.

As it happened, 16 Sutton members met the Fisher family two years previously. It was during their now famous tour, which was organised by former Irish amateur international, Dougie Heather, who, as chairman of the Centenary Committee, admitted to having used Joe's name and reputation to splendid effect in arranging prime fixtures.

These are Heather's recollections of the trip: "We set off for New York on a Friday in early October 1990 and while a few of the lads played Winged Foot that weekend, our first official port of call was Pine Valley in New Jersey. We arrived there on a Sunday evening and, after dinner in the clubhouse, we repaired to the Dormy House, close-by, for a fairly early night.

"There, we were assigned eight double-rooms, simply furnished with a couple of beds, table and with a communal wash-room and showers. A measure of the general excitement in the group was that everybody was up at 6.30 the following morning, getting ready for the day's golf.

"After breakfast in the clubhouse, we played a match against Pine Valley, comprising eight fourballs. Then we had lunch after which most people went out for a further nine holes with Pine Valley members in the afternoon.

"On the following day, we drove to Merion where, through the good offices of Ed Slevin, who is a great friend of Joe's, we again had a match against the members. And we had dinner there that night. All the while, we were conscious that Joe, as centenary captain of the club, was not only a major golfing celebrity but a father-figure to us all. It was quite incredible how our hosts reacted to him. Not only were the players who opposed us hand-picked by the various clubs we visited on the tour, but the majority of them would have been aware of Joe's profile in the game. And among those who weren't, there was soon a deep respect for this man who spoke about great players such as Jack Nicklaus, Arnold Palmer, Gary Player and Sam Snead as personal friends, which of course they were.

"Joe had an excellent, prepared speech, which was used on 11 occasions throughout the tour. And the seriousness with which he approached his duties, could be gauged by the last match, which was at Lake Merced in San Francisco. As last man out, I came into the locker-room to see Joe pacing the floor with notes in his hand. After expressing curiosity as to what he was doing, he explained that he was preparing his speech. Whereupon I found myself saying: 'You have already made essentially the same speech on 10 occasions, so what is there to be concerned about?' No sooner were the words out of my mouth than I had an instant understanding of the professionalism of the man.

"Lake Merced is a Jewish club and our contact there was Shelby Notkin who, in common with the majority of the members, knew relatively little about Joe when we contacted them. Prior to our visit, however, it was clear that Shelby had done a bit of research because he was clearly very excited at the prospect of meeting our captain. As it happens, Lake Merced have since been to Ireland on two occasions, to Sutton and Portmarnock."

Heather concluded: "After our visit to Merion, we flew to San Francisco and John Carr joined us for fixtures against a wide selection of West Coast clubs. We had a match against Sharon Heights before heading for the Monterey Peninsula, where there was the pleasant surprise of meeting Dessie O'Malley, the Limerick politician, resplendent in a Connemara GC sweater. In that marvellous, golfing location, we played Cypress Point and Pebble Beach, which were not matches, but we had a fixture with Monterey Peninsula Country Club and with Pasatiempo, the final home of Alister MacKenzie. Our closing matches were in San Francisco against the Olympic Club, San Francisco GC and Lake Merced."

Joe retains warm memories of that trip, because of what he considered was the signal honour paid to him by his home club. "Being the Centenary captain of Sutton was a terrific honour and I was also delighted to see Hugh Quirke as the president that year," he said. "Hugh was one of those sometimes benign dictators who do invaluable work and Sutton were extremely fortunate in having his services for so many years. I admired him greatly. The marvellous contribution of Brian Wallace is on record and I think special mention should be made of Bill Thompson, for his work on upgrading the course. Without his drive and foresight, it would be nothing like it is today."

He went on: "I've also had a great relationship over the years with our professional, Nicky Lynch. Our company paid for Nicky on tour for a year and I remember back in 1963, when the Open was played at Royal Lytham, I brought him across to meet Jack Nicklaus. The three of us played a practice round together at Lytham and after being well up with Jack for the first four or five holes, Nicky turned to me and said: 'This fellow's not as long as they're making him out to be, Joe.'

"With that, we went down the long fifth where Jack was 15 feet from the pin after a drive and four iron, whereas Nicky was hitting a drive, three wood and a pitch. 'I see what you mean, Joe,' he said to me, somewhat stunned. After the round was over, Jack recommended a special practice regime for Nicky and I remember Dor used to keep an eye on him from a window at Suncroft, to make sure he was following Jack's instructions."

That year at Lytham, incidentally, was the only time that Nicklaus admitted to having thrown away a major championship. He finished with three bogeys to miss out by a stroke on a play-off with Phil Rodgers and the eventual winner, Bob Charles. "I was behind the 17th green when he overshot it in two and failed to get up and down," said Joe.

Against that background, it was hardly surprising that Joe should have made a point of asking Dr Tim Mahony, the owner of Mount Juliet, if there was any chance of getting Jack to come to Sutton during the Centenary Year. Dr Mahony suggested he might do it on the way back to Dublin Airport from a trip to Mount Juliet, where the course he designed was within a year of completion at that stage.

Good as his word, Dr Mahony approached Nicklaus and the upshot was that the helicopter landed at Sutton GC and out stepped the Golden Bear. And he joined Joe and other leading members of the club for lunch. "I considered that to be a very, very great favour," said Joe.

He went on: "Jack and I have been friends since our Walker Cup days. Indeed prior to the US Masters, Dor and myself used to spend quite a bit of time with himself and Barbara at Great Harbour Key in the Bahamas, where Jack had a rondette (a house built on stilts). We'd play golf in the morning and fish in the afternoon.

"I'll always remember one particular trip to Great Harbour Key during the 1960s when I stayed for a couple of weeks. The holiday was followed by the Masters, in which I had been invited to play. And of course Jack was playing. And Roddy, Dor and myself and Jack and Barbara and their two eldest kids, flew to Augusta in his Lear Jet. That was a huge thing in those days."

Joe's relationship with the Mount Juliet owner dates back to 1961 when they were paired in the Barry Fitzgerald Cup (men's foursomes) at Sutton. "Tim had only started the game at that stage and was an absolute beginner," recalled Joe. "As it turned out, we were beaten by my old friend Jimmy Carroll who was partnered by a bank official named Louis O'Connell. But a year later, when I was partnered by Heggy O'Neill, we beat O'Connell and his partner Bob Morrison who, for reasons I can't remember now, was knows as Wet-Leg Morrison."

Returning to the Centenary Year's American tour, he continued: "They were a terrific bunch of guys who reflected all that is to be admired in the Sutton club." During the trip, the Sutton captain met an American named Dick Giddings who asked if he remembered him. "No, I'm afraid I don't," replied Joe. "Well," said Giddings, "I don't blame you. I know I never remember the fellows I beat, only the fellows who beat me."

He then explained that Joe had beaten him in an early round of the 1961 US Amateur at Pebble Beach. Now, aged 68, Joe was playing off eight whereas Giddings, who was 78 was playing off five. So they had a match at Cypress Point in which he gave Joe three strokes and beat him by 4 and 3.

Afterwards, the American enthused: "Won't it be something to tell my buddies that I had the great J B over here and I gave him 10 years and three shots and beat the tail off him. They'll all be delighted."

Earlier on the trip, Joe played the son of Bob Cochran, whom he thrashed in the final at Royal Portrush in 1960 when capturing his third British Amateur title. Though they kept in touch during the ensuing years, Joe hadn't seen Bob since and he was now meeting his son at Merion. And young Bob beat him by 4 and 3, whereupon Joe enquired: "Where's old Bob?". On being informed that he was at home, Joe phoned him. The conversation went like this: "Hello Bob, Joe Carr here." "Oh, yes..." "It's taken you 30 years to get your revenge. This son of your's has given me a thrashing." And they both laughed heartily.

In less salubrious circumstances, there were other matches, against Shandon Park and South Herts who, according to Joe, sent over their drinking team. And essentially the outcome of these clashes hinged on whether or not Joe won. Which he usually did.

Meanwhile, an extended series of annual matches between Sutton and Cork GC had a perfect launch at Little Island in March 1963. The top match was between Joe and Jimmy Bruen, who was an international selector by that time and considered to be past his competitive best by about 10 years. It was only their second meeting, the previous clash having been in 1955 when Joe won by 2 and 1 in a friendly match between teams representing Leinster and Munster.

This time, however, an attendance of about 500 turned up to watch these legendary figures of Irish amateur golf. As it happened, Joe covered the 18 holes in two under par for a one hole win, after Bruen's putt for a half slipped past the target.

On the following morning, the report of the match in the then Cork Examiner, now the Irish Examiner, read: "Joe Carr had to go all the way at Cork Golf Club yesterday to defeat James Bruen in one of the most talked about golf matches played in the south for many years. However, the victory was of no benefit to Sutton and they were well beaten by Cork in this inter-club challenge, the final margin being a surprising 7 to 2.

"In the clash between Carr and Bruen, only the second time they have met, people were surging around the last green to watch as Bruen narrowly failed with a 10-yard putt to save the match. Carr was ahead all the time from the seventh, being three to the good at the turn, but he had to withstand a storming recovery from Bruen which clearly indicated that the man, who is now a selector, is still very much a force as a player.

"In addition, it was only the Corkman's fourth game since last August. The figures, despite a six each on the first nine, were good, Carr being two under par 73 for the 18."

It went on: "Bruen was short at the par-three seventh and then missed a two-foot putt to lose the hole and go one down. At the eighth, Carr, after watching Bruen leave a great approach two inches from the pin, holed out a 40-yard eight iron for a winning eagle two.

"Obviously shaken by this, Bruen temporarily lost his golden putting touch at the ninth and took three putts to lose again and turn three down to Carr. But then started the recovery which kept the rapidly growing gallery scurrying frantically for vantage points."

We are informed that after Bruen had cut the deficit to one hole after 14, he went on to lose the next to go two down once more. But a huge drive and a 10-yard putt on the 16th, gave him a winning birdie. They then halved the 17th in par and after both of them had reached the 18th green in regulation, Joe made a solid, two-putt par for the match.

But there was compensation for the Cork fraternity. As the Examiner reported: "In the morning, Bruen had been in even better form playing with George Crosbie and blitzing Carr and Mick Fitzpatrick to the tune of 5 and 4. He played some exceptionally long shots, including one beauty at the 11th and was putting magnificently. Crosbie, too, was in his best form here and between them they gave the visitors no chance at all. They were level fours when the match finished."

As a personal reflection on that foursomes match, Crosbie, in his book, The Bruen Loop, wrote: "We were playing the 11th hole, which is a very long par four of 460 odd yards, against the wind. Both Michael Fitzpatrick and I hit rather indifferent drives, but mine was on the fairway. Jimmy (Crosbie's partner) took out his driver and hit one of the most colossal shots I have ever seen, straight into the middle of that green from a position none of us thought was possible.

"Joe Carr was so intrigued with this shot that he decided to drop a ball at the same place to see if he could emulate it. This, of course, was possible as this was but a friendly, inter-club match. However, although he tried two or three times, Joe didn't get within 20 yards of the green and he admitted afterwards that it was a fantastic shot."

Jimmy Carroll, who was never averse to a bit of roguery, was invariably one of the central characters in these Sutton performances. And as has been indicated elsewhere in the book, he was a great friend of Joe's. And a master fixer. In this latter context, Joe has special memories of a particular day when, while driving home from Dublin in his 4.2 Jaguar, a garda squad car pulled out in front of him. Both vehicles were travelling at about 40mph, and it was raining. Anyway, at a critical moment, a funeral happened to pull out of a side road, causing the squad car to brake sharply. Given the proximity of the two cars, Joe couldn't avoid hitting into the back of it. Whereupon one of the gardai emerged from the squad car and proceeded to read Joe the riot act.

In Joe's view, it was clearly the sort of situation which required Carroll's intervention. Making a clean breast of things, he said to his friend: "Jimmy, you wouldn't believe how stupid I was. I went into the back of a squad car." Unfazed, Jimmy responded in his soft Louth accent: "Ah don't worry Joe. These things happen to the best of us."

Carroll then enquired as to whether Joe had had the presence of mind to take the number of the squad car. On being told "yes", he wondered if his friend had also got the number of the driver. That, too, was furnished. "That's Paddy Kelly," Carroll exclaimed. "I'll give him a ring."

This was a time when, apart from a large range of women's garments, the House of Carr also made children's clothes. Anyway, the conversation went something like this: "Paddy, it's Jimmy here. How are Mary and the kids? I'm glad to hear it. And I hope those clothes you got from the House of Carr fitted the children. They did? Good. By the way Paddy, you backed into a very good friend of mine this morning."

So it was that while Joe was sitting in the house the following night, Carroll arrived on the scene with two colleagues in plain clothes. And pointing to the other two members of the force, he said: "Joe, these are the two idiots who backed into you." Joe smiled quietly to himself, thinking that these were the sort of things which could only happen in Ireland.

With all the success Joe had had, there was a huge level of expectation in Sutton every time he played. But it didn't create any additional pressure for the simple reason that, as Joe put it, he himself expected to win every time he played. Meanwhile, it was the influence of clans such as the Lauders, Hogans, the Fitzpatricks and the Carrs which created the family atmosphere which visitors to the modest little links talked so much about.

When Joe bought Suncroft, the course had become a 28-acre playground, where he could do just about anything to further his golfing career. "We had the first driving range in the country there, with five bays," he recalled. "And I had two, 1,000-watt bulbs beaming down on the second green. Even allowing for my success, there aren't many clubs which would have permitted me so much latitude."

Joe went on: "Then at Christmas, there were children's parties and members' parties. Lots of celebrating. New Year's Eve was also a very special night. Remember, there was no television in those days, so the club became the focal point of all our social activities. We played golf and went to the pictures three times a week. Life was simple."

He concluded: "What really pleased me about the Joe Carr room was that when they decided to honour me, they did it properly. That's the Sutton way."

❖

Chapter Eleven
A Leader Of Men

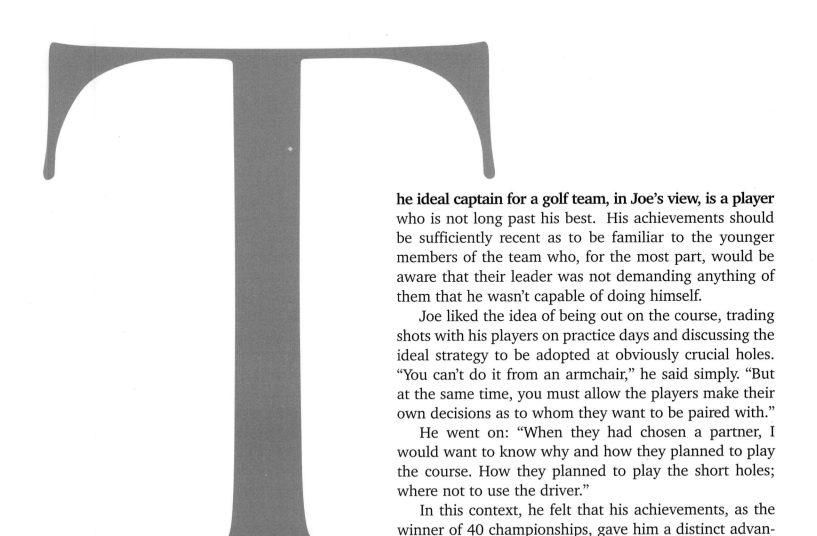

The ideal captain for a golf team, in Joe's view, is a player who is not long past his best. His achievements should be sufficiently recent as to be familiar to the younger members of the team who, for the most part, would be aware that their leader was not demanding anything of them that he wasn't capable of doing himself.

Joe liked the idea of being out on the course, trading shots with his players on practice days and discussing the ideal strategy to be adopted at obviously crucial holes. "You can't do it from an armchair," he said simply. "But at the same time, you must allow the players make their own decisions as to whom they want to be paired with."

He went on: "When they had chosen a partner, I would want to know why and how they planned to play the course. How they planned to play the short holes; where not to use the driver."

In this context, he felt that his achievements, as the winner of 40 championships, gave him a distinct advantage. His qualifications for the role were also enhanced significantly by the tremendous experience gained as a player under such an outstanding captain as, for instance, Gerald Micklem. And he also learned much from playing under bad captains.

"I remember a situation in the Walker Cup when the players were arguing heatedly about tactics, as if I weren't there," he recalled. "By way of restoring a little sanity to the situation, I said: 'Anybody who has won one championship stand up.' Half a dozen players stood up. 'Anyone who has won two?' Fewer stood. 'Anyone who has won three?' Fewer still. 'Anyone won four, five, six?' No reply. 'Anyone won 30?' Okay, this is what we'll do."

It was a measure of Joe's acute sense of reality and indeed his innate humility, that after being honoured with the Walker Cup captaincy, he was quite prepared to come through the ranks in the Irish system, starting as non-playing captain of the Leinster team. From there, it was entirely natural that he should progress to the captaincy of the Irish team, a role he filled from 1979 to 1981.

For a variety of reasons, it was a period of considerable difficulty, innovation and excitement. The difficulty was posed by the seemingly endless civil strife in Northern Ireland which led to the cancellation of the Home International Championship, scheduled for Royal Co Down in 1979. As a welcome challenge, though from a competitive standpoint they were obviously a poor substitute, friendly matches were arranged with Wales.

Innovation came in the form of international squad-training sessions which Joe arranged for Sotogrande on Spain's Costa del Sol. There, the Irish panel members had the opportunity of playing the wonderful old course, along with the neigbouring Las Aves stretch which, with the nines switched around, would become Valderrama, one of the most celebrated venues in Europe. Even then, it was widely acknowledged that both courses represented some of the best work done by the celebrated American golf-course architect, Robert Trent Jones, in the area. And they introduced a number of Irish players to a quality of parkland terrain which was entirely new to them, especially the slippery quick greens.

Some memorable achievements from those sessions were a course-record 67 by Ronan Rafferty at Sotogrande Old in 1981, and a hole-in-one by Enda McMenamin on the sixth (now Valderrama's 15th) at Las Aves, where a three-iron tee-shot popped into the cup. It was clear that the Irish players benefited enormously from this Carr-inspired venture.

The excitement was generated by the prodigious talent of Rafferty and Philip Walton, who would go on to secure places in the 1981 Walker Cup team at Cypress Point. Yet for Joe, the talent was accompanied by torment. "When I looked at Rafferty I saw a wonderful golfing brain, but he was extremely difficult to handle," said Joe. "In fact I ended up having great sympathy with Arthur Pierse who, as his foursomes partner, was on the receiving end of much of Ronan's behaviour."

Joe went on: "Ronan was a complex young man, who had many sides to his character. For instance, I remember in the Quadrangular Internationals at Portmarnock in 1980, we were playing Sweden who had whitewashed us in the previous meeting. And I was determined we'd get our own back. Anyway, the five singles were in progress and we were up in four. Rafferty was the only one down. And out on the course, I told him the situation, before adding: 'Don't worry, Ronan, nobody can beat this guy.' Whereupon he turned to me and said: 'I'll f...ing beat him.' And he did.

"Then there was another, less attractive side to the lad. Like the one he exhibited by refusing to wear a tie on a visit to Aras an Uachtarain (the Phoenix Park residence of the President of Ireland) until we actually forced him to do it. And I was very close to sending him home from St Andrews during the European Team Championship of 1981. I was angry because, in my view, he had ruined my team. With our best-ever line-up in the event, we were virtually guaranteed to win the Europeans, and he ruined it."

Joe explained: "There were disciplinary problems, largely to do with the big ball/small ball situation. Remember, this was a time when either ball could be played in amateur representative matches and championships generally, before the big ball eventually became mandatory.

"I saw Ronan and Arthur Pierse as a very good foursomes combination but unknown to me, all this ball non-sense was going on behind my back: while Arthur was playing the small ball, with my approval, Ronan insisted he wanted to play the big one. That was bound to be disruptive. Anyway, when matters got to a head, Ronan tried to hide in a bathroom but I ordered him to come down and face his team-mates. He came down eventually. Meanwhile, my fellow Walker Cup selectors called me and pleaded: 'Joe, don't do it.' I had told them I was dropping him, a leading Walker Cup candidate, and they said: 'You can't do that. We've all made mistakes as kids.'"

The captain's patience reached breaking point when Ireland lost 5-2 to England on the opening day of match-play. In the top foursomes, Pierse and Rafferty were beaten 3 and 1 by Peter McEvoy and Geoff Godwin and in the top singles, McEvoy beat Rafferty on the 19th.

In any meaningful sense, Ireland were effectively out of the championship at that stage, but as captain, Joe still felt he had to make a point. So, in announcing to the newspaper scribes at the end of play that Rafferty had been dropped from the Saturday match against Denmark, he said: "Ronan has got to learn that when he is playing for Ireland, it is a team effort. I feel that his performance in foursomes against England lacked the necessary discipline and I have no option but to leave him out. His attitude does not seem to me to be 100 per cent behind the team." Joe added: "We must remember, of course, that he is only 17 and at that age, perhaps my attitude was not as mature as it is now."

The skipper's disappointment was entirely understandable, given the quality of the players at his disposal. Apart from having Rafferty and Walton together for the only time at European level, there were the short-game skills of Mark Gannon, the burgeoning talent of Pierse and Garth McGimpsey and the established quality of Declan Branigan, who would go on to win three championships that year.

For years afterwards Rafferty remained extremely bitter about that particular episode in his amateur career. Yet from a captain's standpoint, Joe had worked a masterstroke. He had publicly reprimanded the player without jeopardising his chance of making the Walker Cup team, which was announced the following Monday.

Though Joe claims that Rafferty is quite friendly towards him these days, there was a deeply upsetting aftermath to those events at St Andrews in that the captain was left with the impression that he had made an enemy for life. This, in his view, was not deserved. Meanwhile, with the exception of Jack Magowan of the Belfast Telegraph, who had always enjoyed a special relationship with the player, Irish golf writers were treated with profound suspicion, even antagonism by the Rafferty for the remainder of his productive, playing career.

When I tackled him about the matter during the British Open at Muirfield in 1992, he agreed that it all stemmed from those fateful days at St Andrews. And he went on to assert that his main complaint with the media was that nobody bothered to ask him for his side of the story. Mind you, with such a respected figure as Joe Carr in command of things, it was hardly surprising that those reporters present did not feel the need to seek the views of a 17-year-old.

Ironically, Joe had always been a great admirer of the player's talent, though the pair had clashed from as far back as the 1980 Home Internationals the previous autumn at Royal Dornoch. As I have indicated, by way of easing the transition to the adoption of the big ball on this side of the Atlantic, the R and A permitted either the big or small ball to be used in competition. Indeed McEvoy continued to use the small ball during the Walker Cup the following year.

But with his eyes set firmly on a professional career, Rafferty was totally committed to the big ball, which he wanted to play in all circumstances. On the other hand, his international partner, Pierse, had yet to be converted. So, it was perhaps inevitable that the foursomes would create a problem, which they duly did, with either half of the same pairing wanting to play a different ball. A crucial factor, however, was that Carr had insisted the small ball be used, to which Rafferty rebelled. This was the same problem which carried over to the European Championship at St Andrews.

It wasn't the first serious problem that Joe had encountered as a captain. When he skippered Britain and Ireland in the Eisenhower Trophy in Mexico City in 1966, the locals became aware of problems in previous events with captains who hadn't stayed behind the fairway ropes, so blocking the view of spectators.

So the Mexican Golf Association and the USGA decided at a meeting that on this occasion, the captains would not be permitted inside the ropes. When Joe heard this, he went to the US captain, Jess Sweetser, and said angrily: "I've come more than 7,000 miles to captain my team in this tournament and I'm not going to start waving at them from 50 yards away. It's not right. I'm going to protest." Sweetser agreed.

With that, the rival captains went to Joe C Dey of the USGA who insisted that there was nothing he could do about it. Whereupon Joe said that he was making an official protest on behalf of the R and A. The upshot was that they had another meeting from which Dey emerged with a little red rose. And he said to the British and Irish skipper: "There you are, Joe. This rose entitles you to go inside the ropes." But he added with a sly smile: "It also entitles the Mexican Golf Association to tell the R and A how to run all their future competitions." From that point onwards, Joe and the USGA official became the best of friends.

As it happened, Joe's last assignment as Irish skipper was in the Home Internationals at Woodhall Spa in September 1981. It was an event that would become memorable for two, main reasons. Rafferty delivered a highly significant singles victory by becoming the first player from these islands to defeat England's McEvoy after an unbeaten run of 25 international matches. And Joe's son John made a marvellous international debut.

In a golfing context, John Carr was a late developer, who was still playing off a relatively high handicap during his late teens. Yet with his father's genes and the example of his older brother Roddy, he always had a burning desire to succeed.

This is how he described his rise to international status: "I suspect like my brothers, I was intimidated by the fact of who dad was. I liken it to climbing a mountain and getting to the top and not having any fear any more. My brother Gerry, for instance, has always been totally intimidated by playing with the Old Man. You tried to hit every shot the way you thought he'd want you to hit it, rather than the way your natural instincts dictated.

"My personal view is that dad's great gift was the gift of application and desire. These are very special qualities which I didn't have in anything like the same measure, except for one, special winter. I had been to Henry Cotton for tuition and I remember going out every morning and practising my heart out.

"With Henry's help, all of the key elements were in place to make things come together in my golfing career, but it still didn't happen until relatively late. As a consequence, I was a one-handicapper when I went to the British Amateur at St Andrews in 1981. And I had got my first Leinster cap at Rosses Point only a month previously, under the captaincy of Mick Craddock.

"We won the Interpros that year and my dubious claim to a share in the credit was that I was beaten by Paddy O'Looney in our victory over Connacht, the only match I got. Hardly what one might describe as a very inspiring debut!

"But there was no qualifying in the Amateur at that time, so I felt I had nothing to lose. I went over with Arthur

Pierse and my challenge was special from a family point of view – being at St Andrews which had been such a memorable stage for Roddy and dad. And Roddy insisted that if I was going to do it, I should do it right. That was when he decided to set me up with Tip Anderson as my caddie.

"Dad gave me the advice which he applied when winning the 1958 Amateur: concentrate on driving the ball well and hitting wedge-shots well and nothing else really matters. Still, though I was always a good driver, I went there pretty much as a raw, 25-year-old with my one match for Leinster and a win in the Dundalk Scratch Cup. But I knew I could play the game, even if my course management was never what it should have been.

"So I went out with Tip for a couple of practice rounds and his influence was tremendous. It was the first time I had met him and I soon became aware of his extraordinary wisdom, not only regarding the Old Course, but of the game of golf itself. And I was aware of a kind of family familiarity about the situation, which obviously made me feel very much at ease.

"When I got through to the third round, dad phoned me, as he would do every day, and said 'You're doing great. Keep your head down. I'm on my way over.' And I remember ringing my brother Gerry and telling him: 'Look, the Old Man is coming over. Please tell him to stay away from me.' My fear was that if I used the wedge in a particular situation, he would be thinking that I should have used the putter, or vice versa. Things like that. So I was still intimidated at that stage by the notion of playing the game the way I suspected he'd want me to play it.

"But he came over just the same. And it must have been heartbreaking for him, dodging behind bushes and mounds and watching from a distance through binoculars. I was through to the last 16 at that stage and while I was pleased that he came, there was no real communication between us in a golfing sense.

"I remember being very focused to the extent that after a morning round, I would go into the member's bar and read a book. Tip took all the pressure away from me which meant that I had no fear of facing opponents with impressive reputations. Players like Malcolm Lewis and Geoff Godwin. I simply treated it as an experience to be enjoyed, though I have to admit that it was a crushing disappointment to be putted off the course by Philippe Ploujoux in the semi-finals. That was on Friday afternoon and when it was over, I went home with dad instead of waiting for the presentation, which I regret a little bit now.

"It was only on my return home that I discovered my whole world had changed. I remember going to Portmarnock and the golf-course designer, Robert Trent Jones Jnr happened to be there in the company of the captain, John Fitzgibbon. And I was treated like a minor celebrity, even to the extent of being offered preferential tee-times.

"Two weeks later, I won the 72-hole Waterford Scratch Trophy, with Ronan (Rafferty) in the field. Then I was brought into the Irish international panel, which led to a rather bizarre situation. I began to get letters from dad, addressed: 'Dear panel member etc.' And while he could have handed them to me, he obviously preferred the formality of sending them by post, just as he did to all the members of the panel.

"After the Amateur, the Europeans were in St Andrews later that month and the Irish team had already been picked. But I played in the Home Internationals at Woodhall Spa later that year, when dad was captain for the last time. That was a very proud experience. By rights, I would have been fairly low in the pecking order but dad took a bit of a flier on me.

"People who remembered the events of Friday at the Europeans in St Andrews, would have been surprised to note that I roomed with Ronan at Woodhall. But I was chosen to partner Arthur (Pierse) in the foursomes while Ronan played with Philip Walton in a repeat of their highly successful Walker Cup partnership the previous month.

"Arthur and myself found ourselves two down with five to play against England's crack pairing of Peter McEvoy and Peter Deeble. But we took the match to the 18th, which was a par five. That was where I holed a 20-footer across the green for a birdie and they needed to hole a 15-footer to halve. And Arthur took a leap in the air and danced on the green, embracing me. The following morning, the 'Daily Mail' reported that Arthur had cavorted around the green like an ostrich that had lost its head. But we had beaten England.

"Against the odds, I got four and a half points out of six, which I know made dad extremely proud. Then the following year I played in the Quadrangular International matches in Halmstad in Sweden and after that in the Home Internationals at Royal Porthcawl in 1982."

John concluded: "As a captain, dad was incredibly enthusiastic, a player's man who instilled confidence in us by his very presence. He wanted us to be the best-dressed team with all our equipment in top shape. And we had to know all the yardages. Though he was clearly a tough task-master, I don't remember him being critical of the players. Instinctively, he understood what we were trying to do."

Team golf had always appealed to Joe, in whatever format it happened to take. And it was said by British observers that he and Harry Bradshaw made foursomes performances appear so effortless as to be no more than child's play. They were also admired for the modest manner in which they carried their honours.

Plaudits were bestowed in abundance at the Gleneagles Hotel in Perthshire in October 1955 when, as the back-markers off plus-two, they won the Gleneagles-Saxone Amateur-Professional Handicap Foursomes. Conceding a stroke in the final to the British partnership of scratchman Bill Sharp, a Penrith haulage contractor, and Syd Scott, a Ryder Cup player, they coasted to a 4 and 3 victory.

Sharp was a reinstated amateur, having flirted with paid ranks as an assistant professional. Yet he and Scott were unable to deprive The Brad of his second win in two weeks, following on a repeat victory in the Dunlop Masters. With the two victories, Bradshaw brought his earnings for the fortnight to £1,000.

Christy O'Connor Snr, who also experienced considerable success in Bradshaw's company, notably in the Canada Cup of 1958 in Mexico City, remembered another foursomes match at Gleneagles, where he and his Irish partner, a Dr Brady, were opposed by Joe and The Brad. "We were receiving two and a half shots, which, of course was as good as three shots," O'Connor recalled. "And I remember we were all square playing the 15th, where the doctor and myself were both down the fairway, receiving our last half-shot.

"Joe had knocked his drive just into the edge of the rough but it was lying OK. So I knocked my second onto the green, which meant we were on in one and a half. But as things turned out, they were just inside us in two. Anyway, we putted up stone dead and were given the putt. But Joe proceeded to hole his putt for a three and we eventually lost the match by a hole. They were some partnership."

Eric Brown also had first-hand knowledge of this fearsome duo. It was acquired when the Scottish Ryder Cup player was one of their victims in An Tostal Amateur-Professional Tournament at Hermitage in 1954. On terrain which was firmly established as being very much to their liking, they triumphed, as everybody expected they would, beating Jim Mahon and Brown by 3 and 1 in the final.

Indeed a measure of Hermitage as a most productive stomping ground for Joe and The Brad was that they captured the annual Foursomes Tournament there on no fewer than eight occasions, from 1940 to 1954. And he was a three-time winner of the Killarney Scratch Foursomes with Noel Fogarty, in 1961, 1962 and 1966.

Then there was team golf of essentially a family nature. As in the inaugural Kerrygold Classic at Waterville GC in October 1974 which, as it happened, was only a month before Joe's heart attack. "If there was to be a competitive swansong to my career, I could hardly have wished for better than this," he said.

It was the occasion when Roddy, then in professional ranks, finished runner-up to Liam Higgins in the main tournament, for a reward of £1,250. And when Joe had a hand in earning him further cash.

In fact it was a memorable day for the Carr family in that Roddy headed a team in which the three amateurs were Joe, Jody and Gerry. And their winning effort ensured a further prize of £750 for Roddy, from the pro-am section of the 72-hole tournament.

Meanwhile, John O'Leary found that Joe also cast a large shadow over his amateur career. As we established in an earlier chapter, O'Leary's first amateur prize was the Joe Carr Trophy for under-15 boys at Laytown and Bettystown. And as a 21-year-old, he had his first experience of playing competitively with Joe, as his foursomes partner with Leinster in the 1970 Interprovincial Championship.

"Joe was extraordinarily generous in what he gave of himself," recalled the Ryder Cup representative of 1975. "The shots he could play then were shots I couldn't even dream of, at any stage of my career. I particularly remember the way he would hit a four wood out of the rough. His divots flew almost further than my wedge shots."

He added: "It was a dream playing foursomes with him because if he happened to drive the ball into rough, he would say 'Just knock it out on the fairway and we'll make par.' And generally we did.

"While his flair was staggering to me, I noted that he was also keenly aware of the percentages. When I thought about it, I concluded that he had clearly learned priceless lessons from playing with the top professionals. Yet for all that, he succeeded in retaining a wonderfully cavalier approach to the game."

Interestingly, the generosity of spirit to which O'Leary alluded, was very much in evidence at Royal Lytham during the climactic stage of the Lytham Trophy in May 1981. And it stood as an emphatic response to later suggestions that Joe was not as well disposed towards Rafferty as he should have been, given the youngster's undoubted talent.

On the second day, the weather at Lytham was unbelievably foul, causing the tournament to be reduced to 54 holes. Yet I watched Joe, then aged 59, out on the course in torrential rain, urging Rafferty to stick to his task. And it was due to no lack of encouragement from Joe that he lost a play-off for the title to his close friend, Roger Chapman. While the Irish skipper could be formidably tough in word and deed when a player in his charge fell below what he felt were reasonable standards, the events of that day at Lytham, showed him to be essentially a player's man.

In the opinion of leading figures in the game, it was a talent which remained vibrant despite the passing years. Which would explain why, six years after being honoured with the captaincy of the Royal and Ancient, he received a fascinating letter from the US, offering him a key role in the inaugural Ouimet Cup, to be organised by the magazine, Senior Golfer. They clearly recognised that Joe's ability to get on with people made him a superb communicator.

The tournament, whose title commemorated the first amateur to win the US Open in 1913, was to take the form of a match between Britain and Ireland and the US for players aged 55 and over. Interestingly, Francis Ouimet shared a distinction with Carr in that in 1951, he was the first American to be honoured with captaincy of the R and A.

With 12-member teams, the event would be played on similar lines to the Ryder Cup and Joe would be non-playing captain of the British and Irish line-up. And with beautiful timing, the approach was made to him in 1997, on his 75th birthday.

"It's great that they still remember me, even now with time running out," said Joe at the time, with a typically hearty laugh. "I no longer like to be reminded of my birthday but this has come as a particularly pleasant surprise." Later, he found himself saying: "For reasons that I was never informed about, the project fizzled out, which was a pity because it would have been a wonderful opportunity to renew old friendships."

So, from a team perspective, 1981 was to be his finale as an international captain. And perhaps it was appropriate that things should have ended that way, with his own son in the Ireland line-up.

Chapter Twelve
Designing Heads

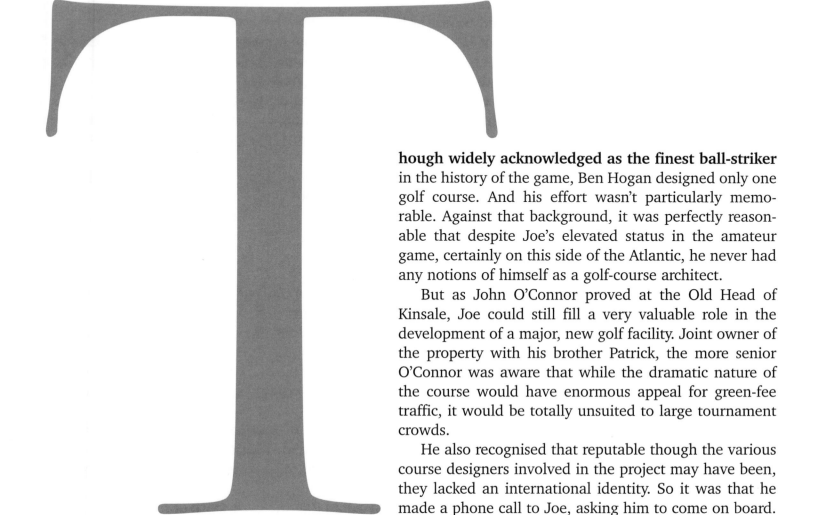

hough widely acknowledged as the finest ball-striker in the history of the game, Ben Hogan designed only one golf course. And his effort wasn't particularly memorable. Against that background, it was perfectly reasonable that despite Joe's elevated status in the amateur game, certainly on this side of the Atlantic, he never had any notions of himself as a golf-course architect.

But as John O'Connor proved at the Old Head of Kinsale, Joe could still fill a very valuable role in the development of a major, new golf facility. Joint owner of the property with his brother Patrick, the more senior O'Connor was aware that while the dramatic nature of the course would have enormous appeal for green-fee traffic, it would be totally unsuited to large tournament crowds.

He also recognised that reputable though the various course designers involved in the project may have been, they lacked an international identity. So it was that he made a phone call to Joe, asking him to come on board.

And by that stage, Joe's profile carried the priceless, additional status of captain of the Royal and Ancient.

Mind you, any American golfing aficionado worth his or her salt, would have known about the charismatic Irishman, who won most of the major awards the amateur game had to offer. Indeed the great Sam Snead once said of him: "He has easily the best temperament of any golfer I've ever played with."

Yet initially, Joe found it difficult to understand why he had been invited to become a key member of the Old Head team. "When John (O'Connor) got in touch with me, I contacted Roddy and more or less told him that I didn't want to get involved in the design of a golf course," he recalled. "What the hell did I know about such matters? Eventually, Roddy and I reached a compromise: I would become a consultant on the project and he would act as my manager."

With typical candour, Joe went on: "I had never designed a golf course and from my experience in the game I could see that it was a very specialised skill. Sure, I could recognise a good golf hole from an unfair one and a layout which was sympathetic with its surroundings, as against one which was simply imposed on the terrain. But even people like Jack Nicklaus had to learn the craft from other, experienced hands. In Jack's case, it happened to be Pete Dye, but I had no experience at all."

It was only when reflecting on his honorary membership of 60 golf clubs world-wide, that Joe began to see the sense in O'Connor's thinking. His role would be one of judge, rather than creator.

"Though I was the holder at one stage of 17 course records, only one of them has survived," he recalled. "That is the 64 I did at Gullane No 1, which has yet to be beaten. All the others have fallen victim to the dramatic improvements in golf equipment, quite apart from the huge developments in agronomy."

Then the shot-making experience, which would be applied in telling detail at the Old Head, came to the fore. "My favourite Irish course is Royal Portrush, where a player's shot-making skills are subjected to the ultimate test," he said. "Portmarnock, which I grew to love from an early age, is the fairest test, but Portrush demands greater shot-making.

"I suppose I'm prejudiced, having won my third Amateur there in 1960. Apart from shot-making skills, Portrush also presents a severe test of a player's temperament in that you won't necessarily get what you deserve there, whereas the good shot is almost invariably rewarded at Portmarnock. If you don't use your brain and keep your emotions in check while playing the magnificent Dunluce Links, you're going to be dead as a dodo. But having said that, if there was only one course I could play for the rest of my life, it would be St Andrews. For very special reasons, I love the Old Course above all others."

Joe went on to describe with obvious delight, the way the elements conspire to have the Old Course play differently every day. And Muirfield is also dear to his heart. "I think Muirfield is magnificent, mainly because of its dramatic changes in direction," he said. "Royal Birkdale is also a wonderful links. In fact, there are very few of the major British links courses that don't hold a special appeal for me."

He went on: "I never had the same love for parkland courses, but let me quickly emphasise that I wouldn't place the Old Head in that category. Its location, with the wind being such a crucial element, calls for much of the shot-making expertise that I would associate with links terrain."

Looking towards the US, he spoke of the pleasure and privilege of playing courses like Augusta National, Seminole, Shinnecock Hills, Pine Valley, The National on Long Island and Winged Foot. He expressed a particular admiration for The National, close by Shinnecock, which he considered to be closest of all the American courses to the British and Irish style of pure links.

Though he wasn't really conscious of it, Joe would readily admit that the experience of playing such celebrated venues must have influenced his thinking at the Old Head. Still, when he applied myself to work on the rugged, windswept promontory, he tried to imagine each hole as the start of a new experience, being aware all the while, of the wonderful potential of the place.

With a wistful smile, he said: "As I looked over those spectacular views, I was reminded of parts of Cypress Point and there were obvious elements of Pebble Beach, where I reached the semi-finals of the US Amateur." Warming to an area of California which was clearly dear to his heart, he went on: "When I was in that part of the golfing world, I always played Cypress. Sandy Tatum (later president of the USGA and a close friend of Tom Watson's) was a great pal of mine. It is, in fact, my favourite course on the Pacific coast: I wouldn't put Pebble in the same league.

"Anyway, when I eventually satisfied myself that it would be possible to build a course on the Old Head, I knew deep down that there would be no golfing stretch quite like it anywhere in the world, not even if, through some miracle, one could combine the best golf holes on the Monterey Peninsula. And this was a wonderful revelation to me, because the truth is that in my competitive days, I saw nothing of nature, not a flower nor a bird. All I saw was the tee and the green and the key elements that made a particular hole difficult."

Now, however, in his 81st year, golf is a far more gentle pursuit. On buggy-assisted rounds with friends at Portmarnock, there is ample opportunity to appreciate the beauty of nature. And in common with most other golfers these days, he uses metal woods and finds them very forgiving.

Yet in applying his playing experience to golf-course design, he often wondered if modern equipment made as big a difference as some statisticians would have us believe. Either way, he found it relatively easy at the Old Head to plan for the general capabilities of the handicap player, even those who would extract the maximum advantage out of ball and club. On more technical matters, he relied on the expertise of established golf-course architects, Patrick Merrigan and Ron Kirby, who eventually became the dominant designers on the project.

As Joe recalled: "I told Merrigan 'You do the designing, Paddy, and I'll do the fine-tuning. If you make a mistake, I'll see it and stop it.' And, quite frankly, I felt that mistakes were being made, notably with the contours of greens and the location of bunkers. The exposed nature of the site meant that it was absolutely crucial to take the wind-strength into account. This was one of my primary considerations."

He went on: "I repeated this to John O'Connor. And though I emphasised that I didn't consider myself to be a course designer in the accepted sense, I assured him that no serious nor costly mistakes would be made. That it would be a fair and playable test all the way, even in hostile weather. And I believe that's what he now has."

Roddy Carr was already acquainted with the site before Joe came on the scene. This stemmed from the Carrs' friendship with Nicklaus. Indeed Roddy was largely responsible for getting the Bear to Royal Dublin in July 1986 for an exhibition match against Seve Ballesteros, promoted by Toyota Ireland. And, as it happened, Toyota Ireland chairman, Dr Tim Mahony, hit on the idea of getting Nicklaus to design Mount Juliet, as a direct result of that venture.

Interestingly, all of these factors would come into play at various stages of the development of the Old Head. In the event, Joe vividly recalls his first visit to what was then a bleak, forbidding headland, down the road from the picturesque, seaside town of Kinsale. "Though it looked as if it had been overgrown for hundreds of years, I could see straight away that it would make a marvellous golf course," he said. "The problem would be to get the right design."

As a memento of what became a fascinating adventure for all involved, Joe's wife Mary retains an album of photographs which were taken on his early visits there, when the site was still crude and in no way resembling a golf course of world-class potential.

In a modern, golfing sense, the pain, frustration and potential danger involved in the struggle to achieve the correct routing, had resonances of 19th century explorer Sir Richard Burton's protracted search for the source of the Nile. And at times, it was no less dangerous. For his part, however, Joe persevered with his brief of co-ordinating the design imput of architects Merrigan and Kirby. And he proved to be a hard task-master. For instance, there were times when he would look at holes and insist: "No. That is not playable." And he would brook no argument until appropriate changes were made.

Those who knew Joe would have expected nothing less. Wonderful company off the golf course, he was never noted for his affability on it. And so it was at the Old Head.

Then, just as Roddy had been responsible for bringing his father on board, it was Joe who persuaded Kirby to become involved with the Old Head, after the American had completed his commitments with the Nicklaus design-team at Mount Juliet. As things turned out, it was a move which led ultimately to the satisfactory completion of the project.

For his part, Joe now acknowledges that he could never even hope for the chance of working on another development quite like it. Nor would he want to. "I have refused to take any further assignments, simply because I invested so much of myself in the Old Head," he said. "I have no hesitation in saying that if it had the same sort of weather as the Monterey Peninsula, it would be the best course in the world."

Then, typically realistic, he continued: "When assessing its overall strength, one obviously has to be aware of the limiations posed by Irish conditions. But it reminds me of the Old Course at St Andrews in how it changes almost every time you play it, due to the way the wind switches around. It offers situations in which you could be hitting a driver for distances ranging from 90 to 350 yards. And my instincts tell me that such stark contrasts in playing conditions are certain to add enormously to its appeal as a golfing experience."

"The horrific events of September 11th, 2001, obviously had a profound effect on the Old Head from a tourist standpoint," he went on. "But when normality returns to international travel, which it surely will, I believe it is set to complement Ballybunion as one of the great golfing attractions of Ireland's south-west.

"Indeed, any early doubts I might have had on that score were emphatically removed in the autumn of 1998." By that stage, Joe felt the course was sufficiently advanced to do itself justice and that it was time to put out the welcome mat to some pals of his from Pine Valley, where he has been an honorary member for more than 40 years.

As he put it: "Ed Slevin and the boys were playing Ballybunion and from there, they were going to the Old Head. So I had John O'Connor well primed for what I impressed upon him was the arrival of a very influential group of Americans."

In the event, 18 of them arrived for golf on a Sunday and the group included Jack Vickers, the owner of Castle Pines GC in Denver, Colorado, which is home to the high-profile International Tournament on the USPGA Tour, each August. In fact there was a group of 12 from Denver and on Joe's insistence, everyone at the Old Head was primed to give them VIP treatment, even down to having the best caddies on duty, as would be the case for the visit of Tiger Woods and his playing friends a year later.

In common with frustrated Irish hosts down through the years, however, the one thing that Joe couldn't organise was the weather. As luck would have it, the visitors arrived in a steady downpour, which was whipped up mercilessly by a 50 mph gale. "Jesus," thought Joe despondently, "what are we going to do now?"

But salvation was at hand. Within minutes, the rain stopped and to the surprise of Joe and his fellow hosts, all of the visitors, who were no spring chickens, set off and played the full 18.

Joe takes up the story: "We had hot whiskies for them at the ninth to encourage them to keep going – and it worked. And when it was all over, the unanimous verdict was that they had never had a more enjoyable day in their lives. Later on, they were treated to a slap-up dinner and I gather they haven't stopped talking about it since.

"I later got letters from them all, telling me what an unbelievable course it was and raving about the entire experience. And I chuckled to myself in the knowledge that if they had encountered the same conditions back home, they wouldn't have put their heads outside the locker-room door."

Keenly aware that the wind will always be crucial to the enjoyment of players at the Old Head, Joe has emphasised to the management the importance of setting the tees to suit the conditions on the day, an instruction which the greenkeeping staff have taken very much to heart.

The construction of the course readily facilitates such an philosophy, with as many as seven tees on every hole. And wind changes are such that it could be entirely reasonable to have a front tee in use on a Monday and a back tee 24 hours later.

It is an experience familiar to Tiger Woods and leading American colleagues from what have become annual trips to the South-West of Ireland, prior to the British Open. But there was something uniquely special about Tiger's involvement in a visit to the Old Head in July 1999. That was when the greatest six-ball ever to tread an Irish fairway, gave a ringing endorsement to the work of Joe and his design colleagues.

They had been promised an awe-inspiring spectacle; a place of breathtaking beauty. But as a blanket of fog enveloped the Old Head on that memorable Friday, the only thing visible from their helicopter was the ghostly outline of a promontory, through a stubborn cover which showed no signs of lifting.

Meanwhile, the atmosphere around and inside the clubhouse, was alive with a mixture of expectation and concern. One of the young caddies fondled the familiar tiger head-cover, like it was a treasured toy from his not-too-distant childhood. The clubs had travelled by road and Cian Daly was told that their distinguished owner would be along in about an hour.

Inside, John O'Connor darted from one room to another; the almost mandatory look of serious contemplation was a little more intense than usual. In sharp contrast, Kirby, looking every inch the studious architect, sat quietly reading a newspaper, lifting his head on occasions to chat animatedly about his pet project.

The clubhouse clock was nearing noon when the elite six of Woods, David Duval, Mark O'Meara, Payne Stewart, Lee Janzen and Stuart Appleby, completed the 30-minute chopper trip from Waterville, where they were based for much of their Irish stay. And the air was suddenly filled with the distinctly eerie combination of a lone piper playing the traditional Cork melody "The Holy Ground", to the accompaniment of a sonorous fog-horn. Soon, the players and their Irish hosts, financiers Dermot Desmond and J P McManus, were at the clubhouse.

The six-ball then headed for the first tee in what the locals had hailed grandly as the "Shamrock Shootout", with no sign of the fog lifting. But the players didn't seem to mind. Perhaps they anticipated the fog being burned off by a hot sun, as happens regularly with mists off the California coast on the Monterey Peninsula. But this was Ireland where the sun rarely reached that intensity.

Anyway, the caddies indicated the best lines to take. And one got the feeling that the players imagined themselves boys again, clearly savouring the idea of doing something dramatically different from target play at a luxurious country club.

Up the first fairway, the mist came sweeping in from the right, the eastern side of the Head. As they walked down the dramatic second fairway, the cliff-edge was just about visible. And still the mist came in.

For Stewart, who was to die tragically in an air-crash only three months later, it was a return visit to a land which he had first experienced in 1991, when he played in the Irish Open at Killarney, a few days after winning the US

Open for a first time at Hazeltine. Now he was here again having regained the title at Pinehurst No 2.

With no sign of the fog lifting, fears grew that the six would settle for nine holes and rearrange their day so as to play a course where they could actually see what they were doing. But there was no hint of quitting, as tee-shots were smashed down the long 10th. And their patience was eventually rewarded when, on reaching the 12th tee perched on a cliff edge, they could see the 300 foot drop to churning, Atlantic breakers below.

All of the players enthused about the beauty of the place. And I can recall Stewart insisting that it would become "a must of a golfing destination for tourists from my country." He went on: "They're going to love it, especially when the golf course matures. I certainly plan to spread the word......" It is interesting to recall that on the recommendation of Woods, significant changes have since been made to the 18th fairway.

Meanwhile, in an entirely different context, other, fanciful American friends of Joe's have phoned him, seeking to confirm stories to the effect that the Old Head was for sale. They were part of a consortium which already owned four or five rather special courses in the US and were clearly interested in adding the Old Head to their list.

As it happened, John O'Connor was in the US on business at the time of the calls, so Joe rang his brother Patrick, informing him of the inquiry. What should they be told regarding the availability of the property? "Well Joe," replied Patrick O'Connor calmly, "have they got a billion?" Both men chuckled. No further talk was necessary.

"To be honest, I didn't expect any other answer," said Joe. "John and Patrick have obviously decided not to part with their baby for all the tea in China." With that, Ireland's most distinguished adviser in the complex field of golf-course design, permitted himself a quiet smile before adding: "And I can't say I blame them."

Chapter Thirteen
First Among Equals

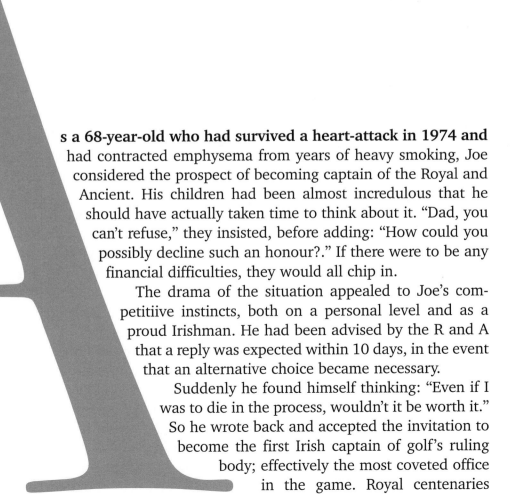

As a 68-year-old who had survived a heart-attack in 1974 and had contracted emphysema from years of heavy smoking, Joe considered the prospect of becoming captain of the Royal and Ancient. His children had been almost incredulous that he should have actually taken time to think about it. "Dad, you can't refuse," they insisted, before adding: "How could you possibly decline such an honour?." If there were to be any financial difficulties, they would all chip in.

The drama of the situation appealed to Joe's competitiive instincts, both on a personal level and as a proud Irishman. He had been advised by the R and A that a reply was expected within 10 days, in the event that an alternative choice became necessary.

Suddenly he found himself thinking: "Even if I was to die in the process, wouldn't it be worth it." So he wrote back and accepted the invitation to become the first Irish captain of golf's ruling body; effectively the most coveted office in the game. Royal centenaries were scheduled for Adelaide and Durban, which he would be expected to attend. And he would have to officiate and speak at the US Open and the US Masters, quite apart from the Open Championship itself, along with the Eisenhower Trophy and the St Andrews Trophy matches.

"It was marvellous," he recalled. "Apart from the population at large, I was conscious of accepting it on behalf of players like Fred Daly, Jimmy Bruen, Christy O'Connor, Harry Bradshaw, Eamonn Darcy and Des Smyth, and all the other fine Irish competitors who had distinguished themselves over the years."

His good friend Michael Bonallack, the then secretary of the R and A, had further advised him that he would be invited to every dinner of the four Home Unions. And that he would probably find he had 560 invitations for the 365 days of his year in office. All acceptances had to be monitored by the R and A which Joe quickly discovered was very much to his benefit.

"The first time I went over to St Andrews during that particular year (1991) was for the Spring Meeting," he said. "I had a speech specially prepared for me by public relations man, Tom Savage, whose help I had sought. On reading it, I thought it was absolutely superb.

"While travelling by car with Portmarnock colleagues, Donal McAleese and Bobby Cuddy, I went over the speech again and again. It had to do essentially with golf as a unifying force in Ireland, North and South. Grand. And I remember when I was announced as the captain for 1991/92, I whispered to Michael 'When do I speak?' And he whispered back: 'September.' And both of us laughed heartily."

On returning home, Joe went to see an old friend and namesake, Bunny Carr, a communications expert who concluded that he spoke far too quickly, especially for foreign audiences. "I knew Bunny very well from the time he worked in banking," said Joe. "He married the sister of Ray McInally, who was a leading player and an old pal of mine in Sutton. That cemented our friendship. Bunny was doing part-time work in radio at the time when he asked my advice as to which career he should pursue and I told him to leave the bank as quickly as he could and concentrate on working in radio."

Joe knew that the manner of his own speech was fine for Irish audiences, but representing the R and A abroad was an entirely different matter. In delivering speeches lasting upwards of 20 minutes, it was obviously important that he should make himself clearly understood.

An outline diary of his engagements indicated trips to Australia, the United States, South Africa, New Zealand, Continental Europe and all over Britain. It was certain to be an onerous undertaking but he saw this as being more than offset by the enormity of the honour. For one glorious year, his address would be the Home of Golf, which had always been so close to his heart. And to be the first Irishman to receive the honour would make it all the more enriching.

As he put it, rather poetically: "All my life, I had felt a romantic attachment to the Old Course and the prospect of marriage, however temporary, was too good to decline."

Whatever the situation may have been beforehand, the impending honour made it imperative that Joe be featured prominently in the programme for the Walker Cup matches, when they were staged at Portmarnock in 1991 to mark the centenary of the Golfing Union of Ireland. An obvious choice to write such a piece was John Redmond who, as golf correspondent of "The Irish Press" group of newspapers, had followed Joe's career since the 1960s. And it helped that golfer and scribe also happened to be good friends.

For the purposes of the article, Redmond arranged an interview in Joe's office where he proceeded to divulge a dark secret. "I told Joe that I had written his obituary," he recalled. "In fact I went on to explain the circumstances which prompted me to write it and that I had carried it around in my pocket since then."

The circumstances were Joe's heart attack in 1974. "Given his status as one of the country's leading sportsmen, I decided to be prepared for the worst," said Redmond. "On explaining this to Joe, I reached into my pocket and pulled out a grubby, wrinkled, foolscap sheet. And when I asked if he'd like to read it, Joe laughed heartily. So I gave it to him; and he read it and proceeded to burst into laughter once more, while exclaiming 'Imagine that. My obituary.'"

Redmond concluded: "Instinctively, I knew that Joe was the only man I could have had such a conversation with." And for his part, Joe has since delighted in the story, telling people, myself included: "Do you know that I've read my own obituary?"

Meanwhile, when Bunny Carr had set to work by taping his pupil, Joe was stunned to discover that he couldn't understand himself when it was played back. So the teacher got a metronome with which he beat out a pace of speech considerably slower than Joe's normal delivery. "Then he warned me never to speak unless I had a prepared script," he said. "I should also check the amplification system to ensure that it was in perfect working order. And that I should be aware that I was talking to a disparate audience."

The entire process took Joe from January until September, when he was ready to take office. He enjoyed it enormously and was grateful for enlisting the help of Savage who guided him through all aspects of protocol, while supplying appropriate anecdotes for individual audiences. All of these things were memorised under headings as a guide. Soon, the big day arrived.

Incoming captains facing the ordeal of the traditional, club drive-in, may take some comfort from the knowledge that even the great ones have been made to suffer. As in the words which Bonallack confided to Joe, shortly before he was about to do the deed as captain of the R and A.

As part of the clubhouse banter before the big event, the then secretary turned to his one-time rival and said with a wicked grin: "Now Joe, you know, of course, that no captain has driven out of bounds here since the R and A was founded in 1754." Even on the first tee at St Andrews, looking towards the spread of Europe's widest fairway, it still conjured up horrific images. Especially with the prospect of hundreds watching.

Even royalty didn't escape a gentle barb. For instance, when the Duke of York, who would later become King George VI, drove in as R and A captain in 1930, Bernard Darwin observed in The Times of London the following morning that he thought the caddies stood disloyally close to His Royal Highness.

So, the one-time proud holder of the amateur records for both the Old and the New course, but then a rusty 69-year-old, took the precaution of heading for the beach, where he proceeded to hit 20 balls into the North Sea, while his children Roddy and Marty and son-in-law Declan Branagan were in swimming (the tide was out and they had to walk "miles" to reach any worthwhile depth of water). The entire family stayed in a guest house up from the Scores Hotel.

September 19th 1991 was a lovely, autumn morning and a crowd of about 500 townspeople gathered for this annual ritual on the Thursday of the Autumn Medal. Twenty-two past-captains of the R and A were there, along with John Panton, the club's official professional, who dutifully teed up the ball for Joe and then stepped back. As Joe walked down the steps and shook hands with Panton, the former captains looked on.

Though he had supplied his own golf ball, the R and A secretary gave him the gold sovereign with which he would reward the caddie who retrieved the ball. "We ordered a stock of them at a cost of Stg£85 each, as far as I can remember," said Michael Bonallack. "The procedure is for the incoming captain to give the sovereign as a reward to the caddie who retrieves the ball. In keeping with tradition, Joe had to pay for it. And he was invoiced a further Stg£200 as payment for the silver casting of his golf ball which, with his name and the year of office on a strip across its centre, was then added to the captains' balls (a magnificent trophy, comprising a silver club with balls attached to it by silver links, which is kept in the R and A clubhouse at St Andrews). The original ball was then returned to him."

In the event, as the big, clubhouse clock struck 8.0 am, the cannon sounded and Bonallack instructed: "Go." And feeling as much at ease as one could reasonably expect in such circumstances, Joe discharged his duty with admirable proficiency, starting the shot down the left from where it cut back to the heart of the fairway. "I hit a blocked slice, which is the safest of all drives," he explained later. "You would normally use it towards the end of a match which had become very tight and which might involve the danger of out of bounds."

Then, by way of illustrating how much thought he had given to this ceremonial drive, he went on to recall that the safe shot for professionals with, say, out of bounds left or right, was a driver from the deck, declining a tee. And it was hit hard. "I remember when I played Billy O'Sullivan in the semi-final of the Irish Close at Royal Dublin in 1940," he recalled. "We were all square with two to go and Billy knocked it out of bounds to the right of the 17th and I knocked it out of bounds after him. And he beat me on the last green. That was something that stayed with me for the remainder of my golfing career. The stupidity of doing something like that."

Fifty-one years on, when the so-called symbolic stroke was safely executed, the past-captains came over one by one to congratulate him. And while he was still on the tee, the fortunate caddie who had correctly anticipated the flight and distance of the ball, like a would-be bride catching a wedding bouquet, brought it back to him and was duly rewarded with gold. With that, it was time for champagne in the secretary's office, where a crowd of about 80 friends, relations and well-wishers had gathered.

All of Joe's six children were there, along with Bill Thompson who was captain of Sutton that year. Roddy takes up the story:

"Never having seen an R and A captain's drive-in before, I was fascinated by it. I suppose the most impressive aspect was the simplicity of it all. Splendid simplicity, you could call it. There was no hype. The setting and the personnel didn't need embellishment.

"When the cannon went off I almost jumped in the air with the shock. There were about 30 caddies, all spread out, most of them to the left side of the fairway, over on the 18th. Naturally, they were waiting for the ball which tradition ordained would carry a reward of a golden sovereign.

"Our old pal Tip Anderson, who caddied for pop, myself and my brother John at St Andrews, was there, but didn't join in the scramble. 'I'm a wee bit too old for that,' he later remarked to me with a quiet smile. I was standing over towards the 18th green when J B hit his shot. After a bit of a waggle, he let it go. It was a blocked slice, about 220 yards and I thought 'you sly old fox'. He had picked the safest shot in the book.

"After it was over, a select gathering went to the secretary's office by which stage one lucky local caddie had already traded the ball with J B in return for a sovereign. Tradition further dictates that a replica of Joe's ball is cast in silver and, having been engraved, is attached to the Silver Club which goes on permanent display in the R and A clubhouse.

"While tucking into a breakfast of champagne and scrambled egg, I suddenly thought: 'Oh my God, the sovereign. I must have it as a memento of the day.'

"I wasn't too sure how much it was going to cost so I had a quick whiparound among the family only to discover that we couldn't raise more than £100 between us. That wouldn't be enough. It was then that I approached Jim O'Malley, an old friend of the family who had travelled all the way from Pittsburgh for the occasion. He gave me Stg£500. I remember thinking at the time that I would go the full extent of that sum, if necessary, to land the sovereign. So, I slipped quietly out of the R and A clubhouse, my heart thumping with excitement, and went directly to the caddie-master in his hut behind the 18th green. 'I'm Roddy Carr,' I said. 'I know who y'are', came the reply in a clipped, Scots accent. 'Then you must know why I'm here'. 'Indeed I do. The young man is waiting for you.'

"There, behind the hut I met with a young man in his late twenties. Though he wore a typical, caddie's cap, he was very much a modern member of his craft, clean cut and in a windcheater jacket. A knowing grin indicated that he was expecting me."

Stories abound of the skulduggery which caddies get up to when being rewarded for the return of the sovereign. Apart from hugely inflated prices, they have been known to actually acquire additional sovereigns from the bank and then sell them to relatives of the newly-installed captain, as if each were the original coin.

Joe's man, however, was satisfied to make a modest profit. As Roddy went on: "I explained that I had to have the sovereign. 'Indeed sir,' he replied. 'You can have it for £139, the same as I would get from Barclay's Bank down the road.' I offered him more but he wouldn't hear of it. 'That's the price, sir,' he insisted.

"Since I had no single notes, he ended up getting £140. A £1 tip, whether he liked it or not. And when he placed the sovereign in my hand, I felt a strange sensation. As I stood there in a place steeped in golfing history, it seemed so appropriate to have this link with the past. It was weeks later before I told J B I had bought it."

As a 69-year-old at the time of his captaincy, Joe made a point of telling his fellow captains that any future holder of the office should be in his early sixties, at worst. He considered it to be too onerous a role for anybody in their late sixties or seventies.

There happened to be quite a few royal centenaries during Joe's year in office and he attended them all. As an additional assignment, there was the annual dinner of the Association of Golf Writers, of which he was and remains a vice-president, at Muirfield. And he found that having a public profile in the game was a considerable help in Australia and the US, even though it had been 22 years since his last championship win.

He had an audience of about 600 at Royal Adelaide – and therein hangs a tale. After Joe had decided to accept the honour, his only daughter, Sibeal, made up her mind to be supportive in every possible way. Indeed she had regularly partnered him to golfing functions in Ireland and though now married with four children aged eight, six, four and two, she had agreed with her husband, Declan, that at least one extended trip abroad with her father, would be possible. Indeed desirable. That trip took in Adelaide.

She recalled: "Everything about the captaincy was new to me, including the journey to St Andrews for his drive-in. Other than being a champion's daughter, I really had no involvement in golf. I always suspected that had I taken up the game, nothing short of becoming a member of the Irish women's golf team, or winning a championship, would have sufficed for a Carr. And I rejected that as being too intimidating.

"When I saw his drive and the caddie collecting the ball, I must say I was really, really proud of him. There was a regal air about the whole thing; obviously a very special occasion. It also struck me that, in a sense, he had become an active golfer once more, having had to go through the pain of no longer being competitive. I could see that that had been difficult for him.

"Though I wasn't really aware of the history of the ceremony, it was clearly a great honour. Funny thing, I had never previously been in St Andrews which I had always thought of as a ski resort. Now, all I could see was golfers all over the place. And it struck me as being incredibly beautiful. Absolutely magnificent. The R and A put him up in an apartment overlooking the 17th green.

"After the drive-in, he showed me an itinerary of the various places he would be expected to attend in his capacity as captain. Prior to that, I tended to go to functions with him simply as support. It seemed entirely natural for me to do so because, though people don't realise it, my father is essentially a shy man. And he would have been a bit nervous about going on his own.

"When I looked at the itinerary, we discussed it and I singled out the trips I could realistically go on. Declan (her husband) was okay with it. We had a live-in au pair and Declan would have been at home as well. So I had no reason to worry about the children.

"When it was decided that I would be travelling, I could see that in one sense, my father was delighted with the prospect of having me along as company, but on the other hand, he would have been thinking that I'd end up bossing him. But the important thing was that he felt secure, physically and emotionally.

"During that year, I went to St Andrews quite a few times for a night or two, generally when he was speaking at some dinner. Abroad, I went to Royal Adelaide and then to the US Masters at Augusta National, having stopped off for a holiday in Hawaii on the way. Declan came over to join me. That was three weeks in all. There was another trip to Royal Durban in South Africa. That was it as far as I was concerned.

"The most striking place of all was Augusta National, mainly, I suppose, because I was a woman who was not involved in golf. I noticed the respect that the older members, his contemporaries, showed my father and the whole place was absolutely beautiful, a bit like St Andrews in the way it was linked to the past, yet very different at the same time.

"While we were away on those trips, I became aware of just how shy a man my father could be. I also became aware of his innate humility when meeting people, whatever their station. And I could see that the entire process wasn't easy for him. Most nights, when he was preparing a speech, his main concern was that he would speak slowly.

"Adelaide happened to be my first trip to Australia. And we had a stand-up row there over the fact that he wanted me to be off meeting people, day and night. From the time we got off the flight, even after 36 hours' travelling, he wanted to go straight to work, as it were.

"The man who drove us to our hotel said he would take us to the golf club in an hour. That was fine with dad but I put my foot down, saying that both of us were wrecked and that we needed some rest. 'But we have to go,' he insisted. And I was just as insistent that we didn't have to. From then on, he would come into my room in the morning and ask me in mock seriousness what my programme was for the day and I'd promptly tell him to feck off. I was prepared to do anything after five in the evening, but not before.

"Though I clearly wanted to protect him, I could see it was an uphill battle. His over-riding concern was to represent the R and A to the best of his ability. And while that impressed me, it also worried me. He wasn't as strong as he had been and I was concerned that he would overdo things.

"As for his speeches: the thing that I took most from them was his pride in being Irish. Of the fact that while projecting our traditional warmth and friendliness, we could also be a successful, modern country."

This was evident from the outset. In fact Joe's first official engagement as captain of the R and A was on October 18th 1991. The occasion was the annual dinner of the Lancashire Union of Golf Clubs at the Park Hall Hotel, Southport, not far from Royal Birkdale, where he had participated in the 1951 Walker Cup, and Royal Lytham and St Anne's, where he was an honorary life member.

Frequent bursts of laughter from an enthralled audience, greeted a typically witty speech which was delivered at an unusually slow pace for Joe: Bunny Carr's voice coaching had clearly paid off. And towards the end of it, Joe said: "It's nice to win championships, but what lasts are people and friendships. As Bob Jones put it, friends are a man's priceless treasures."

He went on: "Golf changed my life, introducing me to a world that I might otherwise not have entered. It is a bit like having a second passport: the official one gets you into different countries but for me, the golf passport gets you through a door marked friendship, camaraderie and enjoyment. Through all the success I've been fortunate to have in the game, I don't think I've received anything to compare with the telegrams and letters of congratulations I've received since becoming captain of the R and A.

"This is the first time I've worn this famous (red) coat outside of St Andrews. I got it in Southport. I had to go there to have it made, thanks to Dr David Marsh (his predecessor as R and A captain). On the day after I was nominated as captain, David showed me his schedule for the first six months and I exclaimed: 'How did you manage it, David?' To which Michael Bonallack interjected: 'Easy. All his patients are dead.'

"This (red) coat involved three flights and several fittings. Being in the rag-trade myself, I could only settle for the best. And after all, only the best is good enough for St Andrews, which is the source and inspiration of all that is great in golf.

"As you know, we still have our share of troubles in Ireland, but one thing I can tell this audience tonight is that they stop magically on the first tee of every golf club north and south in the country. That, for me, is a tiny ray of hope. Golf can help develop friendships and respect which transcend borders and barriers."

He concluded: "During this term of office as captain of the R and A, I have committed myself to focusing on golf as an international language of peace and friendship." And with that, he proposed the toast of the Lancashire Union.

Two months prior to taking over the R and A captaincy, Joe had a particularly pleasant assignment at Mount Juliet. And given that the invitation had come from a long-standing friend, Dr Tim Mahony, he was delighted to accept.

As owner of the magnificent complex built in the former estate of Major Victor McCalmont, Dr Mahony was staging an exhibition match between the course designer, Jack Nicklaus, and legendary Irish professional, Christy O'Connor Snr, to mark the official opening. And Joe would be match referee.

That was when Nicklaus expressed concern to Joe that 66-year-old Christy might not be able to handle the back tees on this championship-standard layout where the lush terrain offered precious little run on the ball. Perhaps they might play off forward tees. Anxious not to offend his good friend and former Walker Cup rival, Joe donned his diplomatic hat to suggest, quietly, that Jack should have no fear: even after reaching pensionable age, Christy was eminently capable of taking care of himself.

Which, of course, was absolutely true. Indeed after the concession of a Mulligan at the first, where his blocked, opening drive was lost in trees on the right, Himself went on to card a round of 71, beating the Bear by a stroke.

"Being there was an opportunity to thank Tim for arranging Jack's helicopter visit to Sutton GC the previous year, when I was the centenary captain," said Joe. "And it was also a chance to show my appreciation to Jack for his various kindnesses to me and my family over the years."

The K Club, which was designed by the enduring partnership of Arnold Palmer and Ed Seay, and which will be the scene of the 2006 Ryder Cup, was also officially opened in early July, 1991. So it was that Joe became an honorary life member of both it and Mount Juliet, within the space of a week.

Indeed honours continued to come his way a year later, when he was made a doctor of laws by Dublin University. Though he takes tremendous pride in the distinction, to the extent of having a photograph of the conferring in his hallway, he has never formally used the prefix.

When Dr Mahony had acquired the 1,000-acre estate, Major McCalmont moved to another residence closeby, on the banks of the River Nore which traverses Mount Juliet. As a gesture to its former owner, he was made the inaugural president of the club. And when Major McCalmont died in 1993, Dr Mahony asked Joe to succeed him. In fact the owner's niece, Ita Slattery, was lady captain that year and the men's captain was local businessman and former Leinster provincial player, Tommy Duggan. Joe has been president ever since.

Meanwhile, Joe's horizons broadened in other directions. With the help of fellow Howth resident, Robert McConkey, he became a keen painter. Indeed a McConkey painting of Ireland's Eye, hangs in Joe's livingroom while some prospective Carr masterpieces also adorn the walls.

"Having got to know Robert, I took lessons off him," said Joe. "In fact I also arranged for lessons for a golfing friend of mine, Paddy Hillery, when he was President of Ireland. I took it up during the 1980s, which my family rather unkindly described as my blue period, and was pretty handy at it at one stage. But my interest in it comes and goes and though I once put on an exhibition of 10 landscapes, it's a subject you've got to keep at and I'm afraid I've become a bit rusty."

He added: "I've never sold anything; I wouldn't be so presumptuous. For me, the attraction was always in the doing." And by way of further illustrating his diverse interests, he also admits to having indulged in transendental meditation for about a year.

And all the while there are new friends and new experiences. Like Father Gerry O'Brien, a Catholic priest from Woodenbridge, Co Wicklow, who prides himself on having a laugh, so loud and distinctive that it would embarrass a donkey. Anyway, he wanted to play Pine Valley, which Joe promised to organise for him.

"At around that time, we had Ed Slevin, who happens to be a board member of Pine Valley as well as being an overseas member of the R and A, and his friend Sir Ronnie Hampel from Augusta National over here playing Portmarnock and I arranged for Gerry to play with them," said Joe. "The upshot was that they got on so well together that the two boys invited Gerry over to play Augusta. Which he did, twice. Staying in the club, no less.

"He then went to Pine Valley where he played the course and stayed in the Dormy House for two or three days. Then they took him to Merion. Then on to Long Island and home. And when he got back, he rang to tell me how he had got on. 'Jaysus Joe,' he enthused, 'it was better than a pilgrimage to Rome.' "

Despite fierce, chilling winds sweeping Ireland's east coast, Joe attempted to celebrate his 75th birthday with a round of golf at Portmarnock. "Fortunately, when I rang the club they advised me it was too miserable," he said. Instead, 24 hours later, he settled for his regular Wednesday fourball as the partner of Willie Grant against Jimmy Joy and Bobby Cuddy.

This was the same Willie Grant who had the distinction of getting a lesson, of sorts, from Henry Cotton. It was arranged by Joe who despaired that his good friend would ever become even reasonably proficient at the game. Later, Cotton requested payment of £15 for the lesson, reminding Grant, who was an eminent ear, nose and throat specialist at the time, that this was his profession and that professionals charged substantial fees. To which Grant replied: "I know, Henry. If you came into my rooms and opened your mouth and said 'Ah', I'd charge you £50. So the fee sounds reasonable."

As a concession to the advancing years, Portmarnock permitted Joe to use a buggy, on medical grounds. As Joe recalled: "When I produced a doctor's letter to the honorary secretary, Moss Buckley, he said 'It's a hearse, not a golf cart you need.' That was the extent of the sympathy I got."

And it was a jolt to him that his long-time caddie at Portmarnock, Peter Maguire, passed away. "Peter became a great personal friend and caddied for me over a period of 30 years," said Joe. "He had a heart of gold and the Americans loved to have him on the bag."

Among the hundreds of stories told about Maguire, Joe remembers two in particular. The first one concerned the King and Queen of Malaysia, both of whom were keen golfers who arrived at Portmarnock with an entourage.

Given their status, Joe decided that they deserved a caddie of the highest rank, so he asked the caddie-master, Brendan, to make sure that Maguire got his highness, who was also likely to give Peter "a few extra bob." .

Said Joe: "Though myself and the Portmarnock members could understand Maguire's highly individual way of speaking, outsiders generally found his Dublin accent difficult to decipher. Anyway, word came back to the clubhouse that after 12 holes, the Queen was heard to remark to the King: 'How did Maguire learn our language so quickly?'" "Absolutely true," Joe insisted with a broad smile.

Then there was the occasion when Maguire was caddying for an American visitor who dumped his tee-shot into the well short of the green at Portmarnock's par-three seventh hole. "Is this casual water?" the visitor enquired. "Oh no sir," the caddie replied. "You can't drink that water. It'd f...ing poison you."

Meanwhile, Joe's competitive instincts remained very much in evidence, even in the gentle pursuit of social golf. "I now play off 10 – well kind of," he said as a 75-year-old, without much enthusiasm. "The truth is that I hate playing badly. In fact only the other day I went to the practice ground and hit about 300 balls to try and get my game into some sort of shape. I honestly feel that with about three weeks' of solid practice, I could get down to six."

The challenge of handicap reduction, however, was the furthest thing from his mind after a weekend in Mount Juliet in June 2000. A severe attack of emphysema had been brought on by fluid in his lungs to the extent that he was rushed to Beaumont Hospital in Dublin at about 6.0 in the evening and taken to the intensive care unit, where he was barely able to breathe.

"I found myself struggling so hard for breath that had there been an on-off switch to decide whether I lived or died, I would have turned it off," said Joe. "You've no idea what a frightening experience it is not to be able to breathe. I thought I was a gonner."

Among the specialists attending him was cardiologist Dr John Horgan and after about four hours' treatment, the crisis began to pass. In the meantime, his children Sibeal and Gerry came in to visit him, an event which became the cause of considerable hilarity when they gathered with their siblings for Joe's 80th birthday two years later.

Gerry was so shocked by the state of his ashen-faced father, with a variety of tubes attached to him, that he couldn't disguise his concern. Yet despite his own struggle, Joe had no wish to see his son distressed, so he signalled to Sibeal that he wanted to tell her something important. Whereupon she dutifully leaned over to his mouth. Then, unable to think of a gentle or suitably diplomatic way of easing his son's concern, he whispered the memorable line: "Get Gerry to hell out of here."

Though he would subsequently concede it to have been very ill-advised, Joe actually attended the Millennium Open at St Andrews a few weeks later, when among the celebrated contemporaries he met was the late Sam Snead, with whom he was photographed. "I should never have gone there," he said. "It took me a few months to get over that attack."

Such memories and the people who made them, dominated the weekend of his 80th birthday, on Monday, February 18th, 2002. The occasion was celebrated with a family dinner at his home in Howth on the Sunday night in the company of his six children – Sibeal, Jody, Roddy, John, Gerry and Marty – and his wife Mary.

It is a home, incidentally, where a stretch of wall was once shared with a dwelling of the poet, William Butler Yeats. And from the terrace, there is a glorious view of Howth Harbour and Ireland's Eye and beyond that, the ancient linkland of Portmarnock, which remains a source of much pleasure.

The presence of his children on that memorable weekend, got Joe thinking about how he must have appeared to them in a competitive context. "I suppose they expected me to keep winning," he mused. "I taught Jody and Roddy how to play the game. They were the ones who got all the attention because they were the older members of the family. Then John came along and Roddy and he were both bloody good players. The others got into the game later on."

He went on: "Roddy was sent to Pine Tree (in the US) where Jack Mulcahy (who later owned Waterville) took him under his wing. He also went to Jamaica and would go down to Penina and spend a month with Henry Cotton.

"Dor and I were at St Andrews in 1971 when Roddy played in the Walker Cup and took three and a half points out of a possible four, which was a GB&I record at that time. I remember we were sitting in a stand at the back of the 11th, which gave us a wonderful view of the surrounding holes. And I was at the 18th for his match against Jim Simons on the second day and hoping he wouldn't three putt from the back of the green. And we could hardly contain our excitement when he holed it for a birdie to win his match and help secure a home victory.

He continued: "I remember talking to Mark McCormack about Roddy and as to whether he was too young at 21 to turn pro. And I remember Mark saying that 'if he can play golf I can make him money. If he can't, then there's nothing I can do for him.' And, of course, he was a bloody fine amateur but he didn't quite make the grade as a pro.

"My own Walker Cup record wasn't particularly good (played 20, won five, lost 14, halved 1), yet I beat three reigning US Amateur champions. I always seemed to be playing Frank Stranahan or Harvie Ward or Bill Campbell or some other top American player. And, of course, we were generally struggling as a team.

"Yet the only regret I have about the Walker Cup is that I felt we didn't get enough credit for our achievement at Baltimore in 1965, when we halved with the Americans. And we could so easily have won. It came after 38 years of unavailing effort."

He then recalled John's marvellous challenge for the British Amateur at St Andrews in 1981. "That came out of the blue I suppose, but John was always a good player, even if he didn't quite have the flair of Roddy," he said.

"He was second reserve on the Walker Cup team for Cypress Point that year and I suppose, as an R and A selector at the time, I could have pushed him a bit harder. But unfortunately for John, his effort came too late, even though I felt afterwards that he was as good as some of the players on the team.

"Anyway, St Andrews '81 was when I found myself hiding behind bushes and behind fellow spectators on a balcony of the Old Course Hotel, while John was playing Philippe Ploujoux in the semi-finals. John didn't want me there at all. I tried to tell him that he needed positive vibes from people but he didn't see it that way.

"Meanwhile, my heart went out to him when things went wrong. Which is always the way when you're watching your children in action. It was worse than the toughest match I had ever experienced. And as it happened, I went away convinced that he had been robbed by some outrageous putting from the Frenchman. Indeed I remember Ploujoux sinking a particularly lengthy effort at the 16th, from way over on the second green. He putted John off the course."

Despite the disappointment of that semi-final defeat, John retains a deep affection for the Old Course. In fact he has found that he generally plays his best golf there. This was certainly the case when, on being elected a member of the R and A, he played in his first Autumn Meeting in 1999. At five under par with six to play, victory was within sight, but he had the crushing disappointment to finish 6,5 for a one-under-par 71 which knocked him back into second place.

As John recalled the occasion: "Later, I was standing in the lobby with dad, both of us in formal attire, going to the dinner. And we sat down together. And people who had seen "J Carr" on the results' sheet were coming over to congratulate J B. It required a very gentle intervention by yours truly to set the record straight."

John went on: "A tradition on the night of a member's first autumn meeting, is that you have to kiss the captain's (silver) balls. Given that I was aware the trophy now included a silver mould of the ball dad used when driving in as captain of the R and A, I found the ceremony to be the most moving experience I've ever had in golf. To have your father sitting up there in his red coat with all the captains and have your name called out – 'John Carr, who held the course to 71 shots' – was something I will never forget.

"I remember writing a letter to Roddy on my way home and telling him that being a member there, in such circumstances, was one of the proudest moments of my life."

Joe had expected a rather quiet 80th birthday, but without his knowledge, his wife Mary organised a sit-down dinner for 42 at their home. And he reflected proudly: "She fed them all – smoked-salmon starter and then a choice of chicken or steak. Willie Grant, Bill and Anita Thompson, Joe Duffy, my next-door neighbours, the local monsignor.

"After celebrating with a few scoops, I went to bed at 12.30 but I gather it was 4.0 before our guests left." Their presence, along with the goodwill cards, letters and phone calls, indicated that his popularity in the game, especially among his peers, was undiminished.

THE END

Epilogue

During a visit to Auckland, New Zealand for the World Cup of Golf in November 1998, I had a lengthy chat with Robert Trent Jones Jnr, designer of the Gulf Harbour course which played host to the event. Before we parted, he offered me a Christmas gift which he dedicated to his Celtic friends.

It consisted of a poem he had written in celebration of the Old Course at St Andrews. It reads:

Round and round we go
in the calm and in the gale
gentle air suddenly impaled.
Round and round we go
always back as first I came
among true spirits of the game.
A barren, timeless land tolled by bells,
Carved by wind and shepherds on watch,
Given to humble folk by noblesse oblige,
A low links from receding seas;
They walked the crook rounded at the estuary.
By ancient and royal measure, 83 acres without a tree
Evolving to 18 shots of whisky and holes of golf
A field of such complexity;
With but 11 greens and 16 fairways
The Old Course confounds to create,
A profound test for all full rounds.
For half a millennia in all seasons
Inhaling pure air at Sea's end.
In summer full joy at the long solstice light,
In winter girded against the cold wind and early sight
The same friends passed by unrecognised
Except by the manner of the others' swing and stride;
Unseen bunkers evoked anger and mirth
For tall and slim or stout of girth.
Baptised upon our journey begun,
When life and all is lost and won,
Return we from whence we come.
Again the wee burn bids us in faith to cross
To safe home as did St Andrew upon his cross.
Round and round we go
in the calm and in the gale
gentle air suddenly impaled.
Round and round we go
always back as first I came
among true spirits of the game.

Even the more enlightened golfers will be surprised to note that the course is set in only 83 acres, which would be considered quite tight, even for a modest parkland stretch. But it was rendered eminently workable through the device of using double greens and the sharing of fairways. As has been illustrated in the preceding pages, every square yard of it evokes wonderful memories for Joe and his family.

Yet while thinking of St Andrews and the many other major venues he has graced with distinction, he wonders these days whether such memories are enough to justify his existence. "I sometimes get depressed because I'm not doing enough," he says. "I would prefer to be active. I played golf all my life and now I find myself with nothing to do."

He continues: "My success as a golfer is all in the past. That is all gone; finished. The game no longer dominates my life. As to whether it is important to have conquered my own, golfing Everest, I don't look at it that way. I went though life having started with nothing, then I had plenty and then there was nothing again. It's cyclical – all part of living.

"But I feel especially blessed in having the love and support of my wife, Mary. Quite simply, I wouldn't be here but for her. She has been the centre of my life for the last 10 years and it is a marvellous bonus that she gets on so well with my children and my grandchildren. They know that without her I'd be a dead duck."

Though Mary insists on staying in the background, she takes a girlish delight in a photograph of herself and Tiger Woods, which was taken on one of his visits to Ireland, two years ago. Meanwhile, she and Joe travel extensively together. Apart from a Caribbean cruise, there have been visits to the US Masters and Kiawah Island, regular trips to the British Open and visits to St Andrews for the Spring and Autumn meetings of the R and A. As Joe put it: "I have been most fortunate in Mary and Dor, the two women in my life. They have been very special."

Then, on a personal level, he went on: "In the tough years, when the business failed, my self-confidence took a bad knock. I could no longer stand up and talk of my achievements, not like in the old days. And I found that there were times when my religious beliefs could be shaken.

"My Catholic faith has always been important to me. In later life, however, I have developed the philosophy that while continuing to pray to God, one takes the precaution of rowing away from the rocks. I find myself hoping there's an after-life and while I can't actually visualize it, I look forward to being part of it.

"As to what I will be leaving behind, it pleases me that I have made my mark; that I've enriched people's lives in some way. I certainly believe that I've touched people – for the better. There are those in various areas of golf, who wouldn't be where they are, only for me.

"Perhaps that's my reward."

Much of this influence on the lives of others, was achieved through the help of contemporaries who were also greatly gifted – with words. John Stobbs of the Observer once noted: "As an Irishman put it to me in the small, eloquent hours of a snowy morning: 'Joe is that rarest of things, a national idol with feet of gold.'" And the greatest of these craftsmen of golf, Pat Ward-Thomas, acknowledged Joe's remarkable integrity in a deeply perceptive tribute, after the British Amateur Championship was won for a third time at Royal Portrush in 1960. It read:

"Human beings cannot be perfect all the time, although many in the public eye are often unreasonably expected to be so. It is hard therefore to criticize a famous player for having exactly the same faults as other people, without their opportunity of concealment.

"It is difficult to retain a sense of proportion when adulation, in the modern, absurdly exaggerated forms, is heaped upon one; it is no small achievement to be normal, balanced, modest and kind in private, when multitudes worship in public. It is exceedingly rare therefore, to find a man whose qualities as an individual have never been impaired by his fame as a golfer.

"Such a man is Joe Carr."

CHAMPIONSHIPS
BRITISH AMATEUR
Winner (3) – 1953 (Hoylake), 1958 (St Andrews), 1960 (Royal Portrush).
Runner-up: 1968. Semi-finalist: 1951, 1952, 1954.

IRISH AMATEUR OPEN
Winner (4) – 1946 (Royal Portrush), 1950 (Co Sligo), 1954 (Royal Dublin), 1956 (Portmarnock).
Runner-up: 1947, 1948, 1951, 1958.

IRISH AMATEUR CLOSE
Winner (6) – 1954 (Carlow), 1957 (Galway), 1963 (Killarney), 1964 (Royal Co Down), 1965 (Co Sligo), 1967 (Lahinch). Runner-up – 1951, 1959.

WEST OF IRELAND (AT CO SLIGO)
Winner (12) – 1946, 1947, 1948, 1951, 1953, 1954, 1956, 1958, 1960, 1961, 1962, 1966.

EAST OF IRELAND (AT CO LOUTH)
Winner (12) – 1941, 1943, 1945, 1946, 1948, 1956, 1957, 1958, 1960, 1961, 1964, 1969.
Runner-up: 1944, 1946.

SOUTH OF IRELAND (AT LAHINCH)
Winner (3) – 1948, 1966, 1969. Runner-up: 1946.

BRITISH OPEN
Leading Amateur – 1956 (Hoylake), 1958 (Royal Lytham). Best finish: 8th in 1960 (St Andrews).

IRISH PROFESSIONAL OPEN
Leading Amateur – 1946 (Portmarnock), 1948 (Portmarnock), 1950 (Royal Dublin), 1953 (Belvoir Park).

DUNLOP MASTERS
Tied second (with Norman Drew) – 1958 (Portmarnock).

US AMATEUR
Semi-finalist – 1961 (Pebble Beach).

BRITISH BOYS' CHAMPIONSHIP
Semi-finalist – 1939 (Carnoustie).

BRITISH VICTORIES
Birkdale Bowl (1951), Golf Illustrated Vase (1951), Gleneagles Trophy (1955), Berkshire Trophy (1959), Formby Hare (1962), Antlers (1970 at Royal Mid-Surrey).

NOTABLE OTHER IRISH WINS
An Tostal Golden Ball (1953). Team event in Kerrygold Classic (1974 at Waterville). Scratch Cups: Carlow

(6) – 1950, 1951, 1953, 1954, 1962, 1963. Mullingar – 1963. Waterford – 1960, 1963. Rosslare (4) – 1950, 1951, 1952, 1954. Dundalk – 1965, 1966. Kilkenny – 1965. North West – 1965. Hermitage – 1969, 1971. Woodenbridge – 1964. Grange – 1947. Castletroy – 1961, 1967. Killarney Scratch Foursomes (with Noel Fogarty) – 1961, 1962, 1966. Hermitage Pro-Am (with Harry Bradshaw) – 1940, 1941, 1942, 1943, 1945, 1947, 1948, 1953. Milltown Mixed (9) – with Nicky McIntyre 1939; with Dor Carr 1949, 1953, 1955, 1956, 1961, 1963, 1964, 1967.

COURSE RECORDS (18)
St Andrews Old Course (67), St Andrews New (67), Sutton 61 (with Jimmy Carroll), Royal Lytham (67), Royal Portrush (68), Royal Dublin (65), Portmarnock (67), Royal Birkdale (69), Co Louth (67), Clitheroe (67), Birr (67), Delamere Forest (67), Mullingar (66), Waterford (66), Woodbrook (67), Gullane (64, and still standing), Howth (69), Milltown (64).

INTERNATIONAL MATCHES
Walker Cup (11) – 1947, 1949, 1951, 1953, 1955, 1957, 1959, 1961, 1963, 1965 (non-playing captain), 1967 (playing captain).

IRISH INTERNATIONAL TEAM
Home internationals – 1947 to 1969 incl. European Amateur Team Championship – 1965, 1967, 1969. Quadrangular internationals – 1968. Overall record – P 157, W 92, H 12, L 53. Non-playing captain and selector – 1979, 1980, 1981.

EISENHOWER TROPHY
1958, 1960, 1964 (non-playing captain), 1966 (non-playing captain).

ST ANDREWS TROPHY
(Britain and Ireland v Continent of Europe): 1954, 1956, 1964 (playing captain), 1966 (non-playing captain), 1968.

INTERPROVINCIAL CHAMPIONSHIP WITH LEINSTER
1938, 1956, 1958, 1960, 1962, 1963, 1964, 1968, 1970. Overall record – P44, W29, H6, L9.

ALL-IRELAND CUPS AND SHIELDS WINNING TEAMS (WITH SUTTON)
Irish Senior Cup (6) – 1948, 1949, 1950, 1956, 1958, 1963, Barton Shield (3) – 1946, 1949, 1950.

AWARDS
Association of Golf Writers (1953), Bob Jones (1961), Walter Hagen (1967), Caltex Trophy (1960), Irish Golf Writers' Distinguished Services (1972), Legends of Golf (1992), Honorary PhD from Dublin University (1993).

ADMINISTRATIVE
Captain of Royal and Ancient (1991/'92), Captain of Sutton GC (1948, 1949, 1990), President Sutton GC (1985, 1986), Walker Cup selector (1979 to 1986), President Mount Juliet GC (1993 –), Life Vice-President Association of Golf Writers, Trustee Golfing Union of Ireland, Trustee Darren Clarke Foundation.

First published 2002
by Poolbeg Press Ltd.
123 Grange Hill, Baldoyle,
Dublin 13, Ireland
Email: poolbeg@poolbeg.com

This edition published 2002

Design: Stephen Ryan
Cover photograph: Alan O'Connor
Illustrations: David Rooney

1 3 5 7 9 10 8 6 4 2

A catalogue record for this book is available from the British Library.

ISBN 1 84223 153 7

Colour separations and scanning by Pre-Press Repro, Richmond Road, Dublin 3.
Printed by Colour Books Ltd, Baldoyle Industrial Estate, Dublin 13.

www.poolbeg.com